How to Deal
with Emotionally
Explosive People

Also by Dr. Albert J. Bernstein

Dinosaur Brains
Neanderthals at Work
Sacred Bull
Emotional Vampires

How to Deal with Emotionally Explosive People

Albert J. Bernstein, Ph.D.

M c G RAW - H ILL

NEW YORK   CHICAGO   SAN FRANCISCO   LISBON
LONDON   MADRID   MEXICO CITY   MILAN   NEW DELHI
SAN JUAN   SEOUL   SINGAPORE   SYDNEY   TORONTO

1 2 3 4 5 6 7 8 9 0   AGM/AGM   0 9 8 7 6 5 4 3 2

ISBN 0-07-138569-X

McGraw-Hill books are available at special discounts to use as premiums and sales promotions, or for use in corporate training programs. For more information, please write to the Director of Special Sales, Professional Publishing, McGraw-Hill, Two Penn Plaza, New York, NY 10121-2298. Or contact your local bookstore.

The purpose of this book is to educate. It is sold with the understanding that the author and publisher shall have neither liability nor responsibility for any injury caused or alleged to be caused directly or indirectly by the information in this book. While every effort has been made to ensure the book's accuracy, its contents should not be construed as medical advice. Each person's health needs are unique. To obtain recommendations particular to your particular situation, please consult a qualified health care professional.

 This book is printed on recycled, acid-free paper containing a minimum of 50% recycled de-inked paper.

Library of Congress Cataloging-in-Publication Data

Bernstein, Albert J.
  How to deal with emotionally explosive people / by Albert J. Bernstein.
     p. cm.
  Includes index.
  ISBN 0-07-138569-X (pbk. : alk. paper)
  1. Emotions. 2. Panic attacs. 3. Anger. 4. Sadness. 5. Adjusment
(Psychology) 6. Impulsive personality. I. Title.
  RC455.4.E46B47 2002
  158.2–dc21   2002010571

Acknowledgments

First and foremost, I would like to thank the clients who allowed me to use their stories to illustrate my points.

I could not have done this project were it not for Arlin Brown, M.D. His help was invaluable in presenting organized and accurate medical information.

Thanks go out also to my esteemed psychological colleagues, Luahna Ude, Ph.D., and Robert Poole, Ph.D., who helped me smooth out many of the rough spots in my thinking, and to Mindy Ranik, who offered her customary miles and miles of insight and support.

I am indebted to my editor Nancy Hancock for pointing out the difference between good advice and useful advice. Because of her, I believe that readers will find my good advice to be useful as well.

Speaking of useful advice, my agent Sheree Bykofsky is a veritable fount. I thank her for helping me through yet another project.

My family, Luahna, Jessica, and Josh have been wonderful at tolerating a husband and father who spends many of his waking hours staring at a computer screen. Thanks also to Molly, who sat with me the whole time I was writing, and sometimes licked my hand.

To Connie Bernstein

Contents

PART THREE: EXPLOSIONS INTO SADNESS 143

PART FOUR: EXPLOSIONS INTO ANGER 201

Part One

Emotional Explosions

Chapter 1

The Blast Zone

All of a sudden your friend's breathing changes into ragged gasps. You turn toward her and see her eyes wide with terror. "Are you okay?" you ask, feeling your own heart begin to race.

"I've got to get out of here now!" she chokes out, and you start plotting a route to the nearest exit, hoping she can make it that far.

* * *

"I need to talk to you," a coworker says as she pulls your office door shut. Her tears burst forth even before she sits down. You hand her a Kleenex and wait while she pulls herself together enough to speak. A minute seems like a year when you're watching another person suffer.

"I'm a terrible person," she says finally. "I never manage to do anything right."

* * *

A customer storms in and slams his statement down on the counter. "I want to talk to the idiot who put this late charge on my bill!"

WHAT DO YOU FEEL when someone explodes into emotion? What happens inside you when another person bursts into tears, flies into a rage, or collapses into a writhing heap of formless anxiety? Do you feel frightened and want to run away? Do you feel concerned and want to help? Or do you feel irritated and wish the whole situation would just go away and leave you alone? If you're like most people, you feel all of the above. And more.

The world is full of walking time bombs who explode into sadness, anger, and fear. Fragile as they seem, they can still drag you into the middle of their outbursts, whether you want to be there or not. Getting *enmeshed* is the psychological term. You try things that would help a reasonable person calm down, only to discover that reasoning just adds fuel to the explosion.

This is the *blast zone.* You've been there before, and you will be again.

Next time someone's emotions blow up in your face, it can be different. This book will teach you how to stay calm, to think clearly amidst the sound and fury, and to understand the psychology of emotional explosions well enough to exert a little productive influence.

For almost 30 years as a clinician working with intense emotions, I've helped people gain control over explosive fear, anger, and sadness in themselves and others. The techniques I use are not particularly difficult—when you stop yourself from reacting and try to understand what's going on. That first step is the hardest. Once you've mastered it, the rest is easy.

What Are Emotional Explosions?

The term *emotional explosion* as used here covers a wide array of events that occur at all levels of intensity and for hundreds of different reasons. They can be dangerous, frightening, painful, or merely annoying. But despite the diversity of causes and effects, emotional explosions have several elements in common.

DISORDERS MAY BE DIFFERENT, BUT EXPLOSIONS ARE THE SAME. People are accustomed to thinking of explosions into anxiety, depression, and anger as different entities, falling into different diagnostic categories and requiring different responses. The closer you look, however, the more illusory the differences become. Perhaps the most significant difference is our reaction. We want to help people who are frightened or sad; angry people make us want to fight or run away.

All explosions, regardless of which emotion is being expressed, are caused by rapidly escalating physiological arousal. The arousal is the problem, not the content. There are times when it is beneficial to listen to what people have to say about what they're feeling and why, but the middle of an explosion is not one of them.

Our first goal is to calm people down. There will be time for talking things through later.

EXPLOSIONS ARE FAST. They happen so quickly that there is little time to analyze what's going on and think about what to do in response. The speed leads to the illusion that emotional explosions just appear out of the blue and are totally unpredictable. Not so; it *feels* that way, but your feelings are reactions, and as such are seldom the best indicators of what is actually going on. Understanding requires calm, and the ability to slow your perception of events enough to see the chain of causes and effects more clearly. This feat does not require an altered state of consciousness, it's actually a side effect of how your brain operates. The more familiar you are with what you're seeing or hearing, the more slowly it appears to move. Foreign languages, for instance, always sound faster than the one you speak.

Consider this book a primer in the language of emotion, which will help you understand and communicate with people who are having a difficult time understanding and communicating with themselves.

EXPLOSIONS ARE COMPLEX. They are composed of a number of events occurring simultaneously, at many different levels of experience, both for the person exploding and for you. Emotional explosions are made of words, thoughts, feelings, hormones, neurotransmitters, and electrical impulses. To deal with explosions effectively, you must consider what is being said, what people are thinking as they say it, and what physiological reactions are going on in their bodies. At first the speed at which everything happens makes this seem a daunting task. You may be surprised, however, to discover how much you already know.

Most of us, especially parents, are more effective in dealing with the explosions of preverbal children than we are with those of overly emotional adults. The explosions themselves are remarkably similar, but our expectations about them and our feelings of efficacy in handling them differ vastly. With adults, we tend to pay far too much attention to words. We sometimes attempt to talk people out of their emotions, explaining why they shouldn't be feeling what they're feeling. Nobody would try something so futile with a small child.

I'm not suggesting that you should deal with emotional explosions in adults by picking them up and giving them a bottle, or changing their diapers. I'm suggesting that you do the same sort of thinking when adults explode as you would on hearing a baby cry. Pay less attention to the squalling itself, and more to the internal discomfort that's causing it.

EXPLOSIONS ARE INTERACTIVE.   They're social events that require the participation of another person. Even when explosions occur in privacy, the audience is there in the mind of the performer. In a way, emotional explosions are like the sound of a tree falling in the forest. If nobody's listens, there's nothing there but a disturbance in the air. Unlike falling trees, however, explosive people will sometimes continue to disturb the air until someone does listen.

It is not possible to merely witness an explosion. Whether you want to be or not, you are involved. How you respond will at least partly determine what will happen. That said, let me point out that doing absolutely nothing may be the most eloquent and effective response. Often the most obvious reactions—exploding back, or explaining to the person why he or she should not be upset—will make the situation worse. *Doing nothing is always acceptable, especially when you don't know what else to do.*

EXPLOSIONS ARE A FORM OF COMMUNICATION.   No matter how incomprehensible the message, when people explode, they're trying to tell you something. Generally, they don't have the appropriate words to describe what's going on, so they use their behavior to evoke the same feelings in you. If you can let them know that you understand what they're feeling, you can sometimes prevent them from having to demonstrate.

When you're at the blast zone, you may feel you're being manipulated—that is, forced into doing something you don't want to do. But thinking in terms of manipulation is not helpful in understanding or dealing effectively with emotional explosions. It's a judgment, and manipulation is generally considered a bad thing to do to someone (despite the fact that people pay therapists to manipulate them). In fact, judging anything renders you less able to understand it.

If you think of an emotional outburst as a devious attempt to take advantage of you, you're looking at the situation from the wrong direction. To handle explosions effectively, you must always look at events from the other person's point of view. Explosive people are thinking of themselves, not you. They're displaying their distress in the hope that someone will do something to make them feel better, though they often don't know what that something is, nor do they care that the someone who does it is you.

I'm not suggesting that explosive behavior doesn't make you feel things you don't want to feel or do things you don't want to do, only that such behavior is almost never the result of conscious intent. There is no first person form of the verb *to manipulate*. People may do it, but they're not aware of what they're doing. Nothing enrages explosive people more than attempts to make them take responsibility for what someone else believes are their unconscious intentions.

One of the most effective tactics for dealing with emotional outbursts is to ask explosive people what they want you to do. And it's unlikely that you'd even consider asking if you believe they already know what they want but are unwilling to admit it.

EXPLOSIONS ARE REPETITIOUS. They are not single events, but a series of outbursts that typically expand in both intensity and duration as they repeat. As we will see throughout this book, repetition is a key element of most emotional explosions. Most strategies involve subtly disrupting a repeating pattern. You may not be able to stop an ongoing explosion; you may just have to brace yourself and concentrate on preventing the next one.

EXPLOSIONS FOLLOW PREDICTABLE PATTERNS. Though irrational, emotional explosions still have a logic of their own. They are usually attempts to get something—relief, safety, or perhaps revenge. This book will help you recognize the typical patterns and respond to them with techniques designed to minimize the damage to all concerned.

DEALING EFFECTIVELY WITH EXPLOSIONS IS AN UNNATURAL ACT. Doing what comes naturally makes emotional outbursts worse. Explosions themselves, and our instincts for dealing with them, are products of biologically simpler times. The internal programs that tell us to protect the fearful, comfort the sad, and fight or run from the angry are useful in the face of physical danger, but are less so when the threat is psychological.

Our instincts make us see frightened and confused people as powerful and dangerous. Kindness may persuade us to take care of people who should be encouraged to care for themselves. Reason betrays us in unreasonable situations. In our logical attempts to be helpful, we may find ourselves calmly explaining to terrified, furious, or disconsolate people that what's bothering them is only a figment of their imagination and that they really shouldn't be feeling the way they do. Our competitive urges may lead us to define emotional outbursts as a struggle in which there is a winner and a loser in situations in which if anybody wins, everybody loses.

The goal of this book is to help you understand and respond to other people's emotional explosions in ways that are good for both of you. The people we discuss here may occasionally engage in behavior that is frightening or annoying, but they're family members you love, friends and coworkers you care about, bosses and customers with whom you need to maintain working relationships, along with the occasional dangerous stranger. The best way to protect yourself from harm and undue stress is by helping them. Bear in mind, however, that helping them seldom means giving in, or giving them everything they want when they want it.

To deal with emotional explosions, you must be kind, caring, and courageous, but not nice. For people accustomed to being nice, the techniques in this book may require a leap of faith. Don't use them without a safety net of belief that they are the correct and loving thing to do.

The strategies you'll read about often involve disrupting familiar patterns. They may feel uncomfortable, but they will not harm explosive people; they will help. I believe this, but I'm not the one who matters. You must judge for yourself before you can use these approaches with a good heart.

Case Studies

More than a treatise on the nature of emotional explosions, this book is intended as a practical guide. Let's see what happens when we apply a few theoretical constructs to the examples from the first part of this chapter.

Before we go further, I'd like to point out that the examples in this book are of real people who have given me permission to write about them. The stories are presented a little piece at a time rather than as case studies, with a fictitious name, age, occupation, diagnosis, marital status, and number of siblings. I think that this is a more realistic and compelling approach, and a good deal more interesting to read. My aim in presenting them is to demonstrate the huge importance of tiny moment-to-moment details.

What people said to these explosive people made a difference. I chose them for that reason. In case you're wondering, most of them get better in the end, but it wasn't because they had a brilliant therapist. It was the changing reactions of the people around them—family, friends, coworkers, and sometimes even enemies—that made the difference in these explosive people's lives.

I encourage you to put yourself into the picture as you read these case studies. Think about what you would say, do, and feel if you had to deal with people like these, or if you were like one of them yourself.

An Explosion into Fear

Remember the friend whom we left at the mall, gasping and trembling at the beginning of a panic attack? Let's call her Jane, and take a closer look at what's going on in her mind and body as she explodes into fear.

What's happening is called the *fight or flight response*. At the physio-logical level, Jane's panic attack is caused by gratuitous activation of the autonomic arousal system that protects her from physical danger. You're probably familiar with this system both from your reading and from per-sonal experience. You know what it's like to feel a sudden rush of adrenaline on hearing a loud noise. Immediately, everything changes. Your heart pounds, your muscles tense, your senses frantically scan for the source of the sound. If you see real danger, your body is already primed to get away as quickly as possible. If, on the other hand, you discover that the noise is nothing to be alarmed about, the alarm system shuts down. The adrenaline in your bloodstream takes a while to wear off, but in a few minutes you're back to normal. This is how the fight or flight response has worked since the days when it protected your ancestors from saber-toothed tigers. It's one of the main reasons they lived long enough to become ancestors.

Jane panics because her fight or flight system is not working correctly. It switches on for no reason. As she walks through the mall, her body gives her a sudden but needless jolt of adrenaline. It feels just the same as the jolt in response to a loud noise, but it has no external cause. Jane's heart speeds up, her muscles tense, and she scans the environment for a danger to fight or flee. She finds nothing, but this makes the situation worse, not better. Her brain, seeing no outside danger, looks inward to the physical signs of arousal, thinking they are the *cause* of her fear rather than its result. She convinces herself she's having a heart attack, which in this day and age is considerably more perilous than the threat of tigers.

The first time this happens, there's no way Jane can know whether it's a real heart attack or merely panic. Nor would you know, if you were with her. You need to get a medical opinion quickly. Your own fight or flight response will help you dash to a phone to dial 911.

Panic attacks are usually recurrent, however, so there's a good chance that on this trip to the mall both you and Jane know that she's experienc-ing a panic attack, not a real threat to her life. But knowing that there's no danger doesn't necessarily help either of you to deal with the situation more effectively. Human brains are not programmed to deal differently with imaginary dangers, so you're both likely to follow the same patterns of thought and action as if you were in the presence of a real threat. This all but ensures that Jane will have more and bigger panic attacks in the future.

Even though she knows she's not having a heart attack, Jane will still be feeling intense dread that is probably focused on her own physiology rather than an external threat. Most people in the throes of a panic attack believe that they will either pass out, have a stroke or heart attack, or at least wet their pants if they don't do something to decrease their anxiety immediately. Rarely do any of these things actually happen, but panicky people seldom stay with their fear long enough to find out. Instead, they try to escape to a place of safety—either physically, by running away from wherever they are, or psychologically, by turning off the internal stimulation with something they get from a doctor, or by medicating themselves with drugs or alcohol. The problem is, running from imaginary danger makes the fear worse the next time, because the only coping strategy the person has learned is to escape.

As we will see throughout this book, escaping from negative emotion is a powerful and dangerous motivator. It teaches people to mindlessly repeat whatever they did to achieve it, without regard for long term damage to themselves and others. The desire to escape from pain is itself the cause of emotional explosions, and of why they're repeated. Indeed, it's the dark engine that runs most psychological disorders. Many of the difficult situations described in this book are the result of misguided attempts to escape discomfort that lead people into greater pain.

On that philosophical note, let's go back to Jane's panic attack at the mall. Unless your heart is made of stone, you probably want to help her. But how? Your own fight or flight response is by now clanging away, encouraging you to aid in her escape. I'm telling you that will make her worse. What do you do?

How you respond depends on how close you are to Jane. If she's merely an acquaintance, you might want to do just what she asks. Get her home as quickly as possible, and cross her off your list of shopping partners. The immediate relief procedure is how they treat panic attacks in emergency rooms, giving people a shot of something to calm them down and sending them somewhere else for real treatment. It's not a bad solution if you're never going to see the person again.

But if Jane is a close friend or family member, you might want to try another approach, one that involves helping her face her fear rather than running from it. Unpleasant and difficult as this sounds, it is far easier to handle than the results of continued running—either regular trips to doctors and emergency rooms—or seeing Jane narrow her life to avoid malls, crowds, stores, and anything more threatening than her own living room in the mistaken belief that the fear lives there rather than in her own mind. This response, by the way, is called *agoraphobia*, which is commonly thought to be the fear of open spaces but in fact is the desire for the false safety of shutting out the frightening.

The way to deal effectively with anything scary, whether it's Jane's panic or your discomfort, is one step at a time. Giving Jane a lecture on the virtues of facing fears will not accomplish anything. Though you both may be convinced that it's the right thing to do, you may not know how to do it.

We'll go into this throughout the book, looking into a number of strategies for dealing humanely and effectively with frightened people. For now, here are a few rules of thumb to remember:

THINK FIRST.   Before you deal with Jane's panic attack or any other emotional explosion, stop and think about what's going on and what you're trying to accomplish. None of the people we'll discuss are bleeding or in need of CPR. They will not get worse if you take a minute to think. In fact, as we'll see later, they may get better. Explosions are interactive. When another person's emergency alarm is going off, just being nearby will set yours off as well. That doesn't mean the situation is in fact a life and death emergency. If you respond as if it were, your agitation increases the overall sense of danger. If you take a minute to stop and think, whether you come up with a good idea or not, you are nevertheless setting a good example.

CONSIDER THE ALTERNATIVES AND PICK ONE.   The typical response to emotional explosions is to attempt several different, often incompatible, actions at the same time. Your feelings are likely to be mixed and confused, but your behavior should not be. Nothing beats having a plan, so do nothing until you have one.

Consider the alternatives. If you suspect Jane is experiencing a real threat to her life, call 911 and let the paramedics sort things out. Don't accept "I'll be okay, just take me home" as an excuse if you're in doubt as to her safety.

If the problem is panic, the best possible outcome is that Jane get some control of her emotions and stay at the mall rather than running home to hide from her fear. Obviously you can't make such a decision for her, but if you're a friend, you may have influence, so you should know what (in the opinion of most therapists) will help her most. There are other possibilities, which we'll examine in the chapters on people who explode into fear, but the thing to remember now is to think about what you want to happen, and to let this goal determine your actions.

Panic attacks are usually recurrent events that you can plan for in advance. If Jane is a friend with a history of panic, it will help to devise an attack plan before you go out. Unfortunately, your plan will not work as well as you think it should. People like Jane will rarely be grateful to you for encouraging them to face their fears. Even if you've discussed and agreed upon a strategy beforehand, at the time of the attack, they will often act as if your refusal to rescue them is the result of gross insensitivity rather than kindness.

KNOW YOUR GOAL. If you and Jane decide to stay at the mall and fight the panic, much of what you must do will go against your instincts and gut feelings. That is as it should be, however it might seem in the heat of the moment. The idea is not to stop the attack, but to help Jane endure it. The more Jane tries to make the panic stop, the longer it will last. There are, however, some things you can do to minimize duration.

DON'T RUN AWAY, BUT DO KEEP MOVING. If *you* were frightened over nothing, you might consider sitting down, taking a deep breath, and waiting for the feeling to pass. This approach will not work for a panic attack. Don't tell Jane to sit down and relax. Remember that the problem is excess adrenaline, which should be burned off rather than waited out. One of the reasons Jane feels as if she's going to faint is that she is *hyperventilating*. Her arousal system is causing her to take in enough oxygen to support vigorous activity, regardless of how fast she's actually moving. Too much oxygen makes people dizzy, and can cause fainting, though it rarely does. Your best bet is to increase Jane's activity level to conform to the amount of oxygen she's inhaling. She will feel that she's not getting enough air, but she really needs less oxygen, not more.

Increasing activity level is far more effective than some of the more passive techniques for controlling hyperventilation, like breathing into a paper bag. As we'll see in the section on fear, unless you know exactly how to administer them, these passive techniques can make the hyperventilating worse.

Getting Jane up and moving is the fastest and safest way to shift her physiological state back to normal.

TALK HER THROUGH IT. Jane's internal alarm system is telling her she's in danger, but you know she isn't. The only thing she has to fear is fear itself. Tell her.

As you dash around the mall, remind her that it's just another one of those pesky panic attacks, and that she'll be fine. Encourage her to observe the panic rather than respond to it. A good way to do this is to get her to compare this panic attack with others she's experienced. Ask how she'd rate it on the Richter scale.

Don't forget to talk yourself through it too.

IGNORE PROTESTS AND CATASTROPHIC EXPECTATIONS. Throughout this process, Jane will probably be saying things like, "I can't take it! I feel like I'm going to die! I've got to get out of here or I'm just going to explode!" She may also resort to giving orders, like, "Take me home this instant!" or attempt to play on your sympathy by saying things like, "If you really cared about me, you wouldn't be playing this silly game." If she says things like this, it means you're doing it right.

Jane may sit down and refuse to budge, in which case you should just walk on until you're out of speaking range but still in sight. Wait where she can see you, but don't look at her unless you want to see a heart-wrenching display of distress. Jane will most likely catch up when she realizes you aren't coming back.

It's possible that Jane will make a run for the car. If she does, just take her home and discuss it later.

DEBRIEF WHEN THE INCIDENT IS OVER. After the attack, Jane will feel really stupid. She'll be embarrassed about losing control in public, and remorseful about all the snippy things she said and did when you were only trying to help. She will probably suggest that you'd have to be crazy to want to go shopping with her again.

Maybe you'd have to be, but that's up to you to decide. If you're going shopping with her again, tell her that instead of apologies, you'd like to talk objectively about what happened and what you both can do to make the situation go better next time. Be sure to point out that facing fear is still an act of courage, no matter how silly you may look or feel while you are doing it.

In the section on explosions into fear we'll examine Jane and her panic attacks in more detail, including how she finally cured herself with a little psychotherapy from me, and a lot of courage. We'll also look at many other fear-related explosive conditions, including phobias, worry, generalized anxiety, and post-traumatic stress.

An Explosion into Sadness

Now that Jane is more or less taken care of, let's go back to that tearful coworker—call her Rachel—whom we left sitting in your office, Kleenex in hand, saying that she's a terrible person who never does anything right. Let's look at what goes on between you and Rachel as she explodes into sadness.

Rachel, like Jane, is in the grip of the fight or flight response, but in her case there is an external cause for her arousal, albeit small, rather than random malfunction of the system. Explosions into sadness are usually a response to a feeling of loss. In Rachel's case, let's say she made a mistake and was criticized by her manager. A loss of face like this would be difficult for anyone, but for Rachel it is devastating because her mind can turn a small setback into the harbinger of losing everything she values.

Like all explosive people, Rachel blows things out of proportion, which means she responds to her fantasies of what *might* happen instead of what is actually going on. This overresponse starts as a protective measure. In the case of physical danger, the first indicator is usually something small—a sound, a smell, or a movement in the periphery of vision. The fight or flight response sharpens the senses so they can scan for signs of danger. In explosive people like Rachel, the scanning process itself becomes the danger. Here's how it happens:

Rachel is criticized, and her brain gives her a dose of adrenaline to help her protect herself. Her senses sharpen, but there's nothing to see because the external event has already passed. Like Jane, Rachel looks inward to find the danger. She begins to generate worst-case scenarios in her mind. A little mistake becomes the cause for losing her job, and in the blink of an eye she's homeless, starving in the snow.

Everyone engages in this process to a certain extent. The common name for it is *worry*. A little worry is a good thing; it leads to contingency plans for dangerous events that are real possibilities. Too much worry, however, can create more problems than it solves. Our brains can't tell the difference between reality and fantasy, so every time we imagine a dangerous possibility, our bodies immediately prepare to deal with it. Most of us are able to stop the process when we recognize that it's no longer useful. There are, in fact, circuits in our brains that help us apply the mental brakes automatically.

For Rachel, and all the rest of the explosive people we'll discuss, these braking circuits are not working correctly. There are many reasons, both physical and psychological, for this malfunction. Later, we'll examine them in greater detail. For now we need to understand that in emotionally explosive people, normal worrying takes on a life of its own and becomes *rumination*, the internal replay of imaginary dangerous situations, which expands and increases arousal with each repetition. Virtually all emotional explosions involve rumination. Explosive people differ in the kinds of dangers they imagine and especially in their tactics for protecting themselves. People who explode into anger want to fight; people who panic want to run away. People like Rachel, who explode into sadness, see the battle as already lost and are crying out to surrender.

The technical name for Rachel's condition is *depression*. The term refers to a specific set of psychological and physiological symptoms, of which sadness is only the most visible. Depressed people think and act in a predictable manner that tends to keep them sad regardless of what is going on around them.

Rachel regularly overestimates the probability of negative events and underestimates her competence to deal with them. She replays scenarios of failure in her head until she feels totally overwhelmed and completely lost. That's when she comes to you for help. What she wants is for you to supply what she has lost—the capacity to control her own thoughts. Unless you want to become a permanent appendage to her brain, you need to help Rachel find some control within herself. Here are some ideas:

THINK FIRST.   As with all emotional explosions, the first thing you need to do is switch off your automatic pilot. You want to help Rachel, but as we have seen with Jane, helping doesn't necessarily mean doing exactly what Rachel or you *feel* like doing. To be truly helpful, you have to step outside of social conventions and do the unexpected.

The expected response—being nice—might be to sit there and listen while Rachel complains, hoping that if she gets the emotions off her chest she'll feel better. When she finally winds down, you might try a little reassurance, explaining how whatever she did isn't all that bad, that everybody makes mistakes. You might consider pointing out some of the positive things she's accomplished on the job and in the rest of her life, and giving her a little advice about what she could do to make her situation better.

Big mistake. Whatever you say, Rachel will think of a reason why it isn't true or won't help. The conversation that you hoped would last a few minutes can drag on for an hour and never seem to go anywhere. Eventually, Rachel will start to feel better, but your kindness and understanding may become addictive, making it likely that she'll be back the next time she needs a shoulder to cry on. Somehow, her problems will become your problems.

And you were only trying to help.

Even if this is the first time Rachel has appeared at your door in tears, when she sobs out that she never does anything right, you can be pretty sure that whatever happened has already become a part of the endless series of failures and disappointments already playing in her mind. To help her in a meaningful way, you need to get her to stop the cycle of rumination and focus on the specific situation. You can't do this by passively listening.

IGNORE TEARS.   This is easy to say but hard to do. Tears have instinctive power to command action. But just because they command, it doesn't mean you have to obey. When people cry, we want to protect them as if they were hurt children, or honor their sadness by listening. Both of these responses will encourage Rachel to recount the whole list of everything she feels bad about. But repeating that list to herself is what keeps her feeling bad. It may give her some temporary relief to retell her tale of woe to a sympathetic listener, but in the long run it will only make her and you feel worse. And the last thing either of you need is for Rachel to decide that your office is a safe place to come when she needs to cry.

Don't wait for Rachel to finish crying, and don't try to get her to stop. Just hand her another Kleenex and ask her about the specific situation that has her upset. Your goal is to move her off her self-imposed trail of tears and in the direction of solving her own problems.

DON'T TRY TO MAKE HER FEEL BETTER.   I'm not suggesting that you be cold and uncaring, only that you *can't* make her feel better. She has to do that for herself, or it won't work for more than a few minutes. As we will see throughout this book, temporary solutions only lead to more problems.

INTERRUPT TO KEEP HER FOCUSED.   Rachel deserves to be heard, but try to restrict your listening to one issue presented one time. Recitation of the litany of misfortune is the essence of depression. When Rachel starts repeating herself or dredging through her history for other sources of pain, it will actually help if you interrupt. Do it gently; say: "Maybe we should deal with one thing at a time." Try to keep her focused on the specific problem and what she's going to do about it, rather than letting her make herself feel worse while you sit there being polite. Certainly there are times that talking about problems helps to make them better, but repeating the same talk generally makes them worse.

SET LIMITS BEFORE THE CONVERSATION BEGINS.   Just because someone else defines a situation as an emergency doesn't mean that it is. Rachel has been struggling with depression long enough that a few minutes more are not going to make a big difference. It may actually help her pull herself together if you tell her that you can talk to her in half an hour. Delays often require people to mobilize their own internal resources while they're waiting to be rescued.

When you begin talking with Rachel, let her know in advance how much time you're willing to spend. Fifteen minutes is usually enough to help, if you stay focused. More time usually accomplishes less. If the situation warrants, you can extend the time, but the important thing is that you stay in control of what you're offering.

ASK WHAT SHE WANTS YOU TO DO. Before you engage in a heavy-duty conversation, make sure you both know what you're trying to achieve. You want Rachel to think about what she wants rather than just allowing her to dump her feelings on the floor and have you sort through them looking for an answer.

Know in advance what role she expects you to play. If she just wants you to listen, fine. Do so for the time limit you've set; fifteen minutes was suggested above. If she's looking for a solution, you can steer the conversation in that direction from the start.

ASK FOR SOLUTIONS, DON'T OFFER THEM. The most important thing you can say to a person like Rachel is, "What are you going to do about it?" In one simple sentence you are defining the situation as a problem to be solved rather than a disaster, and stating that it is her responsibility to come up with the solution. Often it helps to ask someone like Rachel what she's done before to deal with such problems. If it worked in the past, maybe she should try it again.

NEVER ACCEPT "I DON'T KNOW." Count on the fact that the people described in this book will answer most questions with "I don't know." They typically prefer that you come up with all the ideas and explanations, so they can tell you what's wrong with them.

Never skip over an "I don't know" and just move on to another topic. Stop right there and keep asking questions until you find something the person does know.

IDENTIFY OTHER SOURCES OF SUPPORT. You're probably not trained to do psychotherapy, and even if you are, you shouldn't do it without an appointment in the middle of a workday. If you feel you're in over your head when dealing with a person like Rachel, tell her. Ask with whom she usually discusses these issues, and suggest she contact that person. Preferably after work. Be prepared to hear that you're the only person in the whole world that she can talk to. Let her know you're flattered but that you don't feel qualified, and spend the rest of the conversation steering her in the direction of somebody who can do more to help.

GET HER TO TAKE RESPONSIBILITY.   Call it psychological first aid, or just trying to keep someone else's monkey off your back, your best bet for getting through an explosion into sadness unscathed—and Rachel's as well—lie in getting her to take responsibility for her own problem. Needless to say, that's no small task. The place to defuse emotional explosions is in the moment-to-moment choices you make in conversation. This book will help you with pragmatic strategies that encourage people who are falling apart to get their acts together. They may not always be easy, but they will work.

An Explosion into Anger

Now that we know the basics about how emotional explosions operate, we're ready to take on Brandon, the guy we left yelling about the idiot who put the late charge on his bill.

If you're like most people, angry explosions are the hardest to handle because they're most likely to activate your own fight or flight response. Obviously, it's difficult to think clearly if you're frightened or angry, but even when you feel relatively calm, the primitive urge to fight back or run away has a way of slithering into even the most reasonable comments. What feels like pouring oil on troubled waters can turn out to be more like throwing gasoline on a fire.

To deal effectively with anger, you have to look at the situation not from your own point of view, but from the point of view of the angry person. As Brandon stands at the counter glowering at you, there are two questions that are absolutely irrelevant to productive action: whether the late charge is justified, or whether you are the idiot who put it there. Jumping into a discussion of either of these is guaranteed to make Brandon angrier. To know why, we need to understand what's happening inside an explosively angry person.

From the outside, explosions into anger appear sudden, but what you're seeing is only the rapid expansion of the same cycle of rumination and escalating arousal that causes outbursts of fear and sadness. The outside behaviors are different, but the internal process is quite similar. It begins, as always, with the brain's inability to distinguish between physical and psychological threat. The late charge on Brandon's bill hits him like a slap in the face. Immediately, his brain pours him a shot of adrenaline to brace him up for defending himself.

Explosive patterns are psychologically addictive because they make complex situations easier to understand. Nothing simplifies better or faster than anger. Once his hormones are pumping, Brandon doesn't have to think about the natural consequences of unpaid bills. His anger changes him from a deadbeat to a hero defending his principles. This transformatory power is one of the features that makes anger so popular. It is also what makes it so utterly futile to try and convince an angry person that he or she is wrong.

Holding reality at bay requires sustained effort. Brandon has to keep up a head of steam as he lumbers toward your office. This is where rumination comes in.

When we experience strong emotions, we're programmed to check them out with other people to see if they're valid. Brandon circumvents the social part of this programming by talking to himself. Inside his head he lists his reasons for being angry, confirms their righteousness, and concludes that somebody should be made to suffer as much as he has. By the time he reaches you, he's run through the story about 400 times, becoming angrier with each retelling. Once Brandon starts this sequence of internal repetition and escalation, it's hard for him to stop. The braking circuits in his brain don't work very well. He shares this characteristic with the other explosive people described in this book, and it explains why the same sort of medications (SSRIs, or selective serotonin reuptake inhibitors) are used to treat panic, depression, and irritability. Unfortunately, putting Brandon on Prozac is not an option in the current situation.

Later, he'll probably admit that he got a bit carried away, but now he stands before you primed and ready, an explosion waiting to happen. All it will take is the slightest affront to set him off.

It's your move. Here are some ideas about what to do:

THINK FIRST. You face Brandon with your mind aswirl. Your primitive brain is screaming to fight back or run away, while more rational centers suggest you should merely explain to Brandon why he has no right to be angry, unaware that this is just a civilized way of hitting him over the head. At another level, you wonder if the problem is a computer glitch that should be handled by a technical person. None of these responses will help you. Instinctive attempts to fight or flee will confirm Brandon's view of the situation, and he will press harder.

The most important thing you can do when faced with anger is to think before you speak. If you don't know what to do, do nothing. Brandon won't get any angrier if you ask for a minute to consider the possibilities. Anger relies on immediate action to keep going. Slow the pace. Use every opportunity to break his rhythm.

If you stop and think, it gives you an important edge. Angry people may be mean and menacing, but they are rarely smart. There's a physiological reason for this: If you're using the part of your brain that thinks, and Brandon is only using his primitive programming, you have him by about 50 IQ points. If you can't win with odds like this, you ought not to play.

Above all else, make sure, however, that you know what winning means.

KNOW YOUR GOAL. Regardless of what your primitive brain centers tell you to the contrary, your goal is to calm Brandon down. Until you accomplish that, there's no point in discussing the late charge. People who are ranting or yelling can't listen to reason, so there's no point in trying to reason with them. Instead, get Brandon to lower the volume, not by accusing him of yelling, but by asking softly for something unexpected that he'd be hard-pressed to refuse.

Introduce yourself and offer to shake hands. You don't want him to see you as a nameless cipher. Ask him to sit down, or come back to your office where it's quieter—an audience will make it more difficult for him to back down. If you're uncomfortable being alone with him, invite a coworker, but make sure that only one of you does the talking. If he feels that you're ganging up on him, he'll have to fight more vigorously. Offer him a glass of water; it will be hard for him to continue yelling at someone who's treating him like a guest.

At the instinctive level, Brandon expects you to fight back or run away. Anything you do that doesn't conform to that expectation will force him to use a higher brain center to evaluate it. The whole point is to trick him into thinking.

The techniques for defusing angry people are easy to learn; we'll discuss many. The only hard part is staying calm enough to use them. We'll discuss that too. For now, remember that in dealing with angry people like Brandon, your goal should determine your actions, rather than the other way around. You may be able to get Brandon to calm down, but do not believe for an instant that you will ever get him, or any other angry person, to admit that he is wrong.

AVOID PROVOCATION. The last thing you want is for Brandon to get angrier. This means you'll have to pay attention to your internal dialogue as well as his. Keep reminding yourself that your goal is to mollify him rather than to make his behavior conform to your standards. The fewer lines you have to draw in the sand, the better.

Often it is a cost-effective solution to write off a reasonable charge rather than having to spend the emotional energy to defend it. If you think this means sacrificing principles, you may be confusing reflexive competitiveness with character.

In business settings, angry people can often gain control by using profanity. If you are compelled by your standards or by company policy to interrupt if Brandon starts cursing, there is little chance of anybody getting calmer. This is not to say that anyone should have to listen to objectionable language, only that there is a price to be paid for not having to do so.

If you have to make an issue of his language, let him know that there's something in it for him if he complies with your wishes. Say, "I'm willing to help, but not if you use profanity. If you want me to listen, please pay attention to how you talk to me."

LISTEN. Emotional explosions are a form of communication. One way or another, you will hear what Brandon has to say. He's been rehearsing all the way to your office, so you might as well get the performance out of the way as soon as possible. Listen quietly, and resist the impulse to correct his facts. The goal is to have him empty his head of the material he's been using to stay angry.

Don't give him anything new at this point, he'll only misunderstand. Try to avoid answering questions. Angry people in the midst of their initial rant often ask things like, "How would you feel if someone robbed you?" If you say you'd be upset, Brandon will take it as an admission that the late charge is robbery. If you tell him he isn't being robbed, he'll have to explain why he is. You can't win. It's better to defer his questions with statements like, "What I feel isn't important. I'm more concerned with what you feel."

Eventually, you will have to interrupt, or Brandon will merely shift into an external version of the self-stoking he's been doing internally. The time to make your move is when he starts repeating himself or ticking points off on his fingers. This is a sure sign that he is no longer talking to you but has gone back to fueling his internal fire.

The best way to interrupt is by restating what he's been telling you..

ACKNOWLEDGE HIS RIGHT TO BE ANGRY. Bear in mind that the tirade you're hearing began as an attempt to answer the question, "Do I have a reason to be angry?" The question is still on the table, and you must answer it in the affirmative if you want the harangue to stop. This does not mean that you have to agree with Brandon's interpretation, only that you affirm his right to be angry. Everyone has the right to be angry. Say something like, "I can see why you'd be upset over a late charge." Bear in mind when you're validating that angry people seldom call their emotional state anger, since that is a pejorative term. You seldom go wrong validating emotional states using the terms upset or concerned.

The simplicity of this technique often causes people to underestimate its importance and leave it out. Until you acknowledge his suffering, Brandon will resist any attempt to end it, even by writing off the late charge on the spot. To most angry people, the validation is more important than having you solve the problem for them.

DO NOT EXPLAIN! To an angry person, explanations sound like, "Unless you're really stupid, you'll see that you have no cause to be angry at me when you're the one who's wrong."

Trying to convince an angry person that something isn't your fault is worse than having it be your fault. Trust me on this.

ASK, "WHAT WOULD YOU LIKE ME TO DO?"   What could be more simple and more unexpected than asking Brandon what he wants you to do? He probably won't know, so he'll have to stop and think. This, at least, is what you want him to do. Some subtlety is required, especially if you're irritated. If you put the emphasis in the sentence on like or do, it's a question. If you put the emphasis on me, it's an insult. Try reading these aloud:

> What would you *like* me to do?
> What would you like me to *do*?
> What would you like *me* to do?

It also makes sense to ask because you really don't know what Brandon wants. Maybe he'll ask you to cancel the late charge, or maybe he'll be satisfied with having you stand there for another couple of minutes while he yells at you. You never know. Even if you're certain that Brandon is trying to manipulate you into removing the late charge, you should still ask him what he wants.

Getting an explosive person to ask for what he wants is a critical step. It moves the situation from an ambiguous display of emotion to a negotiation with a specific and stated goal. If Brandon tells you what he wants, he is making an implicit contract to be satisfied if he gets it. Your role changes from target to the person who can decide whether or not to grant his request. All it takes is one simple question that you wouldn't ask if you assumed you already knew what he wanted.

NEGOTIATE.   With angry people you can be right or effective; take your pick. Probably the late charge is more than justified, but don't let that blind you to the possibility of putting Brandon in your debt by canceling his.

Playing the Numbers

How likely are you to encounter an emotional explosion? It's almost a certainty that you'll encounter one at some time or another.

The National Institute of Health estimates that there are 19 million Americans with anxiety disorders, 22 million with depression, and that one in five people can expect to be depressed at some time in their lives. Of these millions of people, some are likely to be your friends, your family, your coworkers, or your customers.

Anger is harder to track, but according to insurance company estimates 2500 people in every 100,000 have been physically attacked on the job. Two-thirds of these attacks were by customers and strangers, the rest were by coworkers. Then there are the approximately 600,000 incidents of domestic violence reported in an average year.

Sooner or later, somebody's emotions will blow up in your face. When it happens, you'd better know what to do.

In ensuing chapters I'll share my strategies for different kinds of emotional explosions so that in fact you will know what to do when you next find yourself in the blast zone. In the section on explosions into fear, we'll look at techniques for dealing with panic, phobias, worry, social anxiety, and post-traumatic flashbacks. In the section on explosions into sadness, we'll discuss the various kinds of depression, including bipolar disorder. In the section on anger, we'll look at techniques for dealing with all levels of anger, from irritability to violence, including passive attacks by people who don't realize that they're angry.

We'll also continue the stories of Jane, Rachel, and Brandon so you can learn more about their explosive disorders and find out how they finally got control of their lives in therapy.

Chapter 2

What's Wrong with These People?

How What We Know About Mental Disorders Can Help, or Hurt

Jane's husband dashes toward the kitchen shouting. " Honey, guess what! My boss gave me two tickets to the Mariners game. Great seats and VIP parking. Do you think that just this once you might … "

He hopes Jane will be excited, but when he gets to the kitchen, she looks terrified. "I can't," she says, already beginning to hyperventilate. "You know how crowds freak me out."

* * *

Rachel is in the bedroom with the shades drawn, having one of her crying spells. After an hour or so, her roommate cracks open the door. "Hey Rache, I made a pizza. You want some?"

Rachel doesn't even look up to answer. "Not now. I'm not very hungry."

Rachel's roommate walks over and sits on the bed, putting the plate of pizza on the night stand. "Do you want to talk about it?" she asks.

* * *

Brandon bellies up to the bar at Cassidy's. "Better make it a pitcher, Fran, it's been a really stressful day. You wouldn't believe the crap that's coming down on me. I got chewed out at work for my so-called bad attitude, got called a deadbeat, and, on the way over here, this guy cuts in and nearly runs me into the guardrail, then has the nerve to flip me off. I chased that sucker all the way to the university exit, then he changed lanes and got away."

JANE, RACHEL, AND BRANDON are the emotionally explosive folks we met in the last chapter. In this chapter we'll struggle with an important and surprisingly difficult question: What is wrong with these people?

You may think you know. Just a few pages ago I diagnosed them as having panic disorder, depression, and an anger control problem, respectively. What those diagnoses mean is another story altogether, and a confusing one at that. On the surface these disorders appear quite different, but the underlying mechanisms that lead to explosions are surprisingly similar, whether people explode into fear, sadness, or anger.

One major reason that explosions keep happening is because people with psychological disorders are confused about what's wrong with them and what will make them feel better. We bystanders are confused as well, unsure of how to act around them, afraid that something we say or do might set them off or make them worse. Experts in the field are confused as well, and at least some of our confusion arises from theirs. What all of us know about mental disorders has as much to do with values, beliefs, and prejudices as it does with science.

The science behind defining and treating mental disorders is still in its infancy. Nobody really knows enough to say which way is best, but lack of knowledge seldom stops experts from saying anything. It has certainly never stopped me.

The good news for you in your daily dealings with emotionally explosive people, regardless of their diagnoses, is that there are a lot of experts who have all the answers. The bad news is that the answers are all different. Somehow, you have to sort through them and come up with answers of your own. Maybe the way to start is by taking a closer look at some of the more controversial questions.

What are emotional explosions? Are they symptoms of disease or evidence of weakness? If explosions are symptoms, are the diseases physical or psychological? Are mental disorders hang-ups that people should work to overcome, or handicaps that require you to accommodate them?

The best answer is *all of the above*. The problem is, none of us, experts included, is equipped to deal with this kind of complexity. The only way to grasp anything so intricate as the human mind is by looking at one little piece at a time. To the people studying it, however, each little piece seems to be the one that makes sense out of the whole puzzle. Also, when we study the mind, what we try to make sense *of* is the same as what we're trying to make sense *with*. We believe what we see, but we see what we believe. Experts disagree because, like everyone else, they judge new information based on how well it fits with what they already know.

Why should you care about disagreements among experts on the nature and treatment of mental disorders? There are at least three reasons. First, what we think about explosive people, and what explosive people think about themselves, is shaped by what the experts believe. Most of us prefer experts who tell us what we want to hear, rather than what we need to hear, so it makes sense to consider several sources before we make up our minds.

The second reason experts' beliefs matter is that they affect treatment. You're probably not reading this book to learn how to deal with strangers. The explosive people in your life may be friends, family, and coworkers, people you care about and want to help. Or want to *get* help. And what mental health professionals think about the issues raised in this chapter will strongly influence what sort of help they offer, and what results that help will have.

Consider this: A common belief held by many explosive people is that their outbursts are something that happens to them rather than something they do. Some treatment approaches unintentionally reinforce this belief by paying more attention to the reasons explosive people are the way they are than what they have to do to change. Spending six months talking about the dysfuntional families they grew up in, or six minutes a month writing prescriptions to correct chemical imbalances in their brains, can give explosive people the message that they're victims of their history and biology rather than authors of their own fate.

The third reason the different beliefs and opinions of experts must be considered is that emotional explosions are not just symptoms of personal disorder, they are complex social interactions. Regardless of which person is diagnosable, what happens will depend on what *both* of you say and do. Nothing escalates an emotional situation faster than turning it into a struggle between right and wrong. When we think we're right, we have a hard time thinking anything else, which is as true of mental health experts as with any of us. Remember the fable of the blind men and the elephant. Each man knew of only one part of the elephant—the trunk, knee, side, ear, or tail; and each, respectively, thought the whole elephant was like a snake, tree, wall, fan, or rope. We do the most damage when we mistake our beliefs about how things should be for how they actually are.

Here are some of the questions that are up for debate. The answer is *all of the above*; all are correct, but none is complete.

Sickness or Weakness?

By far the most commonly held view, even in this enlightened age, is that mental disorders don't really exist, that overly emotional behavior is caused by a deficiency in character, perhaps lack of willpower. Nobody says this out loud, of course, but many people believe it, or act as if they do. At the gut level, mental disorders still carry a lot of negative baggage. Referring someone to a psychiatrist is like, well, telling him to get his head examined. Think of all the humorous expressions for mental illness—freaking out, losing your marbles, being half a bubble off the mark, or two bricks shy of a load. Speaking of jokes, check your mental health coverage. Or check yourself. Let's put it this way: Would you be as willing to admit to depression as to diabetes? And even if you did admit to depression, would you recognize it as a disorder of perception that causes you to see everything, even your own distress, in the worst possible light, or would you just think of it as lack of willpower?

Jane's Anxiety

People have no trouble believing in mental disorders in the abstract, but when they come face-to-face with symptoms, their belief falters.

Jane's husband looks at the baseball tickets in his hand, then up at Jane. "Honey," he says, "I know that crowds scare you, but there really isn't anything to be afraid of. You just have to tell yourself that you'll be okay, that's all. It just takes a little will-power."

Jane wrings her hands and gasps for breath. "I just can't," she says.

"Why can't you just try?" her husband says. "Maybe you could take one of those chill pills."

People who have never had a mental disorder have no idea what it feels like. They can only draw on their own experience. Jane's husband has had some problems with performance anxiety before making a presentation at work, so he thinks of Jane's fear in relation to that. He talked himself out of it, so why can't she?

Jane's fear feels to her more like she is falling out of an airplane without a parachute.

Before you condemn Jane's husband for being utterly insensitive, let's look at the situation from his point of view. Jane's illness is forcing him to make a choice between abandoning her or missing the game. What evidence does he have that her illness is as real as the knots in his stomach? Jane doesn't look sick; seconds before he mentioned the game, she was fine, and she'll be fine again later that evening. All he actually *sees* is Jane wild-eyed in the kitchen, saying she's afraid.

To make matters more confusing, the experts seem to agree with Jane's husband. The E.R. doctor did prescribe the chill pills, and Jane's psychologist is treating her using *cognitive therapy*, which it seems to him consists of teaching her how to talk herself out of it. If you can talk yourself out of a disease, were you really sick in the first place?

Jane's husband knew better than to think this way, but like everybody else, when he's upset or frustrated, what he feels is more real to him than what he ought to know. More recently acquired information is no match for lifelong beliefs, even if they are prejudices.

Meanwhile, back in the kitchen, her husband's skepticism had a powerful, though unintended, effect on Jane. Though she wasn't aware of it, she felt trapped into defending the integrity of her disorder. To prove she was really sick, she had to get worse. Any effort she might have made to get better could be taken as evidence that there was nothing wrong in the first place.

By trying to make Jane feel better, her husband was actually making her worse. This unfortunate pattern is often repeated between explosive people and those who care most about them. Mental disorders are made of exaggerated emotions. They elicit exaggerated reactions from other people, which in turn elicit more exaggerated emotions. It's hard to believe in an illness whose very nature is changed by whether or not you believe in it.

Jane's husband ended up giving the tickets to his brother and sister-in-law. He resented it, but felt it was better than hurting Jane's feelings by going without her. Of course, he never asked her whether that would be okay with her because she was already upset and he didn't want to make the situation worse.

It was actually several years before Jane's husband learned to navigate emotional cross-currents more effectively. I taught him a trick that's useful to me in doing therapy: *When you get stuck, forget psychology and look at economics.*

Dealing effectively with explosive people is like making a business deal. To know whether it will fly, you have to do a cost-benefit analysis. Ask yourself:

WHAT DO YOU WANT?   In Jane's husband's case, he wanted Jane to go with him to the game, have a good time, and just be normal.

WHAT WOULD IT COST THE OTHER PERSON TO GIVE IT TO YOU?   For Jane, it would amount to a few hours of jumping out of a plane without a parachute. Though her husband cannot feel what Jane does, he knows enough to realize that being in a crowd can be pretty awful for her, even if she doesn't experience a panic attack. She'd like to just be normal too, but doesn't know how. It's a pretty good bet that baseball won't cure her.

WHAT ARE YOU OFFERING?   To Jane, the contingencies are clear. Her husband wants her to suffer through the game to make him happy, or perhaps to avoid seeing him moping around.

Would you take this deal? Jane's husband was a businessman. Had he used a business approach to analyze the deal he was offering , he would have realized that no one in her right mind would take the deal. Jane might have a mental disorder, but she wasn't crazy.

When we reach an impasse with explosive people, often it's because we're offering what, from their point of view, is a really bad deal. This is far more likely when we think we're only trying to help them, not get anything for ourselves. In economics, there is no altruism, so we're forced to look for self-interest at the heart of every action. Most explosive people feel tremendous pressure to get better to please us. Unless we stop and analyze the economics of the situation from their point of view, we're likely to continue offering bad deals and wondering why they don't just snap them up. Problems arise not only from low-ball offers, but, as we'll see later, from offers that are too good to be true.

If the deal you're offering doesn't pencil out, you negotiate. Jane's husband would probably have done better had he told her that he was pulled in two directions — wanting to support her and wanting to go to the game — and asked for her suggestions about a deal that would work. Jane might have told him to go with his brother and have a good time.

Would she have meant it? Who knows? I'm not naive enough to believe that people will always say what they really want as opposed to what they think you want to hear. I do know that it's a step in the right direction to get the deals we live by out on the table, where we can discuss them, rather than assuming we know what other people want. None of us can read minds.

Speaking of moving in the right direction, Jane's husband was able to help her talk herself out of her fear and go places. The trick was doing it one little step at a time. We'll talk more about this in the section on explosions into fear. For now, back into confusion.

Rachel's Depression

Another reason people have a hard time grasping mental disorders is that they don't make logical sense. Remember Rachel, who cried in your office. Depression has been a problem for her since she graduated from high school. Let's look at something that happened back then.

Rachel's mother taps on her door, then enters without waiting for a response. She finds Rachel on her bed, in tears.

Rachel's mother shakes her head. "Honey, what do you have to cry about? Look at this room. Nice furniture, nice clothes—if you'd bend over and pick them up off the floor— your own phone, a TV, a VCR. People would kill for such nice things.

"And you. Don't you have lots of friends, and parents who love you? But all the time you're up here, sobbing as if your heart would break."

Rachel's mother shakes her head again. "I just don't get it."

What's to get? Depression means being sad for no reason. Rachel's mother knows this, but she *really* believes that when you're sad, there must be a reason. Rachel's mother wants desperately to know what the reason is, so long as it isn't her.

But what if it is her? Interchanges like this, recounted in therapy, have convinced countless practitioners that people like Rachel are sad because they have lousy mothers. The idea has become part of our intellectual wallpaper, but that doesn't mean it's true. Being sad for no reason is so hard to imagine that therapists may inadvertently search for a reason in their own beliefs about how things should be. They think, *I'd be sad too if I had a mother like that.* This is not terribly different from Rachel's mother thinking that sadness must be the result of not having something you want. Somehow, the notion of a disorder that causes people to be sad for no reason disappears in a cloud of fuzzy logic.

But wait. Rachel's doctor believes. She prescribes Zoloft, and by ignoring Rachel's mother's issues and other personal problems, turns being sad for no reason into having no reason to be sad. Unfortunately, the deal is too good to be true.

Mental Disease or Psychological Disorder?

Physicians, by and large, see mental illnesses as physical problems to be treated with medication. Psychologists see them as distortions of perception, treated with talk. Every bit of research suggests that they're both right. This does not stop them from arguing over who is "righter."

There's no question that mental disorders have physiological components, but whether they are causes or effects is still unclear. That's only one of many ways mental illnesses are different from other diseases. They just don't fit the model, but it's not for lack of trying. Every few years the American Psychiatric Association puts out a new diagnostic manual in which the names and descriptions of disorders change according to the latest medical theories. The *Diagnostic and Statistical Manual of Mental Disorders*, widely referred to as DSM, is by far the best classification system anybody has ever devised; the problem is with the diseases themselves.

Most of what we call mental disorders have two distinct elements: their symptoms—such as anxiety, depression, or anger—and the patterns of thoughts, feelings, and actions that cause those symptoms to mess up people's lives. In real life, the two are inextricable. In the DSM they are divided into *clinical disorders* and *personality disorders*, as if they were separate, the general wisdom being that symptoms can be alleviated with medical treatment but personalities can't.

The Disease Model

Most physicians believe that mental illnesses are brain diseases—imbalances among chemical neurotransmitters at the synaptic level. (We'll discuss the nuts and bolts of brain function in later chapters.) Different disorders are thought to relate to different neurotransmitters and/or differing structures within the brain. Treatment involves prescribing medications that enhance or inhibit the appropriate chemicals. Solid and convincing as all this sounds, it is still theory rather than fact. Science is not advanced enough to prove it with anything but circumstantial evidence. There is no question that many medications have profound, positive effects on the symptoms of metal disorders, but why they have these effects is still a matter of heated debate.

Perhaps one day biochemical causes and cures will be found for all the symptoms in the DSM, but that day is not yet here. Mental disorders are still more complex than any theory yet devised to explain them, and their treatment still involves art as well as science, and a grasp of both chemistry and personality. Either one by itself is incomplete. Medication is sometimes the only thing that will make painful and incapacitating symptoms go away. But sometimes when you get rid of the symptoms with medication, personality patterns bring them back.

> *Zoloft changes Rachel's life; it feels like opening a curtain and letting the sunshine in. The crying spells stop, she has energy to do things, she can laugh again.*
>
> *Until she starts gaining weight. After a few months, when a size 14 starts getting tight, she stops taking the Zoloft.*

Rachel's depression returns, and it's even worse than before she began taking medication. Zoloft can have withdrawal effects if you stop it too soon or too suddenly. Rachel's mother notices that the crying spells have returned, and after weeks of denying it, Rachel finally admits that she isn't taking her medication.

> *Rachel's mother paces the room, wringing her hands and stepping over clothes. "Honey, how could you stop taking the Zoloft? It made you feel so much better, even if you did put on a couple of pounds"*
>
> *Rachel rolls over on her bed and faces the wall. Her mother gives her tush a little pat. "You know, sweetheart, maybe it's not the medication that puts the weight on. Maybe if you cut back on the ice cream and french fries? A little exercise wouldn't hurt either."*
>
> *Rachel pulls the pillow over her head and sobs. It's always her fault.*

Eventually, Rachel's mother gets her back in to see the doctor.

> *"Every medication has side effects," the doctor says as she listens to Rachel's heart with her stethoscope. "It's unusual, but some people do gain weight on Zoloft. Maybe we ought to try Wellbutrin. She scribbles a prescription and hands it to Rachel. "Try this and come back to see me in a month."*

Rachel is afraid to take Wellbutrin. At least when she's depressed she doesn't put on weight. Her mother finally talks her into taking the medication, but it doesn't help the depression.

Rachel and her mother continue to argue.

"I can't just sit by and watch while my child suffers.....”

"Mom, I'm not a child! Anyway, you're the one who's acting immature and manipulative."

"Oh, so suddenly you're all grown up, and I'm immature and manipulative." Rachel's mother narrows her eyes. "Answer me this, Little Miss Perfect: Which one of us is taking medication for mental illness?"

The disease model is not without side effects. In the medical sense, being depressed means there's something wrong with your brain. If there's something wrong with your brain, how can you ever win an argument?

Also, once you get a mental diagnosis, it tends to become the diagnosis for everything else.

"Rachel, we have some good news," the doctor says. "All the tests are normal. The pain in your stomach is just stress."

The notion that mental disorders are diseases is supposed to free people from guilt. It doesn't work for Rachel. Not only does she feel terrible, but somehow it always ends up being her fault.

Or her mother's.

The Psychological Model

Psychotherapy doesn't work particularly well either.

Dr. Judy thinks Rachel's depression is caused by a dysfunctional relationship with her mother. She encourages Rachel to stand up for herself. Sometimes, it doesn't work quite the way Dr. Judy intends.

"Where does your therapist get off saying that I have problems with boundaries!" Rachel's mother shrieks. "You're my child and

it's my job to take care of you. It has been since you first came out of my body."

The sessions with Dr. Judy help Rachel feel better during the few months they last. At least someone listens to her side of the story. But when the sessions are over, very little has changed. Rachel still feels depressed, and her mother is still as manipulative and immature as ever, in spite of all the time Rachel and Dr. Judy spent talking about her.

For some reason, both clients and therapists seem to believe that talking about parents is the stuff of therapy. We all have unresolved issues with our parents, and it feels good to talk about them with someone who listens, but there's little evidence that this cures anything. We continue to do it because psychotherapy still has some unresolved issues with its own family of origin.

Today's therapies are the children of Freud. Though psychoanalysis has been out of fashion for almost 40 years, it still influences everything we think. Everybody knows that analysis involved "working through issues with parents," so we still do it, regardless of whether it ever accomplished anything.

The psychoanalytic reason for talking about parents was to develop *insight* into the irrational sources of present day perceptions. The real issues to be worked through were in the patient's fantasies about their parents, not with actual parents in the real world.

Analysts examined dreams, early memories, and slips of the tongue, believing that full understanding of where symptoms came from was sufficient to cure them. Sometimes it worked. Psychoanalytic therapy was art. Along with a few masters, there were many who just painted by the numbers. Freud talked about parents, so they did too.

Some patients were cured by psychoanalysis, but many spent years analyzing dreams and talking about how their parents hurt them, lost in the fantasy that they were doing something productive.

Art eventually fell to science. Psychoanalysis was overthrown by cognitive/ behavioral approaches; the pursuit of insight was replaced by the teaching of practical techniques for solving real life problems.

In the shifting of paradigms, however, the baby was thrown out, but somehow the bathwater remained. Therapists still talk about the damage done by parents. They may no longer be quite sure why or how, but they're as enthusiastic as ever, and perhaps a bit more destructive.

Struggles with parents used to be internal. Now some therapists encourage clients to make them into external confrontations. The old name for this was "acting out adolescent fantasies," and even uninspired psychoanalysts would tell you that it made internal conflicts worse. With the demise of analysis, therapy became considerably less internal than it used to be.

We didn't lose the idea that parents cause mental illness, but we did lose 75 years of experience in getting people to pay attention to the implications of everything they say, do, and think. Insight may not cure mental disorders, but it surely helps. It's not a bad thing for therapists to have either.

Psychoanalysis was overthrown because knowing where problems come from is not enough to fix them. Today, therapists teach useful problem-solving skills like assertion, relaxation, communication, anxiety management, rational thinking, and positive self-talk. There is no question that this helps many people, but the approach does have some real limitations.

Consider Brandon's extremely unfavorable opinion of his anger management class.

Fran, the bartender at Cassidy's, sets a pitcher down in front of Brandon as he tells her about his stressful day of being chewed out, called a deadbeat, and chasing an inconsiderate driver on the freeway.

Fran shakes her head. "I guess that anger control class they sent you to didn't do much good."

"Are you kidding?" Brandon says. "That class was the biggest joke I've ever heard. This shrink wanted me to write down my 'anger producing cognitions' in this little notebook every time some idiot got in my face." Brandon rolls his eyes. "Like that's really going to happen."

They both laugh, and Brandon takes a big swallow of his beer.

If you don't think anger control classes are a joke, you haven't been watching late night TV. Cognitive therapists know that it's your own thoughts, not other people's actions, that make you angry. What could be more logical than teaching people how they can use this knowledge to control their anger? Unfortunately, most angry people don't understand themselves well enough to see anger as *their* problem. They think it's the natural reaction when idiots get in your face.

What people like Brandon need before they can learn to control their anger is good old-fashioned insight. Not about where their problem comes from, but about how it works, how their fantasies of strength create a reality of weakness. When you're angry, any idiot can control you. This insight has to be pointed out in a way Brandon can understand before he sees any value in controlling himself. Such communication requires artistry, but art is what therapy has lost. This sad truth is what makes anger control classes so easy to joke about. Therapy consists of two separate phases:

> **Insight:** clearly understanding the nature of the problem, how it works, and possibly where it comes from
> **Working through:** doing something about it

Both phases are necessary; neither is sufficient by itself. They are merely different parts of the same elephant. The problem is that therapists tend to pay more attention to one or the other. Artists focus on insight, scientists on working through. In the world of psychotherapy, artistic scientists who can help their clients clearly understand what's wrong with them *and* teach them what to do about it are about as scarce as, say, normal childhoods.

There are master therapists out there who can put together a synthesis of art, science, and medicine. In a later chapter we'll talk about how to find one. There are also quite a few confused but well-meaning counselors who understand only one part of the process and try to pump it up big enough to make a whole elephant. Their clients may be coming to see *you*.

> *The phone rings a little after one a.m. It's Rachel, in tears again. She says she needs to talk to you because you're the only one who understands her well enough to make her feel better. You brace yourself for a long night.*

Feel Better or Do Better?

Explosive people just want to feel better as quickly as possible. We want them to feel better. Everyone seems to believe that if they feel better, they'll do better, which is what we really want.

Yet another reason mental disorders are confusing is that the things that make people feel better quickest, usually make them do worse.

More than anything else, explosive people need to learn how to feel bad; that is, not to wait until they feel better to do the things that will make them feel better. Teaching them that is an art.

Whatever else they are, symptoms of mental disorders are also dashboard warning lights. They let people know that something important needs to be fixed. Making symptoms go away without fixing their cause is like putting duct tape over the glowing lights.

Emotional explosions are the unintended by-product of this process.

Mental disorders hurt, and the people who have them want to feel better. Brandon drinks beer, and Jane hides from the things she fears, and Rachel incessantly cries out in the night for reassurance. These strategies make them worse, and at some level they know it. But they're unwilling to stop doing what makes them feel better quickest until the pain burns its way through the duct tape. All they can do is display their distress, hoping you will make it go away. Emotional explosions are that display.

"Rachel," you say after half an hour on the phone. "I'm exhausted tonight, and I've got to get up early in the morning."

"That's fine," she says, after a long pause. "I really shouldn't be bothering you anyway. Maybe I should just go someplace where I won't bother anybody."

Rachel hangs up, and you lie there in the darkness, wondering what's going on in her head. Is she talking about killing herself? She wouldn't do that, would she? You begin wondering how many pills she has, and realize that you aren't going to be able to sleep anyway. You dial her number.

Here is your dilemma: If you don't call, she may harm herself; if you do, you make yourself the equivalent of an addictive drug.

In Chapter 10 we'll talk about how to handle suicide threats, but they aren't the point here. For now, I'll tell you that the secret to dealing with this situation is to ask sincere and direct questions, rather than reacting to innuendo. Get it out on the table and let Rachel know that you want her to do whatever it takes to protect herself.

The issue for now is not technique, but the struggle inside you. Imagine the terror of believing, albeit erroneously, that you hold someone else's life in your hands. Even if you knew exactly what to do, you might be too scared to do it. Instead you might spend the whole night reassuring Rachel because it makes *you* feel better. This is the awful struggle between feeling better and doing better. This struggle is the psychological mechanism behind addiction.

Addiction is one of the most basic of psychopathological processes. We all do it to some degree. We all block out the warning lights that tell us we're doing something that will make us feel worse in the long run, and instead we do things that make us feel better now. People use anything and everything to cover the lights, but if they use certain kinds of tape, they have to go to another universe for treatment.

Mental Disorder or Addiction?

The mental health and 12-step universes exist parallel to one another, often as mirror images, separated by law in many states. Some basic parameters differ as well, In one, you're not supposed to treat people for what you have, because you can't be objective. In the other, having the same life experience is as important as formal training.

Explosive people often self-medicate, controlling one disorder by creating another that's even worse. Substance abuse, if present, must be dealt with first. The 12-step model is better than what most doctors order for treating substance abuse. Analysts used to spend years with patients trying to discover the repressed reasons for their drinking, thinking that insight into the cause would make the addiction go away.

Having substance abuse rehabilitation counselors who have been addicted themselves works well on a number of levels. First, they know what addiction is like, and their clients know they know. Psychotherapists often don't have this kind of credibility. Recovering rehab counselors can be sympathetic and still hammer away at the self-deception they recognize from their own experience.

After his second DUI, Brandon lands in alcohol treatment. He thinks he can stop anytime he wants. His rehab counselor thinks he's in denial.

"Brandon, you're just like I was five years ago," the counselor says. "A practicing alcoholic. Myself, I practiced every day. Thought I could quit too. And kept thinking that until I lost my wife and kid, and got canned from my job."

"That's you, not me," Brandon says. "I'm not an alcoholic; I don't need alcohol. I don't have any craving at all."

The rehab counselor smiles and shakes his head. "Hey buddy, that's just your denial talking. I said the same things five years ago."

Rehab worked, Brandon got clean and sober.

Take away the addiction from someone like Brandon and there's still a psychological disorder underneath. The 12-step model works less well with these. Mostly it's because of the very thing that makes it so effective with addictions — the personal experience of the person doing the treatment.

Therapists who identify too strongly with their clients tend to become advocates or prosecutors, or a weird combination of the two, as Brandon discovered when he asked his rehab counselor for advice about anger.

"Hey, I know that scene backward and forward," the rehab counselor says. "Instant a-hole, just add beer. Been there, done that."

"But I've been clean and sober three months now," Brandon says, " and my wife says I still have an anger control problem."

The rehab counselor leans forward in his chair. "How did it make you feel when she said that?"

"I don't know, I guess it kind of ticked me off."

"Did you tell her how you felt?"

"No, but —"

> "Gunnysacking, huh?" The rehab counselor looks directly into Brandon's eyes. "Know what? I think the problem is really low self-esteem. One of your parents was abusive, right?"
>
> "Well, yeah," Brandon says. "My dad used to yell at me a lot, especially when he was drinking."
>
> "It's a well-known fact that people with abusive alcoholic parents have problems with anger. First thing you have to do is get your wife to read this book that tells what adult children of alcoholics are like, so she'll understand. Then you need to learn how to quit gunnysacking and get those feelings out."

A week later Brandon got ticked off at his rehab counselor because he was charged for a missed appointment. He didn't gunnysack; he got his feelings out. His counselor was not impressed—he told Brandon to quit whining.

With the popularity of recovery, the two universes—mental health and 12-step—are leaking into one another. Rehab counselors are treating substance abuse and mental illness bundled together into a dual diagnosis. Psychologists, no longer concerned with overidentification, are declaring specialties in disorders they themselves are recovering from.

Though there are benefits from cross-fertilization between models, it has also created some disturbing mutations, like psychologists who act like press agents for the syndromes closest to their hearts, and portray their clients as victims, deserving of accommodation, if not reverence; or rehab counselors who tell depressed people to get off their pity pots.

Handicap or Hang-up?

Should we treat people with mental disorders as handicapped? Should we make accommodations for them; that is, change the rules or the shape of the playing field so their disability puts them at less of a disadvantage? Or should mental illnesses be treated as hang-ups, distorted perceptions and ill-considered choices, for which people must take responsibility themselves? Do we help most by helping them, or standing aside and letting them face the natural consequences of their actions?

For centuries, mental illness hasn't been considered a disease at all. Today it is moving out from the shadows to take its place among other handicaps; in the Americans with Disabilities Act, for instance.

To people in wheelchairs, accommodation means building ramps and accessible work areas. We consider this their due, and our responsibility.

Some handicapped people may also have hang-ups about their disabilities, perhaps feelings of hurt and anger at their loss of function, or feel badly about themselves because they're different. We see dealing with these hang-ups as something they must do themselves. We sympathize with them as they move toward this important goal, but we don't build ramps to help them get there.

So, are mental disorders more like handicaps or hang-ups? The answer is critical, because accommodating a handicap helps, but accommodating a hang-up hurts. It's called *enabling*.

Can you determine whether the following situation is a handicap or a hang-up?

> *Rachel is going through a tough time with her depression. She's crying a lot, not sleeping well, and thinking of suicide. Her therapist thinks she ought to take a few weeks off work to get her head together.*

I don't know either. The point is knowing that you don't know, so you have to think it through each time to strike some sort of balance between treating people as handicapped or hung up. The only wrong answer is picking one to the exclusion of the other.

Many explosive people come to see themselves as handicapped victims of their disorder. The choice is generally not conscious, nor carefully considered. They already feel controlled by some external force; all it takes is someone to make it official.

> *At his rehab counselor's suggestion, Brandon attends a support group of adults who were abused as children. Part of the group's canon is a list of traits that identify people with a history of abuse, and Brandon has every one of them. He now sees abuse as the real cause for his alcoholism, his irritability, and everything else that's wrong with him.*

This is a breakthrough. For the first time in his life he understands why he is the way he is. In group, also for the first time, he feels he is really part of something.

Brandon joins a group effort to lobby the state legislature for stiffer sentences for abusive parents. He's thinking about going to community college to become a counselor for abused kids.

The last thing Brandon needed was to be part of a group that encouraged him to go after abusive parents the way he used to chase inconsiderate motorists. To be fair, the group did talk about working on internal issues related to abuse, but that part got lost in the shuffle of people marshaling their hurts and angers and sending them on a crusade. What Brandon thought would make him better actually ended up making him worse.

How would you feel if you suddenly learned that the things you'd been feeling guilty about all your life weren't really your fault? This is the kind of insight the psychoanalysts sought, thinking it was the source of healing. It may be; it depends on whether you use the information to change your life. Remember, therapy consists of both insight and working through.

Guilt is painful, and changing your life is difficult. The moment of epiphany is a blessed relief in the midst of an arduous process. Can you blame anyone for wanting to stay in that moment forever? This is the lure and danger of seeing yourself as handicapped. *It's not your fault* can easily be incorrectly taken to mean that it is someone else's.

"Brandon," his wife says. "I think it's great that you're working on your abuse and all, and I'm trying to be supportive, but it just seems like you're never happy. You're so grumpy most of the time."

"Grumpy?" Brandon slams his self-help book down on the table. "I can't believe you said that! You know when you say things like that, you give me flashbacks of my father. It's post-traumatic stress. Did you read about it in the book I gave you?"

Brandon's wife casts down her eyes. "I haven't really gotten to it yet."

Brandon sighs. "You need to understand how it is for abuse victims. We're people pleasers who take care of everybody else's needs but our own. To get better, we have to stand up for ourselves, be assertive. But when I try it at home, you just call it being grumpy. What kind of emotional support is that?"

Brandon's vocabulary has increased, but he's still telling the same old story: His anger is not his responsibility. Now it's because he's a victim of post-traumatic stress, handicapped by perceiving even the most loving criticism as verbal abuse.

Even if he were correct, how would you accommodate him? By never criticizing?

That's how Brandon's wife saw it. Eventually she got sick of it and moved out. It was the best thing anybody ever did for Brandon. For the first time, he became aware that what happened next in his life was up to him. We'll continue his story in the section on explosions into anger.

Being a victim is seductive. We live in an age in which people seem willing to trade control of their lives for the knowledge that their suffering is someone else's fault, and perhaps for the chance to talk about that to someone on daytime TV. Counselors who've been abused, anxious, suffered from post-traumatic stress, or depressed themselves tell us that victims are handicapped and that the appropriate accommodation is to revere them for the suffering they've endured. What they don't tell us is that what goes around, comes around. People who see themselves as victims usually end up unconsciously victimizing other people.

What victims really need is to get a life. Or actually, to realize that they have one and are in danger of losing it unless they pay more attention to what they're doing and less to what's been done to them.

Mental or Environmental?

Maybe it's not illness that causes all the problems; maybe it's just stress.

Stress is insensitive people, screaming kids, ringing cell phones, and not having enough hours in the day. Stress gives us headaches and makes holes in our brains. It makes our arteries less flexible and it inhibits our immune systems. But if your pain is caused by stress, it means it's not really there and you should ignore it, because your doctor will.

Stress causes mental illness, and mental illness is the inability to handle stress. Stress makes us uptight, cranky, and drives us to drink. Stress keeps us awake at night and makes us want to sleep all the time. Stress is a noun, a verb, an adjective, the source of all suffering. And an answer to every question that begins with *What's wrong ...?*

Stress is the external cause for most everything in ourselves and our world that we dislike but do not fully understand. Not too long ago it used to be called *evil spirits*. What used to be called *good spirits* is now called *self-esteem*.

Mental health is famous for coming up with concepts that explain everything. Of course, anything that explains everything means nothing.

Is it stress itself that causes the problems, or is it people's response to stress? All of us can think of stressful events that have destroyed some folks and caused others to grow and change for the better. The difference is, the ones who survive believe, even erroneously, that they have some control over what happens to them. This one simple belief is the source of all healing of mental disorders, regardless of their cause.

So now we're back to the original question: What's wrong with these people? The answers call to mind the fable of the blind men and the elephant, described previously.

No wonder explosive people are so confused, and we are so confused about them. With so many expert opinions about what mental disorders are, where they come from, who should treat them and how, who wouldn't be confused? The important thing is not letting what we already know blind us to what is still out there to learn.

We may never know for certain what the elephant looks like, but we still have to clean up after him, and house-train him if we can.

Part Two

Explosions into Fear

Chapter 3

Basic Calming Technique

The elevator comes to a grinding halt between the 18th and 19th floors. You've heard about this glitch, it's a loose something-or-other that the repair person keeps saying is fixed. Last time, it took about half an hour to get the dumb thing running. The joys of big city life. Another passenger is already grumbling into the emergency phone. You look resignedly at the report you were supposed to present in five minutes. The woman from the office upstairs seems to be gasping for breath.

"Omigod," she says, her voice thin and tight as steel cable. "I'm getting claustrophobia. I can't breathe. I've got to get out of here!"

Now what?

HOW DO YOU CALM SOMEONE who's in a panic? What you say is less important than how you say it, and when.

Panic wells up from brain structures that evolved before words. To understand how to calm a frightened person, we have to go back to that far-off time and look, not at panic, but its opposite.

It is the time of ripening. Even before she sees the first red berry, she can smell them on the breeze, mixed with the scent of dust, leaves, and evaporating dew. She scans for the shape of red berry bushes, marks their location, and plans her route. Soon she is filling her basket with bright, ripe berries, working carefully and quickly, immersed in the feel of the leaves against her skin and the sweet, sharp smell of berries. She is happy.

The opposite of panic is picking berries — quiet focus on a rhythmic, repetitive task. This mental place is where you want the woman in the elevator to go. *Calming* means showing her how to get there.

In technical terms, what you're trying to do is mimic the functions of her *parasympathetic nervous system*, a loop of connected brain centers, senses, and muscles that regulates relaxed activity. The other large feedback loop is the *sympathetic nervous system*, which mediates the fight or flight response we discussed in the first chapter. You know what this one is like — mental alarms clanging, heart pounding, muscles tensing, lungs sucking air, and mind prepared to kill or die. The physiology of explosions.

Speaking of physiology, before we can talk intelligently about how the brain affects emotional explosions, we must first agree on a few terms. The grayish lumps of jelly that make up a human brain go by many names, depending upon the tools people use to study them. The scalpel, the microscope, the test tube, and the PET scan all yield different views of the brain, and these views are often described in what seem to be different languages. How do synapse and sympathetic system relate to *amygdala* or the *cingulate gyrus*? And what do *serotonin* and *norepinephrine* have to do with *right brain* versus *left brain* thinking?

As a psychologist, my tools are rather low-tech. Senses and words. I watch and listen, then use language to try and explain what I see. My own understanding of how the brain works, like yours, is mostly from standing outside and looking in. I don't scan, dissect, electrically stimulate, or prescribe chemicals to adjust function, so I've had to learn from the people who do. I'll do my best to teach you. To make this confusing area clearer, I may have to jump back and forth from one language to another. I promise, at least, to refrain from making up new terms of my own.

We'll look at the brain on four different levels:

NEURAL STRUCTURES.   Physical parts of the gray matter like the amygdala and the hippocampus—which mean "almond" and "seahorse," respectively—were named according to what anatomists thought they looked like, much the same way early astronomers divided the stars into constellations. The stars seem to fit together to make human figures and animals, but seen through a telescope, they reveal themselves as unlikely combinations of near suns and distant galaxies. So too do almonds and seahorses fall apart into separate cells when observed through a microscope or by their electrical activity. Functions in the brain are never localized into one particular structure, and structures are always involved in many different, and seemingly unrelated, functions. Still, it's often useful to think about fear and anger being, at least somewhat, localized in the amygdala and a little piece of the tail of the hippocampus.

CHEMICAL CONNECTIONS.   Though their activity is electrical, brain cells are not physically fastened together like circuits in a computer. The wires in the brain are made of chemicals called *transmitter substances*. That's where serotonin and norepinephrine come in. As we'll see, starting in the next chapter, virtually all psychoactive medications work by affecting the operation of transmitter substances.

The same transmitter, say serotonin, is often the link between many very different structures and functions. This is why a *selective serotonin reuptake inhibitor* like Paxil might legitimately be prescribed for any explosive disorder described in this book.

THEORETICAL SYSTEMS.   Sometimes it's useful to group brain structures according to what they're supposed to do. No one can say exactly where the limbic system is, or what it's made of, but we can think about circuits of cells working together to regulate emotion. Likewise, you'll never see the sympathetic or parasympathetic systems on a map of the brain, but they are still useful in describing how the mind and body work together.

PROGRAMS.   As if knowing the names of the hardware weren't difficult enough, there's still the software to consider. The brain comes equipped with abstract processes like *memory* and instinctive programs, like the fight or flight response and *dominance hierarchies,* all of which we'll discuss in later chapters.

Now that we've defined a few terms, let's go back to our discussion about how to calm explosive people.

The basic maneuver for dealing with emotional outbursts is to tone down activity of the sympathetic system by stimulating parasympathetic activity. In other words, before you do anything else, you have to calm people down. To do that, you have to know where they are mentally and where you want them to go.

Take a few seconds to recall a time when you were frightened or anxious. It's likely that your recollections are intense but vague, a jumble of words, pictures, and feelings without clear connection between events. When the sympathetic system is going, your mind thrashes about from one possible danger to another with no reason or rhyme, and, perhaps more significantly, no rhythm. The music of your experience would sound like the jagged, screeching theme from *Psycho.*

Now think back on a time you were calm. I'm not talking about your trip to Hawaii, when you were so relaxed you could barely lift your mai tai. I'm talking about normal, day-to-day calm. Think of engaging in a hobby, be it a sport, reading, gardening, making something, or scrolling through items on eBay. The music of this kind of experience is more rhythmic. Perhaps you even hum to yourself while you're doing it.

Think of calming as restoring rhythm to the music of experience, and at a deep, intuitive level, you will understand how to do it. The techniques I'll teach you are merely variations and elaborations on the theme that's already playing in your parasympathetic nervous system.

Stuck in the Elevator

There really was a panicky woman stuck in an elevator. I know; I was there too, trying to help her. I've calmed frightened people before, but in a professional capacity, which gave me an advantage that you wouldn't have. This time, I was caught by surprise, just as you would have been. Here's what I did, complete with mistakes.

The woman's voice is tight and shrill. "What's happening? What's wrong with the elevator? Why won't it go?" She pulls at her collar, panting. "Omigod, I'm getting claustrophobia. I can't breathe. I've got to get out of here!"

I look around. Nobody else seems to be doing anything to help her. I guess it's up to me.

"It's okay," I say. "The elevator gets stuck like this. There's some sort of loose thing that they can't get to work right. It just takes a few minutes to fix it. That guy's already called for repair, so we just have to wait while they—"

"I can't take this! Can't somebody get the door open?" The woman is almost shrieking now. "I've got to get out of here. I can't breathe."

She begins to cry, and I realize that explaining the mechanics of elevator repair is not going to work. I take a deep breath, and shift mental gears.

"Hey!" I say, loudly enough to get her attention. "It's going to be okay. The elevator gets stuck like this. You're going to be okay. We're all going to be okay.

"Just take a deep breath." I take one to show her how. "Good. Hold it a second. You're going to be okay."

THE FIRST GOAL IN CALMING IS TO RESTORE RHYTHM.   There are many techniques for doing this, some as old as fear itself. All rely on cadence more than verbal content. The best way to learn how to do them unto others is to experience them yourself.

Imagine a deep, slow drum in a Himalayan monastery beating like the heart of the universe.

Now, adjust your breathing to the beat of that drum. Take a deep breath, hold it until the next drumbeat, then actively blow out all the air until the drum sounds once again. Repeat this ten times, and you'll feel yourself becoming more relaxed.

What you're doing is called *meditating*. It's easy when you know how.

Meditation, like berry picking, involves relaxed focus on a repetitive task. This stimulates the parasympathetic system. Hypnosis and biofeedback work pretty much the same way. All of these techniques take advantage of the fact that the parasympathetic nervous system is wired as a feedback loop in which senses, muscles, and brain are all connected. If you control any part of the loop, you influence the whole thing.

If, instead of me, you happen to be the one stuck in the elevator with the panicky person and all you do is repeat the phrase "You're going to be okay" to the rhythm of an imaginary deep, slow drum, she will eventually calm down. Paramedics often use this simple but effective technique with accident victims.

Restoring the rhythm of experience works better if you start loudly and rapidly enough to catch frightened people's attention. Go where they are and bring them to where you want them to be. When consciously used by hypnotists, this technique is called *pacing*. If you're a parent, you've probably done it a thousand times without knowing that it was a sophisticated psychological technique.

Think about how you'd pat a fussy baby to sleep. You begin by patting hard and fast enough to get the child's attention, then gradually shifting to softer and slower, tapping out a lullaby with your fingertips.

Just thinking of it can make you feel relaxed as well. Countless mothers have been found dozing next to their children's beds, having stimulated two parasympathetic systems for the price of one.

Berry patch, Buddhist monastery, your baby's bedroom, or in the face of an emotional explosion, the nonverbal technique is the same. *Give panicky people something pleasant and repetitive to focus on. Start loudly and rapidly enough to attract their attention, then soften and slow. Go where they are, and gently lead them to where you want them to be.*

> *"Okay, blow out all the air," I say as I demonstrate, hissing like an overheated radiator. She follows my lead.*
>
> *"Good. You're going to be okay. Now take another breath." She does.*
>
> *"Good," I say. "Okay, blow it out. Good! You're going to be okay."*
>
> *Another breath.*
>
> *"Okay, good. Now blow it out. Good! You're going to be okay."*

Often, you can restore rhythm by getting panicky people to control their breathing. Sympathetic breathing is usually rapid, shallow panting, which works well for running or fighting but merely fans the flames of fear when people are standing still. Hyperventilation causes all sorts of frightening sensations. Try it yourself. For the next 30 seconds triple your breathing rate and feel the effects of too much oxygen.

Now that you're over being tingly, dizzy, confused, and generally disoriented, imagine piling that kind of weirdness on top of fear, and you have some inkling of what a panic attack is like. If you know how bad panic feels, it may help you understand how eager panicky people are for relief. Often they're very open to suggestions, and are seldom offended by attempts to help them calm down.

As we saw in the first chapter, the best way to burn off excess oxygen is to get people moving. This is difficult in an elevator, but as we'll see in a minute, not totally impossible.

To help people control their breathing, you might say something like:

You're going to be okay. Now take a deep breath. Okay, hold it while I count to five. One, two, three, four, five (start at about half-second intervals, then move up to a full second between numbers). Now, blow all the air out while I count to five again.

Sounds like yoga class, doesn't it? Focusing on breathing as a way of achieving tranquility is not a new technique, but it's still cutting edge even after 10,000 years. Blowing out is the most important part because people who are hyperventilating inhale more often than they exhale.

You won't have do breathing exercises with every explosive person you deal with, but you should *always* pay attention to the rhythm and cadence of breathing as an indicator of general arousal. The more staccato, the more sympathetic activity.

REWARD SMALL STEPS.   In calming, you're trying to lead people out of emotional arousal to a state of tranquility. If you don't reward them every step of the way, they're apt to get lost. Give them an *Okay* or *Good* every time they do what you suggest. One of the bedrock rules of human behavior is: *actions that are rewarded increase in frequency*. Giving all these rewards will feel weird, because we don't normally tell adults when they're doing something right. If you feel like a preschool teacher, you're probably doing it correctly.

> *"Take another breath," I say. "Good. You're going to be okay. Now blow it out." She's still following.*
> *"This time we're going to tense up like this while we take a breath." I demonstrate. "Okay, good. One, two, three, four, five. Now as you blow the air out, let yourself relax."*

INVOLVE THE MUSCLES IF YOU CAN.   When the sympathetic system is going, muscles are tense and ready for action. It helps to get people moving to burn off excess adrenaline. In an elevator, there isn't anyplace to go, but you can still get the panicky woman's muscles involved by having her tense, hold, and relax. Muscles that are involuntarily clenched relax more easily if they are purposely tensed first. If she responds well to the breathing exercise, having her tighten as she inhales and relax as she exhales will help her to calm more quickly.

> *"Don't you understand?" she begins to cry more loudly. "I can't handle this. I've got to get out of here!"*

IF AROUSAL INCREASES, GO BACK.   Getting explosive people to calm down involves a hierarchical sequence of goals. You must accomplish one before the next is even possible. There are, however, no straight lines in human nature. Explosive people may begin to slow down, then speed up again for no apparent reason. *This is inevitable; it does not mean the calming technique isn't working.* All it means is that you have to go back up in the sequence and bring them down again. Remember that you're standing in for the parasympathetic nervous system until it can take over for itself. The system is a feedback loop that continually adjusts itself to current conditions. So must you.

The woman in the elevator may begin to breathe regularly, then go back to gasping and keening. This doesn't mean you've done something wrong. Just go back up to where she is and bring her down again. Crisis workers like police officers and emergency medical technicians do this dance instinctively. When breathing gets rough, they automatically go back a few steps to regain a smooth, repetitious delivery. It makes sense to follow their lead.

Eventually, after a second try, I got the panicky woman to tense and relax her muscles. If it hadn't worked that time, I would have dropped it and just stuck with the breathing.

DISCONNECT THE ALARM.   So far, we've paid attention to rhythm and cadence more than verbal content, because how you say things is critical to the calming process.

What you say is also important. Words are powerful; they are not only vehicles of communication from one person to another, they also convey thoughts from one part of the mind to another. Many of the brain structures involved in emotional explosions are prelinguistic; they evolved before people could talk. Nevertheless, we use words to communicate, and some-times this makes us think that the whole process is considerably more ratio-nal than it really is.

The sympathetic system is one huge neurological and biochemical alarm, but the way it insinuates itself into people's consciousness is subtle. It doesn't shout *"DANGER, WILL ROBINSON."* Instead, it sends out impulses that are translated by the verbal cortex into reasonable sounding words like: *Your chest is tight. That's a symptom of heart attack. You're going to die if you don't get out of here!* The words are mistaken for reality, because reality, and everything else we know, is also made of words inside the head.

Many of the problems in dealing with emotional explosions arise from paying too much attention to the words the sympathetic impulses are translated into, and too little to the impulses themselves. Somehow, you need to get it across to the panicky people that their alarm systems are malfunctioning, warning them of danger where there is none. You can get badly sidetracked by discussing the specific dangers they imagine, because as soon as you've talked them out of one, they think of another. Focus instead on the alarm system itself.

Calming Techniques

Allow me to demonstrate, using you as an example. Would you actually use the techniques I'm describing to calm someone who's having a panic attack?

If you're like most people, you're thinking, *No way; I just couldn't.*

Before I try to convince you that there is a way, think about how you decided that you couldn't do it. I think your sympathetic system said you couldn't, and you believed it.

How did it get through? Did it say the techniques were stupid? Or that you were too stupid to do them correctly? Or that if you messed up you'd make the situation worse? Or did it simply tell you that someone else would do it? Or that you'd never have to calm a panicky person in an elevator because you always take the stairs? Your sympathetic system creates arguments like these to keep you safe inside your comfort zone. Most of the time you just accept them as an objective assessment of reality. This time, I'd like you to see them for what they really are: malfunctions of your own alarm system.

What is the danger in calming a panicky person? The only real, though slight, possibility of physical harm is if nobody does anything. The poor woman might flail about and accidentally bump into someone. Why then is your alarm system warning you against even thinking about using the techniques I've described?

Let's look at the chapter thus far through the eyes of your sympathetic nervous system. Bear in mind that the system evolved for the sole purpose of protecting you from danger. Since the system evolved, the notion of *you* has expanded from your body to everything contained in your image of yourself, and *danger* has expanded from physical damage to anything that conflicts with how you see yourself. Your sympathetic system makes no distinction between threats to your body and threats to your dignity. It sends the same warning signals for wild beasts and potential embarrassment. The signals come up through the verbal parts of your brain, and are translated into whatever words will convince you to stay away.

Right now, your sympathetic system, in a misguided attempt to protect you, is whispering half-truths and giving you little injections of adrenaline to prevent you from even *imagining* doing something unfamiliar.

The warning system operates smoothly, just below your awareness. Most of the time, you don't even feel afraid. You simply avoid situations without even asking yourself whether there's any real danger. Once you begin paying closer attention to what your sympathetic system is saying, however, it makes less sense. You can argue with it, and since you're much smarter, you can prevail. This sums up the whole theory behind psychotherapy. The awareness is *insight*, and the arguing and eventually trying out of new, formerly frightening actions is *working through*.

Take a minute to read back over the techniques I've written about. They aren't difficult. You've probably used all of them in other contexts without a second thought. Yet, if you think about doing them in an unfamiliar situation, you begin to imagine all sorts of possible disasters. You may even feel a few jolts of adrenaline. Now, instead of just turning away as the sympathetic system wants you to do, listen more closely to what it's telling you. Aren't the dangers a bit farfetched?

When you try these techniques in the real world, you can bet that your alarm system will be making even more mental noise, pumping out chemicals and bellowing that you'll make a fool of yourself or hurt somebody else if you try something you've never done before. When that happens, do the same thing you're doing now. Listen closely and think about what you're hearing. Who is saying what to whom, and for what purpose? While you're doing that, take a deep breath and hold it while you count to five. You might even try humming.

Now that you understand how the sympathetic system distorts reality, you're ready to go back to the elevator and do a little psychotherapy yourself. Relax; the theory is the only complicated part. What you actually do is simple.

Disconnect the alarm by sending contradictory messages. The panicky woman's sympathetic system is telling her she's in danger, and you need to tell her she isn't. "It will be okay, the elevator gets stuck like this sometimes." might be a good place to start, but only after you've got her breathing under control. The biggest mistake you can make is to jump into explanations when people are too agitated to understand them. I did it; you probably will too. If you do, just go back to basics.

Tell her that she's safe, not that she shouldn't be afraid. The idea is to reassure, not argue. Give her new, more accurate information on which to base her emotional response. "Elevators get jammed, and repair people come and fix them. It happens all the time. It may take a few minutes, but they'll get it moving." Her sympathetic system has feelings, but no hard facts to back up its contention of danger. If you supply new information, it may help to stimulate the panicky woman's higher brain centers to override the sympathetic alarms.

Don't lecture. The goal is not to reason her out of being unreasonable. You're simply adding a little more information to the rhythmic, repetitive message you're already sending. Every time her internal alarm bellows, give her something more solid and reassuring to think about. Tell her about positive things that will happen; don't add images of danger by saying what won't happen. Avoid comments like: "The elevator isn't going to fall, and even if it does, it probably won't kill all of us, just break a few bones." You get the idea.

To disconnect the alarm, slowly and steadily add new, more reassuring information and keep repeating until you notice her becoming less tense. Slower breathing and less fidgeting mean you're having a positive effect.

> *The panicky woman and I take a few more deep breaths together.*
> *I reassure her that she's safe and the elevator is being fixed.*
>   *"You're having a panic attack," I say. "Your body is so full*
> *of adrenaline that it's hard to think straight, that's why you need*
> *to take the deep breaths to slow your mind down enough to start*
> *feeling better."*
>   *She nods slightly.*
>   *"Good," I say. "Now take a deep breath and hold it while*
> *I count to five."*

CREATE A VERBAL REPRESENTATION OF WHAT'S HAPPENING.   Ambiguity is the most terrifying experience of all. Imagine what it's like for the panicky woman, her alarm system clanging away, adrenaline coursing through her veins, and not knowing what will kill her first—the elevator falling or her heart blowing itself out. The more agitated she becomes, the further her perceptions of her situation diverge from objective reality. You need to turn this process around by creating a new, more realistic view of what's going on inside her. Again, the theory is more complicated than the practice. Tell her she's having a panic attack.

The words you choose are crucial. As we saw in the last chapter, what you say may inadvertently communicate disbelief in the validity of her experience. There is a world of difference between "You're having a panic attack" and "You're *just* having a panic attack." Nobody who's ever had a panic attack would put that *just* in there. Your words need to display empathy with her terror even when you know there's nothing real to fear.

Try to reframe her experience in a way that will allow her to step outside of it and view it objectively. Her own explanation—that she's having a claustrophobic attack—doesn't accomplish this goal because it isn't actually a representation of her internal state. Generally, when people say they have a phobia, they're asking for external accommodation rather than trying to grapple with what's going on inside themselves. *I'm feeling claustrophobic* means *Let me out of here.*

Reframing allows her to begin *thinking* about the experience of panic rather than just *experiencing* it. You want her to recognize that she's having a panic attack, which is a normal physical response to danger that occurs in a situation that isn't really dangerous. You might say something like I did: "You're having a panic attack. Your body is so full of adrenaline that it's hard to think straight. Taking deep breaths will slow your mind down enough so you'll start feeling better." Blaming adrenaline is often a good tactic because people know that its effects are temporary. Also, when you're trying to induce psychological movement, it's always more effective to talk about where you want people to go rather than where they're coming from. *More calm* is always better than *less afraid.* The sympathetic system only knows from running away; the parasympathetic at least has a destination.

Panic happens in an unendurable, interminable, and inescapable present. You need to remind panicky people that what they're going through has the dimensions of normal experience. That is: It happens with a certain frequency, it lasts a certain length of time, and then it abates. Escape comes from living through it rather than running away. To stimulate this line of thought, ask questions like: Have you ever had an attack like this before? How long did it last? What helped you feel better? You want to set up the expectation that things will get better soon if she just hangs in there.

> "I got locked in a closet when I was a little girl. It was dark and I couldn't get out." The woman's breathing is becoming ragged. "I screamed and screamed, but nobody came. I couldn't breathe. I thought I'd—"
>
> "Okay, take a deep breath," I say once more. "Good. Hold it while I count to five."

INTERRUPT ESCALATIONS. People in the midst of an emotional explosion do not get better by getting things off their chest. Talking about how bad they feel or where their fear comes from only makes them feel worse. Don't be afraid to interrupt. It doesn't help to stand by politely letting people work themselves up when you're trying to calm them down. This rule applies even to angry people, but in that case it must be done carefully. You'll learn how in the section on anger.

Once you begin trying to calm people, you must at least attempt to keep control of the conversation. Occasionally, frightened people will begin asking questions, expecting you to provide answers. Don't get started down this track, because you'll always end up at an awkward point at which you have to lie, admit you don't know, or even acknowledge that people do get squished in falling elevators. Sidestep questions as best you can. Just stick with the dull old repetitions of the same reassuring things you've been saying.

Psychologists are fond of writing about steps and stages as if human experience moved in a straight line. Real life, rather than an orderly progression through stages, is more like a game of Twister, an awkward attempt to maintain balance while stretched between contradictory thoughts, feelings, and beliefs. Nobody is ever in only one psychological place at any given time. Everything is always happening at once.

The steps in calming are sequential—you have to do the earlier ones before the later ones are possible—but that doesn't mean they occur in any kind of orderly sequence. Rather than a journey from here to there, think of them as a dance that involves a good deal of backtracking and waltzing around as you move from one psychological place to another. If you lead, explosive people will follow, even if you feel that you're both dancing in the dark.

IF PEOPLE HARDLY NOTICE, IT MEANS YOU DID IT RIGHT. When you do a good job of calming people down, they think they did it themselves. They did. You only showed them how. Don't expect gratitude, even when the panicky person is someone you know well. Especially then. Beware of explosive people bearing gifts. It may be flattering, but it benefits no one if they require half an hour of your undivided attention every time they need to calm down.

As you can see, calming frightened people is not rocket science. It is, however, an art that demands a bit of timing and subtlety. It's easy to think too much about *what* to say, and too little about *how* to say it, *when*, and *why*. Forget about memorizing phrases. If you concentrate on the music, the words will take care of themselves.

Good.

You're going to be okay.

Chapter 4

Explosions into Fear

Panic Disorder, Phobia, and
Post-Traumatic Stress Disorder

SOME EXPLOSIVE PEOPLE ARE STRANGERS; you can calm them down and walk away. Others you see every day as friends, coworkers, and family. Dealing effectively with these fearful, sad, and angry people will require more than occasional soothing. They'll need your love and support, of course, but more than that, they'll need your wisdom. You'll have to understand their disorders well enough to know what helps them to get better and what makes them worse, even when they don't. Especially then.

Panic disorder, phobia, post-traumatic stress disorder (PTSD), and anxiety disorder are all manifestations of the same physiological process—the fight or flight response, mediated by the sympathetic nervous system. They are eminently treatable, but real recovery requires a stunning feat of mind over matter: the courage to face fear when every nerve and sinew is shouting *Run away!*

The recovering fearful must follow a difficult, and sometimes treacherous, road. They will need you to bolster their courage along the way, and sometimes to gently turn them around and point them in the right direction. If you have to do that, I hope this book will bolster *your* courage.

Fear disorders improve with medication, psychotherapy, and a little help from friends and family, but as with the calming sequence described in the last chapter, the improvements are sequential. One must be achieved before the next is even possible.

The first step is understanding the disorders.

Panic Disorder

According to the fourth revision of the *Diagnostic and Statistical Manual* of the American Psychiatric Association (DSM-IV)*, panic disorder consists of:

1. Recurrent unexpected panic attacks
2. At least one of the attacks has been followed by one month (or more) of one (or more) of the following:
   a. persistent concern about having additional attacks
   b. worry about the implications of the attack or its consequences (e.g., losing control, having a heart attack, "going crazy")
   c. a significant change in behavior related to the attacks

A panic attack is the quintessential explosion into fear. If you've never had one, it will be difficult to conceive of anything so intense. I always think of Carol Burnett's futile attempt to explain childbirth to men: "Imagine taking your lower lip and pulling it over your head."

Some things are simply beyond understanding unless you've experienced them yourself. Suffice to say that a full-blown panic attack is far beyond anything most people would interpret as fear; it feels like certain annihilation.

Let's look at Jane again, whom you'll remember from her attack at the mall and the incipient explosion in her kitchen:

Jane had her first panic attack shortly after her son was born. She awoke from troubled dreams to discover that a strange disease had paralyzed her chest. The muscles were so tight that she could not draw a breath. She was certain she was going to suffocate. In the darkness, she reached out for her husband, hoping to touch him one last time before she died.

Panic attacks aren't fatal, but they probably feel worse than dying. Some people may prefer death. There is a good deal of clinical speculation about the relationship of panic disorder and suicide, but little definitive research because it's so difficult to accurately diagnose people after the act of suicide. What did it, panic or depression? Or maybe they worked together. After the fact, there's no way of saying.

Suicide or not, panic disorder is nothing to mess around with. The good news is that people in treatment, whether for panic or depression, are far less likely to harm themselves. People in treatment who have supportive friends and family are safest of all.

A common response to panic is to avoid any place or situation in which an attack might occur, or help might not be available. As I mentioned in an earlier chapter, agoraphobia is thought by most to mean fear of open spaces. But there's more to it than that. About a third of the people who have panic disorder try to protect themselves by severely narrowing the boundaries of their lives. Many don't go out in crowds, or cross bridges, stand in lines, or use public transportation.

To recover from panic disorder, people need to stop trying to protect themselves. Running only makes things worse. The way to get rid of fear is to embrace it. This is easy for me to say, but, as you can imagine, hard for them to do. They will need help—from their doctors, therapists, and from you.

The most important thing you need to know is that no matter how devastating they are, fear disorders are a hang-up, not a handicap. Accommodating them by standing between the people who have them and what they fear does not help. What does help is the gut-level understanding that though the pain may be real, the danger is not, and letting that central insight determine actions. Your job is to abet and applaud the acts of courage that this process entails.

Phobia

According to DSM- IV, phobia is:

1. Marked and persistent fear that is excessive or unreasonable, cued by the presence or anticipation of a specific object or situation (e.g., flying, heights, animals, receiving an injection, seeing blood).

2. Exposure to the phobic stimulus almost invariably provokes an immediate anxiety response, which may take the form of a situationally bound or situationally predisposed panic attack.
3. The person recognizes that the fear is excessive or unreasonable. The phobic situation(s) is avoided or else is endured with intense anxiety or distress.
4. The avoidance, anxious anticipation, or distress in the feared situation(s) interferes significantly with the person's normal routine, occupational (or academic) functioning, or social activities or relationships, or there is marked distress about having the phobia.

Phobia is essentially a panic attack in response to some identifiable thing, usually something relatively harmless.

Spiders, even the eency-weency kind, cause Neil to go into cardiac arrest. Well, that's what it feels like anyway. His heart shudders, he breaks out in a cold sweat, and he literally shakes with fear. Just a cobweb hanging from the ceiling makes him so uncomfortable he has to leave the room. Neil isn't doing it for attention. He's an engineer, not given to excesses of emotion. When he has one of his outbursts around spiders, it's hard to say which is worse for him, the fear or the embarrassment.

Neil uses his logical mind to figure out all the places where he might encounter spiders. Basements, unpaved outdoor spaces, and rooms that are less than antiseptically clean. He won't go near any of them. There are very few places he will go.

Even though he hardly ever sees one, spiders have Neil trapped in a web of terror.

Most phobias involve violent fear reactions to things that by some stretch of the imagination can be dangerous, but usually aren't. Spiders, snakes, dogs, cats, blood, storms, heights, or bodily functions like choking and vomiting are most common. Few people are phobic of flowers or bunnies. Phobias usually develop in childhood, and almost never involve any actual experience of harm by the feared object. Phobias may be the result of some long outdated programs in the brain designed to encourage our prehuman ancestors to recognize and avoid dangers. Reactions resembling phobias are almost universal in animals.

Blood phobias tend to run in families and may lead to fainting rather than panic. Phobias of doing things—like driving, crossing bridges, and being in crowds or tightly enclosed spaces—tend to develop in the early 20s and are probably the result of panic disorder rather than an ingrained, primordial fear.

Real phobias involve full-blown panic responses; the name is often incorrectly applied to mild to moderate anxiety associated with a specific object or situation. You've probably seen those unintentionally humorous lists of Greek names for every conceivable phobia. They are a relic of the heyday of psychoanalysis, when irrational fears of any sort were considered symbols of the unconscious processes that lay at the root of neuroses.

Unlike people with panic disorder, phobic people don't wonder what's wrong with them; they know they're afraid, but because they can avoid the things they're afraid of, they generally have few attacks. Avoidance, not panic, becomes their biggest problem. Treatment involves helping them face what they fear in small increments. Your job is to support that goal, even when it's easier and less stressful to just let them stay away. A recent study suggests that almost half the families of phobic people rearrange their lives in large and small ways to accommodate the phobia as if it were a handicap rather than a hang-up.

Neil's wife had given up on trying to get him to do anything out-doors where there were overhanging trees or bushes that covered the ground. Just to get him to go on a walk in the park, she'd have to go up ahead under trees and sweep the air with her hand lest he bump into a web. It was a lot of work, but she was willing to do it. What she couldn't endure was the terrified look on his face. It made her feel selfish for asking him to do something that caused him so much pain.

If there is a phobic person in your life, you probably know how hard it is to tell the difference between helping and hurting. Even though you know they should face their fears, pushing them can seem cruel. The secret is to make the steps smaller and more manageable. Before actually *doing* something scary like walking in the park, phobic people can rehearse in their minds until they can at least *imagine* the action without fear. In treatment, Neil's wife learned that seeing the fearful look on his face didn't mean she was being cruel, only that she was asking him to take too big a step all at once.

Post-Traumatic Stress Disorder

According to the DSM-IV, post-traumatic stress disorder (PTSD)is diagnosed when:

1. The person has been exposed to a traumatic event in which both of the following were present:
    a. The person experienced, witnessed, or was confronted with an event or events that involved actual or threatened death or serious injury, or a threat to the physical integrity of self or others.
    b. The person's response involved intense fear, helplessness, or horror.
2. The traumatic event is persistently reexperienced in one (or more) of the following ways:
    a. Recurrent and intrusive distressing recollections of the event, including images, thoughts, or perceptions.
    b. Recurrent distressing dreams of the event.
    c. Acting or feeling as if the traumatic event were recurring (includes a sense of reliving the experience, illusions, hallucinations, and dissociative flashback episodes, including those that occur on awakening or when intoxicated).
    d. Intense psychological distress at exposure to internal or external cues that symbolize or resemble an aspect of the traumatic event.
    e. Physiological reactivity on exposure to internal or external cues that symbolize or resemble an aspect of the traumatic event.
3. Persistent avoidance of stimuli associated with the trauma and numbing of general responsiveness (not present before the trauma), as indicated by three (or more) of the following:
    a. Efforts to avoid thoughts, feelings, or conversations associated with the trauma.

b. Efforts to avoid activities, places, or people that arouse recollections of the trauma.

c. Inability to recall an important aspect of the trauma.

d. Markedly diminished interest or participation in significant activities.

e. Feeling of detachment or estrangement from others.

f. Restricted range of affect (e.g., unable to have loving feelings).

g. Sense of a foreshortened future (e.g., does not expect to have a career, marriage, children, or a normal life span).

4. Persistent symptoms of increased arousal (not present before the trauma), as indicated by two (or more) of the following:

a. Difficulty falling or staying asleep.

b. Irritability or outbursts of anger.

c. Difficulty concentrating.

d. Hypervigilance.

e. Exaggerated startle response.

In post-traumatic stress disorder, the fight or flight response is switched on in reaction to a real threat to the life or the psyche, and doesn't switch off. A part of the person's mind stays stuck in crisis mode.

Trish became a different person after a pickup truck ran a red light and smashed into her car. Nothing in her body got broken, thank God, but something cracked in her mind. She's too frightened to drive; even the sound of traffic makes her jumpy. During the day she feels numb and distant. At night she dreams that the pickup is coming at her but she just can't move herself out of the way. She wakes up screaming.

Awake and asleep, people with PTSD are perpetually on the alert for danger. They tend to be on edge all the time, easily frightened or irritated. Their physical startle responses are far more intense than normal. They avoid situations that remind them of the dangerous event. They tend to feel worn out and numb. Much of their energy is used up in the attempt to keep themselves safe, though the danger that stalks them is only in their past.

So far, this description could, to a greater or lesser extent, apply to anybody who has been through a frightening situation. To warrant a diagnosis of PTSD, however, the dangerous event must involve an actual threat to life or physical integrity—blows to the ego, no matter how painful, do not count. And that threatening event is persistently reexperienced in dreams, fantasies, and physical responses. This does not mean just thinking about the situation and getting upset. Persistent reexperiencing means forgetting where you are and believing you're back there in the literal rather than metaphoric sense. There is no as if about it.

I am not usually doctrinaire about diagnostic criteria, but in the case of PTSD, I am an absolute purist. In 30 years as a therapist, I have seen the initial identification of this disorder in Vietnam war veterans, and its expansion to include people with a history of sexual abuse—remembered or not—the verbally battered, the sexually harassed, and anybody else who has been discriminated against on the basis of anything at any time in their lives. Delayed PTSD can occur years after the dangerous event. It's not that these injured people don't have problems, it's just that diagnosing these problems as PTSD may do them more harm than good.

I believe in helping people with mental disorders to get better. I also believe in helping the downtrodden to gain social, political, and economic power. I do not believe that mental health treatment can accomplish the second goal without sacrificing the first. The overdiagnosing of PTSD is a well-meaning attempt to do the impossible: to help patients both to get well and get back at the people who caused them to be sick.

PTSD is the only mental disorder, other than those resulting from blows to the head, that is by definition caused by somebody else. It is compensable in a court of law, and can be considered a handicap to be accommodated under the Americans with Disabilities Act.

PTSD is also a fear disorder that accommodation makes worse. To recover, people need to see their symptoms as hang-ups to be overcome, rather than handicaps to be accommodated or, worse yet, scores to be settled.

The issue is even more complicated because a necessary step in the treatment of PTSD, especially the delayed type, is recognizing that the symptoms are the result of trauma rather than personal choice. To make matters more confusing, recent research suggests that repeated, unacknowledged abuse actually does damage the brain. In these studies, abuse is narrowly defined as incest, beatings, and physical torture. Outside the laboratory, the definition of abuse has been widened to include pretty much anything that outrages someone in an on-line support group.

Treating PTSD is easier than coming up with an objective definition of abuse. *Anything* is easier than that. By far the most common cases of PTSD relate to recent dangerous incidents like accidents or injuries. The delayed kind is extremely rare.

As with all fear disorders, therapy for PTSD involves helping people approach what they fear and situations that remind them of what they fear. People need to talk about their painful experiences until they hurt less. As you can imagine, some kinds of talk make them hurt more. Your job will be to listen to the talk that helps and do your best to keep from reinforcing the kind that hurts.

The Physiology of Fear

The physical component of all fear disorders is, of course, the fight or flight response mediated by the sympathetic nervous system. The response may start in the amygdala or perhaps in the *basal ganglia*, but since it jumps from one area of the brain to another at warp speed, the Heisenberg uncertainty principle applies. If you pay too much attention to where it starts, you may not notice where it's going and what it's doing.

Though there is no definitive test, it's likely that people who develop fear disorders have an abnormally strong fight or flight response. They're called *autonomic hyper-responders*. The word "autonomic" in this case means "sympathetic." It may be that these people's genetic makeup is different, causing a more intense reaction. We're not talking about a few squirts of adrenaline here, but in some cases a biochemical torrent that affects every part of the body.

An important element in the treatment of all fear disorders is understanding the physiology of fear well enough to know that what it feels like is not necessarily what it is.

Panic, explosion into overwhelming fear. It is unbelievable to people who have panic attacks that their very real agony could be caused by something so insubstantial as fear. They often think they have a serious physical disease. They may, but it's usually not the one they believe they have.

You can't blame them for the mistake. Their bodies tell them they're about to die, or are at least very sick. The symptoms of panic attacks are physical. Sweating, tingling, faintness, dizziness, nausea, chest pain, palpitations, tachycardia, shortness of breath, and severe gastrointestinal distress are all common. Panic can create the classic danger signs of stroke, heart attack, pneumonia, and perhaps even dengue fever. Relatives rush the panic-stricken to doctors, who order tests, take vital signs, and happily announce that they are all negative.

> "Well, Jane," the doctor says as he looks through pages of printouts. "The tests show that you're a perfectly healthy young woman. I think the breathing problems and the dizziness are caused by anxiety. What you have is panic disorder."
>
> "You mean all this is in my head?"
>
> "No, not at all. You see, the anxiety is what's causing you to think … "
>
> The doctor goes on, but Jane isn't listening. She's shocked by the implications of what she thinks she heard: He thinks I'm making it up.

The initial diagnosis of panic disorder is usually made by ruling out anything more dangerous. Panicky patients are more apt to react with suspicion than rejoicing. As they see it, the diagnostic process starts with serious medical tests and ends with being taken less than seriously. They wonder if the real reason the doctor is blaming their minds is that he can't figure out what's wrong with their bodies. Many people with panic disorder pursue a physical diagnosis as if it were the Holy Grail. They shop for doctors who will speak the magic words: You're really sick, but I can cure you. Unfortunately, they find all too many.

For anyone with panic disorder, accepting the notion that their illness is mental as well as physical requires a paradigm shift, a change in perception that is rarely achieved without painful soul-searching. Yet, the success of the entire course of treatment depends upon this single insight. After initial calming and ruling out physical demise, the next step is convincing people with fear disorders that their suffering is caused by the physical correlates of the fear response rather than fatal illness. For that, you need a really good explanation. People like Jane must understand clearly how short circuits in their heads lead to pains in their chests. A busy doctor may have sketched out the process, but it will likely fall to you to elaborate. And repeat. A couple of hundred times should do it.

You must of course believe in the diagnosis yourself. That isn't always easy. Regardless of what you know, mental disease just doesn't feel as real as physical disease. It can't kill you (at least directly), but an undiagnosed physical illness can. You have to trust that the doctor has sufficient acumen to rule out other possibilities. It may be hard to decide if all you have is a frightened person's memory of what was said. If appropriate, it will be helpful to talk to the doctor yourself, go in with the patient, or at least write out a list of questions. Nothing beats an explanation from the person who has actually done the workup.

Short of that, you'll have to understand some basic physiological processes, and improvise.

And, as we have previously stated, the fight or flight response creates instantaneous physical changes to make the body ready to fight back or run away. Heart and lungs rev up to redline. Vascular floodgates slam shut in some places and open wide in others. Blood, supercharged with hormones, is shunted from everywhere else to the muscles. Noncritical functions like digestion are switched off.

As quickly as you can say *psychosomatic*, the body shifts from a resting state to one of readiness for actions that more than likely won't occur. Imagine having your gas pedal to the metal and stomping on the brakes at the same time. It's got to hurt. The sensations in a panic attack are not imaginary; everything the person feels is real, in that it is caused by something that's actually happening in the body. What is imaginary is the belief that these sensations herald impending doom.

Here are some of the more common symptoms, and plausible explanations for why they occur:

SENSATIONS OF HEAT OR COLD.　Heat comes from metabolism, burning food for energy. Blood rushes into the deep muscles, giving them lots of fuel and an assortment of performance-enhancing drugs. The muscles burn up this mixture like an SUV on high-test. They heat up and swell, often causing sweating and flushing. Meanwhile, blood-starved extremities feel cold, numb, and tingly, just as they do when they've been in one position too long and are going to sleep.

Many of the strangest feelings associated with panic attacks have to do with irregularities in breathing and related changes in blood chemistry. A number of studies have shown that people with panic disorder tend to both hyperventilate and hold their breath. The structures in their brain stems that protect against suffocation by monitoring the carbon dioxide level of the blood may be overly sensitive, causing extreme corrections in their breathing rate.

As you learned in the last chapter when you tried it yourself, too much breathing causes all sorts of weird sensations. When you hyperventilate, it decreases the carbon dioxide level in the blood, which raises alkalinity, which increases the excitability of peripheral nerve endings, causing tingling around the mouth, fingers, and toes. The high alkalinity also decreases blood flow to the brain, which can make you feel dizzy and strangely separate from your body.

SHORTNESS OF BREATH. The problem here is not too little oxygen, but too much carbon dioxide. Rapid, shallow breathing and tension in the chest muscles makes it easy to get air in but hard to get it out. This makes the breath-holding and hyperventilating problem worse. Suffocation sensors in the brain stem detect too much carbon dioxide and misread it as a need for oxygen. This causes more hyperventilation, which escalates the cycle further.

A common home remedy for hyperventilation used to be having a person breathe into a paper bag to increase blood carbon dioxide level. Don't try this at home, because it makes the situation worse. Exercise works far better to regulate breathing.

MUSCULOSKELETAL PAIN. Sudden tightening of the muscles hurts, especially if you aren't using them to defend yourself or escape. By itself, muscle tightening can cause excruciating headaches or backaches, or can intensify old injuries, but that's not the half of it. Think of the physics involved—the body is expanding from the inside, but squeezing down into a cringe outside. Blood-engorged muscles take up more space, which can pinch nerves, scrunch organs, and cut off circulation, all of which can cause numbness or *referred* pain. This is pain felt at a different location than the actual blockage. A pinched nerve in the shoulders may cause pain in the chest. Everything in the body is connected to everything else.

DIZZINESS AND FAINTNESS. The change from the resting state to action occurs so fast it can make your head spin. Actually, it's the decreased blood flow to the brain caused by the increased alkalinity brought about by hyperventilation that makes people dizzy, and it causes the weird sensations of faintness and being separate from the body. Changes in blood flow and pressure may also affect the delicate *vestibular system*, the mechanisms in the inner ear and the brain that tell you which end is up.

Muscular tension, especially in the neck, can pull the body off balance and further impair blood flow to the brain. Vision may dim at the edges, leading people to think they're blacking out. Actual fainting is almost nonexistent, except in the case of blood phobia.

CARDIAC IRREGULARITIES.　The heart and lungs have to speed up to get all the fuel-laden blood where it needs to go. Imagine stomping on the gas pedal of your car. If everything is in tune, the change in acceleration will be smooth. If anything is even slightly out of adjustment, there will be bumps and bubbles. Unless you're in superb physical condition, the rapid shift of heart rate and blood volume will be quite noticeable. As the heart beats out erratic rhythms, the muscles in the chest and diaphragm are pulled tight as drums, which creates the percussive effect known as *palpitation*.

GASTROINTESTINAL DISTRESS.　There's no way to put this delicately. When the digestive tract shuts down rapidly, it tries to dump whatever it's carrying from whichever end is closest. Socialization and well-developed sphincters usually prevent indignity, but not without considerable discomfort. People in panic can generate prodigious amounts of gas. They sometimes think they'll throw up or foul their pants, but they almost never do.

Panic Attacks Are Real

There is no question that panic attacks are real, rather than imaginary. Misfiring of the sympathetic nervous system causes actual physical changes that feel terrible, but are not terribly dangerous. The dire implications are the imaginary part. *People with panic disorder must understand that, regardless of how badly they feel, they are not going to die, faint, throw up, go crazy, foul their pants, or otherwise make fools of themselves.* Despite the internal pyrotechnics, panic attacks are almost invisible to the naked eye. You see people having them every day, and never notice.

To help people with any fear disorder, you must both acknowledge that their *symptoms are real* and reassure them that the *danger is all in their heads*. This must be done with almost preternatural sensitivity.

In the middle of a movie, Jane begins to gasp. "I've got to get out of here, I can't breathe."

Her husband gives her hand a squeeze. "It's okay, honey, it's just that hyperventilation again. Let's go out to the lobby and see if we can get it under control." In the lobby, he begins to help Jane through the calming sequence, focusing on her breathing. "It's like the doctor said, honey. You're going to be okay. You're getting plenty of air coming in, but you're not breathing out. Hold your breath a second. That's good. Now blow it all the way out."

Jane's husband acknowledges her symptoms by taking them seriously. He doesn't ignore her or start huffing and puffing himself. He tries to help Jane calm her breathing and return to her activity as quickly as possible. With help, she has been able to do this in other situations.

Doing this sort of thing in real life will not be easy. Psychological disorders are never simple or straightforward.. Symptoms may vary from one panic attack to another. It may be up to you to do a field diagnosis.

Jane clutches her stomach. "Ow!" she gasps. "It's not the breathing. I've got this terrible pain. I think I'm going to faint."

People with panic disorder can also get appendicitis, just as can happen to anyone else.

There will be times that, like Jane's husband, you'll be in a quandary as to whether to continue with the calming sequence or rush the person to the emergency room. If the person has been diagnosed as having panic disorder, and, unless the problem involves audible wheezing, sudden numbness or paralysis, or chest pain in someone who has never experienced it before as a symptom of panic, five minutes won't make much of a difference. Continue the calming sequence and hope for the best.

"Honey, I know it hurts, but panic attacks can cause really bad pains in the stomach too. Let's try to get your breathing under control and see if it helps."

Gastrointestinal cramping takes a while to subside, but if it doesn't get worse, you're probably on the right track. If you have any doubt as to the danger of a symptom, let a doctor decide. If the person has had several different symptom patterns diagnosed as panic, consider delaying a call to the doctor, and instead proceed with the calming, explaining, and reassuring. It helps to have agreed on a panic plan in advance, so both of you know what to expect.

Phobic Explosions into Flight

Everything I've said about panic disorder applies also to phobia. Fear is fear, whether or not you know what you're afraid of. Phobic people rarely have panic attacks, unless they are surprised by their feared object or they find themselves in a situation that doesn't allow escape. In those cases, the calming sequence and explaining how physical symptoms are the result of fear may be helpful.

Most of the time phobic people avoid explosions into fear by staying away or running away. You won't be able to stop a phobic person from running, nor should you try. Your goal should be to try and keep them from running so far that they never have to encounter anything frightening. The process of *generalization* is the most insidious enemy in the fight against fear because frightened people tend to avoid not only what they fear, but anything that reminds them of what they fear—and then anything that reminds them of what reminds them. To help phobics, we must teach them to recognize gradations of fear, encourage them to run only to the place where they can just barely tolerate the internal sensations, then calm them down and help them to move closer. The process is called *desensitization*, and we'll discuss it more fully in the next chapter.

PTSD, Explosions into Numbness and Nightmares

People with PTSD are on the alert 24–7, even in their sleep. Day and night, they are stalked by graphic, real-time, mind-bending, gut-wrenching reenactments of the most traumatic moments of their lives. No wonder they feel depleted and numb!

There is pretty good evidence that PTSD is a disorder of memory. Psychological trauma affects the physiological processes through which the brain stores information.

Memory is a devilishly complex operation, involving areas all over the brain. Rather than listing the theories about how memory works, let me direct your attention to its final product.

Remember what you did yesterday. Unless yesterday was particularly emotional, your memory is an orderly sequence of words, pictures, and sensations that tell you the ongoing story of your life. You may remember getting up out of a warm bed into a cold room, looking out the window to see if it was raining, then walking toward the shower, and so forth. If you pay close attention, you'll notice that ordinary days are stored mostly as words, with a few pictures and sensations thrown in for spice, like photos in a newspaper article. By and large, ordinary memories are a linguistic experience.

Now, remember the most stressful, annoying, or frightening thing that happened last week. You'll notice that emotional events are stored differently than the mundane stuff: less words and more pictures. *The New York Times* of daily existence suddenly becomes the *National Enquirer*, complete with sensational though not completely objective illustrations and conclusions.

Now, think back to a similar stressor that happened at least two years ago. More like *Reader's Digest,* isn't it?

Normal memories are digested by the brain, turned into concise, orderly stories, and filed away according to person, place, and time. Emotional events still stand out, but not in the way they did when they were current events. This is the normal way memories are processed.

The experiences that cause PTSD are like electrical surges that blow circuits in the hippocampus. The connection with higher brain centers goes out; language and reasoning are disconnected. There are no words to explain the experience, and no sense of person, place, or time. All that's stored are raw, unconnected video clips that buzz and crackle with jolts of live emotion. The stuff of nightmares.

The squeal of brakes changes Trish's world. One minute she's pretty much normal, but the moment she hears that sound, even from a distance, she's back there at the instant of impact. She sees the pickup coming at her, the driver mouthing words. She feels a rush of adrenaline, and is absolutely certain that she's going to die. The seat belt grasps her as the truck hits. More adrenaline. Burning coffee from her travel mug sprays every-

where. Classical music is playing, and she can't catch her breath.

The brain demands meaning in order to process memories and file them away. Traumatic memories get stuck at the edge of consciousness until the brain can figure out where to put them. Meanwhile, almost anything can cause them to replay. The sound of brakes, the smell of spilled coffee, or the embrace of a seat belt can turn a car crash into intense and immediate reality. When these nightmares happen in the daytime, they're called *flashbacks*.

People with PTSD are haunted by ghosts of memories too terrifying to be laid to rest in words. Specters stand between traumatized people and everyday reality, turning everything cold and sinister. Is it any wonder that people with PTSD do whatever they can to make themselves numb? Many resort to drugs, alcohol, or other addictions. Some learn to learn to hypnotize themselves into dissociation.

Hypnosis is nothing more than paying close attention to one thing to keep from paying attention to another. A very common way that people with PTSD do this is by getting involved with small irritations.

Trish knows she's being too crabby, but she can't stop herself. People just don't pay attention to what they're doing. Leaving the lights on costs a fortune, but the kids could care less. They don't pay the bills. And look at the mud on the carpet! She marches the kids down to clean it up. Her husband suggests that she's being a bit overbearing. Trish hits the roof.

Exorbitant bills, mud on the carpet, and tiny slights by loved ones become huge to people with PTSD. If you're fighting, at least you don't have to think.

Treatment involves calming the person down enough to approach the traumatic memory and make sense of it so it can be stored. Nonnumbing medications may help, but words are the only cure. Your job is to listen.

People in the midst of nightmares usually believe they're completely alone with their fear. The distance and irritability of people with PTSD often turns this belief into a reality. Your other job is to be there when the going gets tough and reassure them that they are safe and loved.

Medications for Fear

It would seem that if we had a drug that could get rid of the symptoms of sympathetic arousal—panic, pain, dizziness, tense muscles, flooding adrenaline, hammering heart, and ragged breathing—we'd be rid of fear disorders for good. Many would agree, especially some of the people who have them. And drug companies.

Psychiatric medications make people feel better. In some cases the effect is nothing short of miraculous. But as I suggested in Chapter 2, *feeling better* does not necessarily mean *cured*. Explosive people have to feel well enough to do better, but if they feel too good, there's no motivation left to do anything differently. It's a dilemma that must be resolved through careful consideration of all the variables. To consider the role of medications in fear disorders, you'll need a basic grasp of the neurophysiology involved.

The Neurophysiology of Fear

The brain is made of nerve cells, which consist of a cell body with long extensions called *axons* that divide at their tips into terminal fibers. These are the parts that send impulses. The cell body also has rootlike receptive structures, called *dendrites*. Terminal axon fibers and dendrites of many nerve cells overlap in areas called the *synapses*. To make matters more complicated, synapses can be axon to axon or axon to cell body as well.

The firing of nerve cells is a change in the polarity of chemical ions on the inside and outside of the cell that yields a tiny electrical current. That current is propagated from one cell to another by dumping minuscule amounts of chemicals called *transmitter substances* into the synapse. If there is enough of the chemical in the synaptic area, the firing of one cell will cause others to fire.

There are about 100 known transmitter substances (also called *neurotransmitters*), and more are being discovered almost daily. The most famous is serotonin, which we've previously mentioned, as well as norepinephrine. Others you may hear about include GABA and *dopamine*. Transmitter substances affect only cells that have specific receptors to which that substance can *bind*. Each cell has binding sites for many—but not all—of the different transmitter substances. For one cell to fire another, it has to dump enough of the right kind of transmitter substance to bind with enough specific receptors in the other cell to cause it to change polarity. To make matters even more complex, the receptors, in addition to being specific, must be open and in a sensitive state.

Different areas of the brain are composed of cells with relatively more receptors that bind with specific transmitter substances. These brain areas are connected to other areas via transmission pathways called by the name of the substance, as in *serotonin pathways*. To make matters still more complicated, each transmitter substance can serve as messenger in many different kinds of pathways that have different functions and different binding sites in different brain centers. If you increase the amount of one transmitter substance relative to others, there will be effects in virtually every area of the brain. Serotonin pathways are involved in sex, sleep, mood, memory, motivation, emotion, and just about everything else, so increasing available serotonin has effects nearly everywhere, though the effects may vary tremendously among individuals.

You do not need to know all this, but you do need to understand that chemical transmission in the brain is an enormously complicated process that occurs on a molecular level that cannot as yet be directly observed, and that everything connects to everything else in a number of ways, none of which are completely understood.

Psychiatric Drugs

All psychiatric medications operate by manipulating chemical transmission. They work by increasing or decreasing the amount of transmitter substance available, or by blocking or unblocking receptors. Some act on receptor sites like transmitter substances themselves, but most do not because of the *blood-brain barrier*. Though only a few molecules of serotonin are needed for transmission, you could eat a pound of it with little effect because it can't get through to your brain. Psychiatric medications are substances that get through the barrier and, once on the other side, affect the production and metabolism of various neurochemicals. They do many other things as well, but we're not sure what they are.

Virtually all psychiatric medicines in use today began as drugs for other purposes. They were found to have an effect on mental illnesses while being used to treat something else. The basic classes of drugs were discovered serendipitously, and the multitude of medications within the classes were derived by tinkering with the basic chemical structure to yield a substance that was similar, but not enough to infringe on patents. Each variation is, of course, presented as an improvement on the original.

There are two ways to understand how drugs work: from the inside, by knowing what they do physiologically, and from the outside, by observing how drugs make people feel and how they affect their actions. I've learned what psychiatric drugs do by watching and listening to people who are taking them. A few courses, and explanations by many medical colleagues, have helped me understand what I was looking at, but in the end, like you, all I know is what I see. Here are my observations about the drugs most commonly used to treat explosions into fear:

Alcohol

The oldest, most common, and most effective medicine for attenuating symptoms of excessive sympathetic arousal is alcohol. It is no longer pre-scribed because of its dangerous side effects, but is used for self-medication by millions of people.

Alcohol is a generalized central nervous system depressant that acts quickly. It is absorbed into the bloodstream right from the stomach, and enters the brain almost immediately. Alcohol enhances the action of the neurotransmitter gamma-aminobutyric acid (GABA), which inhibits neu-ronal firing in many parts of the brain. The effect is to relax muscles, generally slow things down, and encourage the parasympathetic system to take control. Alcohol also releases dopamine and serotonin, which bind with receptors in the so-called *pleasure centers* of the brain.

Alcohol will stop a panic attack in its tracks, and make a person feel pretty good, at least for a while. The problem is, it gets people drunk, it's addictive, and when it wears off, the panic attacks come back with a vengeance.

Though alcohol is obviously never prescribed for fear disorders, it can help us evaluate the medications that are. When a medication does too much too quickly, it's too easy to depend on it. Our bodies develop *toler-ance*; it takes more and more to do less and less. Addictive substances usually work fast and create tolerance. Most also stimulate pleasure centers.

I have had patients use alcohol successfully as a medication to prevent panic attacks in specific situations, such as flying on an airplane, or having

Thanksgiving dinner with the in-laws. The alcohol is part of a relaxation program that increases confidence more than it physically prevents attacks. Obviously, this works only with people who seldom drink and have not built up a tolerance. In doses of more than one drink, alcohol quickly ceases to be a medicine and becomes a disorder itself.

Most people with fear disorders who self-medicate with alcohol don't talk to their doctors about it. You'll see them more than I do. If the dosage is higher than one drink a day, possibly two, the various side effects are probably canceling out the benefits. If you have the opportunity, gently suggest that the doctor can prescribe something more effective.

Benzodiazepines

These are the drugs you think of as tranquilizers. They include Valium, Librium, Ativan, Restoril, Xanax, Klonopin, Serax, and several others. See Appendix 1 for a listing of generic and brand names of all the medications covered in this text. Benzodiazepines are central nervous system depressants that, like alcohol, enhance the inhibitory action of GABA. They have fewer side effects than alcohol, but still work quickly and well. That is their benefit, and their danger.

Benzodiazepines are a part of a series of drugs that include barbiturates and meprobamate (Miltown), which, though they bind to different receptor sites in the brain, do pretty much the same thing. Each one in its day was the drug of choice for anxiety, and each one has been abandoned because of its addictiveness. The first and most popular of the benzodiazepines were Librium and Valium. In the 1960s they were the most frequently prescribed medications in the United States.

Back then, researchers noted that benzodiazepines bind to different receptor sites than the addictive substances. There was a theory that anxiety was caused by an imbalance in the benzodiazepine-GABA receptor complex. It was thought that benzodiazepines mimicked the action of unknown but naturally occurring chemicals that calmed anxiety. Much was made of the fact that betacarbolines, that do occur naturally in the brain, act on the same receptors as benzodiazepines but have an opposite effect—they cause anxiety. Taking Valium three times a day was supposed to increase the amount of good transmitter substance relative to the bad.

In the 1960s a lot of people were physically dependent on Valium and Librium. You'll remember that to be addictive, drugs have to act fast and create a tolerance. Drug companies keep coming out with new benzo-diazepines, like Serax and Klonopin, each a bit slower and, presumably, a bit less addictive. They couldn't do much about the tolerance. It was also discovered that alcohol, barbiturates, meprobamate, and benzodiazepines develop *cross-tolerance*, which means that tolerance to one makes you tolerant to all. These drugs, when combined, *potentiate* one another. Effects can be augmented to levels that are dangerous, or even fatal.

Benzodiazepines now are seldom used for generalized anxiety, but they are used for panic disorder. In the 1980s, when Congress was holding hearings on the overuse of Valium and Librium, panic disorder was shifted into a separate diagnostic category from other anxiety disorders. The treat-ment of choice was Xanax, a newer benzodiazepine that was pretty much a clone of Valium and Librium. At the time there was some speculation that rapid treatment with benzodiazepines was necessary in panic disorder because of the danger of suicide. This danger has not been supported by research, but it is still very much a part of the folklore that surrounds the disorder. For a few years people who had panic attacks were regularly prescribed Xanax three times a day. Because of the dangers of physical dependence, this practice has all but disappeared.

More than anything else, people with panic disorder want their awful feelings to just go away. If a medication will do that for them, they are apt to take it now and ask questions later.

There is no justification for the prescription of long-term daily doses of benzodiazepines for panic, or any other fear disorder, unless everything else has failed. They are often prescribed for two to three weeks in con-junction with serotonergics, drugs that increase available serotonin, which are safer but take several weeks to work. The justification is that panic attacks are so painful that patients may get worse or even kill themselves if they don't get some immediate relief. This may be true, so it makes sense to be cautious.

Presently, doctors are well-aware of the dangers of benzodiazepines and strictly limit the amount they prescribe. Often they give out only a small supply to be taken, not daily, but as needed to stop panic attacks or prevent them in specific circumstances. This is a reasonable strategy, though it does not seem so to some patients. They shop around for doc-tors who will prescribe them what they want, sometimes using subterfuge.

If there is a person with panic disorder in your life, you should be aware of the dangers of benzodiazepines and watch out for overuse. Ask what he or she is taking, how much, and how often. If you don't know what the drugs are, look them up. Be especially careful if the person is seeing several different doctors. Often, one may not know that another is treating symptoms of the same condition. The best way to have a positive effect is to insist that the patient tell each doctor about all the others so they can communicate among themselves.

Serotonergics

One thing is certain: Drugs that increase the amount of available serotonin in the brain make a lot of people feel better, regardless of what is wrong with them. What is not certain is why this is so. Serotonin pathways go just about everywhere in the brain, and serotonin circuitry regulates most of the processes involved in most mental disorders. Other transmitters are involved as well, but serotonin connects to them all.

(I should note that I use the loose, generic term *serotonergic* to cover a whole class of drugs that work by increasing the amount of available serotonin in the brain. Some also affect norepinephrine, acetylcholine, and dopamine as well. The transmitter substances may be different, but the theory is the same. In writing about psychiatric drugs, I try to use the name you will most commonly hear, usually the brand name. See Appendix 1 for specific classifications and generic and brand names of all medications discussed in this text.)

There is absolutely no mental disorder that hasn't been ascribed to a serotonin deficiency or, more rarely, overabundance. Serotonin is to psychiatry as *self-esteem* is to psychology—both seem to explain everything. To be fair, I must admit that increasing available serotonin is a far more effective treatment for psychological disorders than increasing self-esteem.

Serotonergics were first used for depression, so we'll save the extensive discussion of how they work for that section. For more than 40 years serotonergics have been used to improve mood and motivation. More recently they have been widely and effectively used for other explosive disorders as well. Needless to say, if you improve a person's mood, everything looks better, but I suspect that the effect on emotional explosions is through another pathway entirely.

Perhaps you'll remember from the first chapter that *rumination*—
the continual replaying of unpleasant thoughts—is a component in all
emotional explosions. Rumination has many forms, from the terrifying
apparitions of PTSD haunting consciousness in search of the words that will
lay them to rest, to the much more common replaying of incendiary words—
predictions of doom or assignments of blame—that fan the flames of fear,
sadness, and anger. The common element is the repetition that people
feel is out of their control. It's possible that the automatic replay button
in the brain is in the *cingulate gyrus,* an area implicated in obsessive-
compulsive disorder, which is characterized by uncontrolled repetition
and treated with—you guessed it—serotonergics.

What I have observed in hundreds of patients is that these drugs
somehow make it easier to stop thinking negative thoughts. Countless
times I have relied on this property of medication to help me sneak in a
few positive thoughts edgewise. When you're doing therapy on explosive
disorders, you need all the help you can get.

Serotonergics fall mostly into two classes.

TRICYCLICS.   These are an older form of antidepressant, among the serotonin norepinephrine reuptake inhibitors (SNRIs). Imipramine, the first
drug in this class, is still used to treat panic disorder. Amitriptyline is also
used. As antidepressants, tricylics have two drawbacks: They tend to be
more sedating than newer drugs, and in rare cases they can lead to heart
rhythm irregularities. The sedating part sometimes makes tricyclics especially useful in treating fear disorders.

Amitriptyline, which can be sedating enough to make a normal person sleep for two days, is sometimes quite effective in taking the edge off
panic and acute anxiety without the danger of addiction. Trazadone, a
serotonin antagonist reuptake inhibitor (SARI) somewhat similar to drugs in
this class as well as to those described below, is sedating but metabolizes
more quickly. It is often prescribed as a safe sleeping aid, which is helpful
to people with fear disorders. The chief complaint that my clients have
about tricyclics is that they make them feel groggy and drugged, with a
dry cottony mouth, which comes from anticholinergic effects. Tricyclics
also have some of the same side effects as serotonin reuptake inhibitors.
These will be discussed in greater detail in the section on depression.

SELECTIVE SEROTONIN REUPTAKE INHIBITORS (SSRIs). The SSRIs are the newer, safer, less sedating antidepressants that seem to do just about everything else as well. They increase serotonin by slowing its reuptake by dendrites after cell firing, thus leaving more available in the synaptic area. Prozac was the first drug in this class in the United States, followed swiftly by Zoloft and Paxil.. Though these drugs generally have fewer long-term side effects than tricyclics, the first few days can be very difficult, especially for people with fear disorders. A common side effect as the body adapts to SSRIs is agitation. Clients typically describe the feeling in multiples of cups of coffee. Usually these medications are started at a lower than therapeutic dosage to diminish this effect, and usually the agitation subsides in a few days. But by then people with fear disorders often decide that it makes them worse and discontinue the medication. This is another reason that benzodiazepines are used in the first couple of weeks of treatment.

The effects of SSRIs vary tremendously across individuals. One can make people worse, while another with almost identical chemical properties can work miracles. Nobody knows why. Every doctor has his or her own preferences, but the word on the street is that among the three big ones, Prozac and Zoloft are more activating, and Paxil is slightly more sedating, and thus better for fear disorders. It's as good a guess as any, but the variability of effect across patients is so great that few generalizations hold up. *There is absolutely no substitute for close, regular contact with the prescribing physician.* The usual procedure is to start people on a low dose, have them adapt to it, then raise it in a couple of weeks.

Though studies show that SSRIs increase available serotonin immediately, they generally take at least two weeks to work on depression, and even more before they have an effect on fear disorders. Nobody knows why these drugs take so long to work if their main effect is supposedly achieved by increasing available serotonin. Clearly there are other unknown effects involved. In addition to the big three, there are other SSRIs, like Luvox and Celexa, as well as NDRIs like Wellbutrin, and NASAs like Remeron.

When SSRIs are working well, people taking them don't feel medicated, they just feel better. This can lead them to stop taking the drug because they don't think they need it. Illogical as this may sound, it happens all the time. Common side effects like weight gain and loss of sexual interest are sometimes the underlying reason, but most often people just stop because they think they're cured. If someone in your life is on SSRIs, make sure they talk to their doctors before discontinuing. There may be withdrawal effects. Treatment usually lasts for at least six months.

SSRIs may be prescribed forever for chronic depression because they're considerably better than the alternative. I don't think the case is nearly as strong for lifetime use to control fear disorders. Medication should calm fear enough for people to face it, and ultimately conquer it. Controlling fear with medication makes people feel better, but in the end it's a hollow victory that should only be accepted when all else has failed.

BUSPIRONE (BUSPAR).   BuSpar is a new kind of medication derived from antipsychotics that regulates the amount of serotonin available to receptors and, supposedly, makes them work better. It may also help dopamine receptors as well. BuSpar is not addictive, but its effects are usually not strong enough for use in fear disorders. It may be helpful in generalized anxiety and for some of the things it does in combination with SSRIs. We'll discuss this medication in more detail in other chapters.

ANTICONVULSANTS.   Medications like Depakote and Neurontin, which were originally developed to control convulsions, are being more widely used for fear disorders. These drugs are generalized inhibitors of synaptic transmission that work through several different mechanisms. A few years ago they began to be used to control the manic part of bipolar disorder. The theory is that they inhibit "kindling," and thus keep abnormal neural responses from generalizing throughout the brain. Lately, anticonvulsants are being more widely prescribed for anxiety and fear disorders. They work for some people, but my clients generally don't like them. The chief complaint is that the anticonvulsants make them feel drugged and stupid. Weight gain on anticonvulsants is an even bigger problem than with SSRIs.

Drugs Work

Drugs do work. They make people with explosive disorders feel better. This has led to speculation that the neurochemicals that the drugs affect *cause* the disorders, and the areas of the brain known to contain or be sensitive to these chemicals are where the disorders dwell. You will undoubtedly see drug advertisements in magazines suggesting that the causes and cures for mental disorders are known, and available in capsule form. Please realize that you're hearing only part of the story.

Prescribing medication, like everything else related to mental illness, requires art as well as science. The effects of medications vary greatly from one person to another, even to the point of being opposite. One drug may not work at all, while another that is almost identical works beautifully. Some medications stop working for no known reason. Others work well for things they're not supposed to affect at all. Then there are the side effects. No matter how thorough their scientific training, doctors can only make educated guesses about what will work, and why. Artists among physicians are comfortable with the vast uncertainties of dealing with the mind. Whatever happens, they work closely with their patients to achieve a creative balance between feeling better and doing better.

Art without science to back it up can also cause problems. In health food stores you may hear that certain herbs, vitamins, and supplements affect the operation of neurotransmitters and thus affect the disorders that the transmitters control. The evidence for this is considerably more speculative than the more creative promotions from drug companies, though in some cases the chemicals involved are quite similar. Don't be fooled into believing that because something is derived from "natural sources" it is better, safer, or has less side effects than medicines physicians prescribe. Actual medicines are tested for purity and uniformity of content. The people who prescribe and dispense them have a great deal of training in their safe use. Also, the fact that prescribing and selling are done by different professionals, physicians, and pharmacists is also a source of protection. Caveat emptor.

An Old Wonder Drug

If there is a wonder drug for explosive disorders that does not involve increasing available serotonin, it is *exercise*. Actually, exercise probably does increase serotonin, endorphins, and every other kind life-enhancing chemical, though the research on this is not particularly rigorous. Who cares? Exercise is the one thing that is good for whatever ails you. If there is a fearful, depressed, or angry person in your life, the very best gift you can give is your company in a daily program of aerobic exercise. And it will help you just as much.

Chapter 5

Storming the Tower of Psychobabble

IN THE LAST CHAPTER I outlined the physical components of fear disorders. Now, before we look at the psychological components, I need to define a few terms. Actually, a lot of terms.

If you thought medical concepts were confusing, you ain't seen nothing yet. Doctors have only to name things that are invisible to the naked eye; psychologists have to name things that don't even exist at all, except in people's imaginations. How can you expect us to agree on what to call them? Needless to say, competing views create confusion.

There are two grand traditions in clinical psychology: psychoanalysis and behaviorism. Each has its own language and its own way of doing things. In the 1970s the two approaches went to war. The battleground was the treatment of fear disorders.

Psychoanalysis started about 100 years ago when Freud discovered the unconscious. Before that, life was pretty much what people said it was. Afterward, everything had a *manifest content*—what they said—and a *latent content*, what it really meant. Freud, almost single-handedly, added a whole new layer of complexity to human experience. Unfortunately, the master was a bit rigid. *What it really means* became synonymous with *what Freud said it means*. Analysis was conducted with scrupulous attention to detail, sometimes at the expense of the overall goal.

Freud saw panic attacks as *catastrophic anxiety*, caused when universally repressed, unacceptable desires—like wanting to kill one parent and have sex with the other—escape from the unconscious and threaten to overwhelm the personality. The cure involved accepting the unacceptable, realizing that everybody has Oedipal fantasies, and understanding that thinking about murder and incest doesn't mean you have to do them.

Neuroses develop to protect people from catastrophic anxiety, but the choice of symptom reflects the underlying conflicts. In phobia, the feared object was supposed to be symbolic of those terrifying repressed desires, so a great deal of time was spent figuring out what those snakes and spiders *really* meant. It was this sort of thinking that gave us the list of Greek names for every imaginable fear. Freud himself was reputedly phobic of cocks crowing.

Freud never said anything about PTSD, because it didn't exist as a separate entity in his day. Nevertheless, popular misinterpretation of Freud's theories still haunts our thinking about this disorder. We'll look at some of the conceptual problems later in this chapter.

By the end of World War II psychoanalysis was quite fashionable. An oversimplified version became a part of popular culture. A lot of people thought, and still think, that everything relates to sex, and that remembering repressed memories somehow cures mental illness.

Psychoanalysts did search for repressed memories, not of real events, but of unacceptable fantasies about sex and aggression. Since Freud's time we've discovered that sometimes the fantasies about incest were true. Oedipus stepped out of the unconscious and became a real live monster.

In the shadow of real monsters, many people have forgotten some of the more remarkable psychoanalytic insights, like the notion that the most frightening things in the world are not what happens to you, but the unacceptable parts of yourself. Repression is not so much of events, as of clues that you are meaner, more cowardly, or a more lascivious person than you think you ought to be.

Despite some dazzling insights into the human condition, psycho-analysis didn't work very well. Analysts were often more adept at explaining symptoms than alleviating them. When analysis did work, it took forever, cost a fortune, and required a college education to appreciate its benefits.

Meanwhile, back at the lab, more scientific psychologists were hatching a plot to overthrow analysis and make psychotherapy more effective and available. Until the 1960s, behaviorists were more concerned with running rats through mazes than with treating mental illness. Their goal was prediction and control of observable behavior. They prided themselves on complete disinterest in any sort of internal process that might fall between stimulus and response. Behavior, to them, was shaped solely by its results.

When behaviorists did talk about mental illness, it was in terms of *conditioning*. There was *classical conditioning*, first discovered by Pavlov with bells and dog drool, which explained how physiological processes could be connected to unrelated environmental stimuli. If salivation could be arbitrarily connected to bells, why couldn't fear be connected to snakes?

Then there was *operant conditioning*, championed most famously by B. F. Skinner. The basic idea was that any behavior that is rewarded will be more likely to occur again. Very early in the game behaviorists discovered that punishment was not a useful tool for shaping behavior, because its effects were too unpredictable. *Positive reinforcement* and the many ways it can be administered stands at the center of behavioral theory. There is such a thing as *negative reinforcement,* but *it is not punishment!* Any behaviorist worth his salt would punch you in the nose for saying it is. *Negative reinforcement is a stimulus that rewards by being taken away.* Its effects are far more powerful than mere punishment. Anything that turns off a painful stimulus will be repeated, even long after the pain has passed. This is the reason it is so difficult to get people with fear disorders to face what they're afraid of if they've already learned a means of avoidance.

In the 1960s a few radical behaviorists came up with the idea that mental illnesses had nothing to do with psychoanalytic gobbledegook, that they were merely conditioned responses. Armed with techniques from the laboratory, radical behaviorists set out to topple the mental health establishment by showing that snake phobia was merely a conditioned response that could be cured by *systematic desensitization*.

Desensitization means weakening the connection of fear with anything else; in the case of snakes, for example, by repeatedly pairing snakes with relaxation techniques. There was a short period in the history of psychology during which every graduate program had its own pet snake. You can imagine what the more Freudian professors had to say about that. They also said that desensitization could never in fact actually cure a phobia because the unconscious would merely pick some other symbolic object to fear. *Symptom substitution* was what they called it, and try though they might, the analysts were never able to show it existed. They lost big-time.

Next, the behaviorists gleefully pointed out that any number of psychoanalytic concepts could not pass muster when subjected to research. The analysts protested that their ideas were too complex to be tested by the simple which-technique-works-better paradigms the behaviorists used, but nobody listened. In those days, no self-respecting scientist would do anything but sneer at psychoanalysis. Seventy years of close observations of how verbal subtlety could be used to heal were relegated to the same category as ESP.

Meanwhile the victorious behaviorists were learning that you could pair relaxation exercises with just the *thought* of a snake and desensitization would still work. The black box inside the head opened and revealed that the mind contained *cognitions* that followed the same rules of reinforcement as external behaviors. Clients could learn to think in ways that would make them feel better. *Cognitive therapy* was born.

In those wild wartime days when behaviorism battled psychoanalysis, there arose a third force, which in its time was called the *human potential movement*. It's still around today, now called all sorts of creative names by its practitioners, *New Age* or *Touchy-Feely* by its detractors.

Human potential therapy is simple enough for a flower child to understand. The central idea is essentially *if you express your feelings, everything will be okay*. Most concepts were borrowed from psychoanalysis, then dumbed down and spiced up with gratuitous sex and aggression. There were nude encounter groups, and people settled differences by pounding each other with foam bats until the anger just faded away. Then they hugged.

Human potential techniques were designed to loosen up inhibited but basically healthy people, to help them understand and feel better about themselves. It was never really intended to cure mental illness. This little detail was quickly forgotten because the techniques were so much fun and so easy to do.

Human potential therapy can make mental illnesses worse by encouraging people to get out of their heads and go with their feelings when they desperately need to learn to ignore their feelings and go with their heads.

The human potential movement's gift to the intellectual world was the concept of *self-esteem*, which was also borrowed from psychoanalysis, and invested with near-magical properties. Every disorder known to humanity can be caused by low self-esteem, and can be cured by raising it. Conceit is merely low self-esteem when a person is *in denial*, another Freudian term popularized by addiction treatment.

Today, human potential techniques are practiced mostly at the fringes of psychology, often by people whose qualifications include being in recovery from whatever they're treating and by support group members who have no qualifications at all.

All the competing approaches I've described are still in use for treating explosive disorders. If there's an explosive person close to you, you'll probably hear all of the terms I've defined, often in the same sentence. Thesis and antithesis are trying to combine to form a synthesis, but they haven't quite gotten there yet.

Though the language of psychotherapy is still recovering from the great paradigm shift of the 1970s, the basic elements of psychotherapy vary little from one approach to another. In 30 years, I've had the opportunity to observe hundreds of talented therapists of virtually every theoretical persuasion. What they *do* is remarkably similar, what they *say* about it varies all over the place. Therapy itself is not a vague process, it only gets confusing when you try to explain it. If you're not too confused at this point, we can proceed with describing the psychological treatment of fear disorders.

Chapter 6

The Psychology of Fear

THERE ARE 168 HOURS IN A WEEK, only one of which is a therapy session. The most important work happens out in the real world, often with you. Since you're going to be doing it, you could probably use an overview of what therapy for fear disorders entails.

Steps in Treating Fear Disorders

Psychological treatment of fear disorders is an orderly sequence of interventions designed to help terrified people realize that though their fear is real, the danger it signals is not. The fearful must then be persuaded to use that knowledge, rather than their feelings, as a basis for action.

Step 1: External Control

Before you can hold forth on the intricacies of fighting fear, people have to be calm enough to listen. In Chapter 3, I outlined the technique for basic calming: Restore rhythm, disconnect the alarm, and create a verbal representation of what is happening. This is a form of external control, because you are the one doing the calming, not the fearful person. If there is such a person in your life, especially one with panic disorder, you'll go through the sequence many times, but hopefully not forever.

The overall goal of psychotherapy is to foster internal control of fear. External control is a necessary precursor: the beginning, not the end.

Treatment for fear disorders is usually begun by primary care physicians. After making a differential diagnosis, they attempt to alleviate symptoms, usually with medication. This medication can be a blessed relief, but the blessing is mixed. If the medication works, there's no problem. Treatment begins and ends right there. Nothing else is needed but prescription refills.

If the medication doesn't work, however, if it doesn't cause the symptoms to go away, fearful people may be left with some confusion as to who or what is responsible for making them feel better.

For panic disorder, the usual regimen is a serotonergic, usually a reuptake inhibitor like Prozac, Zoloft, or Paxil, but sometimes a tricyclic like Imiprimine, with a limited course of benzodiazepines until it takes effect. As I said in the previous chapter, benzodiazepines have to be watched carefully because they work too well. Addiction is less of a problem than fostering unrealistic expectations.

> On the night Jane awoke in panic, her terrified husband rushed her to the hospital, where they calmed her with a shot of Valium and told her to call her doctor in the morning. The clearest memory Jane had of that night was the immediate relief she felt when the Valium took hold. That feeling became imprinted below her awareness as the way a panic attack should end, with the fear melting away into a pleasant haze that she mistook for normalcy.
>
> The next day, Jane's doctor, after diagnosing her condition as panic disorder rather than physical demise, prescribed Xanax three times daily for two weeks, until Prozac could take effect.
>
> In Jane's opinion, the Prozac never took effect because it didn't make the panic go away as well as Xanax.

The Prozac was working just fine, and there was nothing improper or unusual about Jane's treatment. It did, however, light the fuse for her next emotional outburst.

The *Make It Go Away* Explosion

> *A week after the Xanax prescription runs out, Jane's husband comes home to find her on the couch, shaking. Her face is streaked with tears.*
>
> *He sits down and puts his arm around her. "What's wrong?" he asks.*
>
> *"The new medicine doesn't work," she says. "I had two attacks today." Jane starts to sob. "I don't think I'm ever going to get better."*

More than anything else, people with panic disorder want their attacks to *just go away*. They long for the lost paradise of simply feeling good. Paradise is never simple, however; and usually it isn't even paradise. Much as Jane may long for it, she can't go back to a place that she's never really been. Panic attacks don't just appear out of nowhere. People who get them usually have a history of anxiety problems, which they've dealt with by putting on a happy face and ignoring the turmoil below. Explosive people are known for taping over warning lights until the engine blows up. Then they want a quick fix.

If there is a panicky person in your life, you will face the *Make it go away* explosion many times. You'll probably feel frightened and helpless yourself as you scramble around, searching for something, *anything*, that will make the person feel better.

Hold that thought and pay attention to what's going on inside you. What you're feeling is the almost telepathic power of an emotional explosion to communicate emotion from one heart to another. *Emotional explosions make you feel what the explosive person is feeling.* That is their purpose, though most often it lies outside the awareness of both sender and receiver.

Since you don't have an explosive disorder, feeling the same raw emotions doesn't necessarily lead to the same response. You may not explode, but your thoughts and actions still reflect your own hang-ups, if you have any. Your first response is not likely to be your best.

Jane's husband feels her pain, and this turns it into a goad for action. His sympathetic system switches on and he chooses to fight. Jane needs a champion to protect her! He rushes to the phone to demand that the doctor prescribe something that will help his wife.

Whoa, big boy!

When Jane's husband feels bad, he *does* something about it. He *fixes* the problem, as any alpha male would. Unfortunately, he is rushing off to fix the wrong problem. Jane's emotion has turned him into a guided missile that merely moves the explosion to another place. He has unwittingly adopted Jane's unrealistic goal of making the fear go away immediately. If the doctor is sufficiently intimidated to prescribe more Xanax, we already know it will make Jane worse in the long run, but everybody will feel better for the moment.

Think for a moment about what you would do in the face of a *Make it go away* explosion. Most people automatically leap into the fray without realizing they're fighting another person's battle. Some will try to hand the problem off to someone else. Others may ignore it, hoping the problem will go away. Others get irritated, hoping the explosive person will go away. Very few think about the long-term implications of what they say and do. I hope you're one of those. If you look closely, you'll see that most of the immediate reactions are variations on fighting back or running away, which we already know is ineffective.

The best response is one that acknowledges the reality of the pain, then shifts responsibility for problem solving from you to the explosive person, and the venue from emotion to thinking. All this can be accomplished with one simple question: *What can I do to help?*

These are magic words that give some responsibility back to the explosive person. Always use them before taking matters into your own hands. In the early days of the disorder you may have to exercise a bit of external control with basic calming. As soon as the person is settled enough to talk, he or she needs to start thinking things through, making choices, and taking responsibility. You can encourage all this by asking how you can help them before you start helping.

The response will undoubtedly be, "I don't know," but who cares? The thinking about the question does the magic, regardless of the answer. If the explosive person doesn't ask for anything, don't do anything. Just sit and wait. *I don't know* is just an unconscious attempt to restate the basic message, which is, "I feel bad, and I want somebody to make me feel better." Stepping out of an unconscious pattern is the most helpful thing you can possibly do.

> *"I can't take it anymore!" Jane shrieks. "I can't go on living this way. I'd rather be dead!"*

Sometimes, stepping out of the pattern can intensify the explosion, but it doesn't make the disorder worse. If you ask what you can do to help and the explosion escalates, regard it as a more emphatic restatement of the basic message. Ask again, and keep asking until the person calms down. *You cannot do harm by asking what you can do to help.* This situation is one in which you can safely ignore talk about suicide. In Chapter 8 we'll look more closely at suicide threats.

> *"What can I do to help," Jane's husband asks, undaunted.*
> *Jane sighs. "I don't know what to do. That's the problem."*

That *is* the problem—not that Jane has panic attacks, but that she doesn't know what to do about them. Now, she and her husband can discuss what both of them can do. If Jane keeps asking for something to make the panic attacks go away, her husband might respond with a refresher course in what drugs can and cannot accomplish in preventing or alleviating such attacks.

Any drugs that make fear go away are addictive, and more dangerous than the fear itself. Serotonergics like Prozac don't cure fear disorders, but often they make a cure possible. Medications can improve mood and give people more conscious control over their emotions. To get better, people have to exert that control a little at a time.

If there are medicated fearful people in your life, their doctors have explained these things to them. You may have to repeat them a few hundred times before they finally sink in. No one will thank you, but you're definitely helping. Medications may make a huge difference, but for emotionally explosive people, they're usually the beginning of the road, not the end.

Step 2: Taking the Measure of Fear

Once people are calm enough to think rationally about fear, they have a lot of learning to do, and unlearning. When they understand what fear really is, they can begin to act as if it doesn't exist. The process isn't quite as confusing as it seems. You already know most of the information; the only problem is how to teach it and when.

Throughout the process you will have to acknowledge that fear and the pain it causes is real. It may originate in the brain, but it is not all in the head. Acknowledging fear is simple; just say: *I know that being afraid* (or having a panic attack, or whatever words the person you know uses) *feels terrible,* and perhaps offer a hand to hold. Then, don't say or do anything that would cast doubt on your previous statement. That's all there is to it, but as we'll see, it may be harder than you think.

The value of recognizing another person's pain runs deep. Intense fear radically changes the way the brain works. It feels more like going crazy than actually going crazy does. People with fear disorders often worry that they are losing their minds. Someone needs to reassure them that they aren't, that what's happening to them is still within the realm of normal human experience. You can do all that by looking them in the eye, taking their hand, and saying, "I know that being afraid feels terrible." Giving the abyss a name makes it less likely that they will fall into it.

At this moment, ready as you are to extend your heart and hand, it may surprise you that one of the biggest problems people with fear disorders face is thinly veiled suspicion that they are faking. Many explosions into fear are unconscious demonstrations of the reality of the disorder that might be unnecessary if frightened people felt their friends and family believed them.

But why would a caring person not believe?

The answer lies in the phenomenon that analysts called *secondary gain.*

Secondary Gain

According to Freud, the primary gain from developing a neurotic symptom is protection from being swept away and destroyed by *catastrophic anxiety*. The secondary gain is that illness gets you out of doing things you don't want to do.

> *Jane's husband shakes his head. "I just don't get why you never have panic attacks when it's time to play bunko with your friends. But if I want you to go to a ball game, you act like I'm some kind of insensitive idiot for even bringing it up."*

* * *

> *Neil's wife comes in soaked and muddy after a cloudburst catches her raking leaves, under which spiders might hide. As she puts down an armload of firewood, carefully swept outside so as to be spider-free, she glances at her husband, warm and dry in front of the TV. Her look says it all.*

Friends and family are at first overly solicitous, then they gradually begin to see what they think is method in the madness. What was once a serious disorder begins to look suspiciously like a stomachache on test day.

If you're ever in this position, please remember: *Secondary gain is not primary purpose.* People don't make up fear disorders to get out of obligations. On the other hand, if doing an unpleasant task brings them nearer to what they're afraid of, why not kill two birds with one stone? Secondary gain is just about universal in explosive disorders; it is almost never conscious malingering. Think about it: Would you trade mowing the lawn for a panic attack? Feeling guilty on top of being afraid doesn't make the situation any better. It makes it worse.

The *You Think It's All in My Head* Explosion

> *His wife's disapproving look chills Neil as surely as an October rain. What kind of man are you? he asks himself. He doesn't*

need an answer. Inside, his guilt combines with his fear and makes it stronger. His fear of spiders grows and the area he perceives as safe shrinks. He now becomes anxious even looking out the window.

* * *

Jane stops going to bunko. Her husband's comments are part of her decision. It does seem unfair that she can go out and do things for herself when she can't do the things he wants her to do, but that isn't the real reason. She began to notice some of the warning signs—racing heart and breath catching in her throat— even while she was having fun with her friends. She thinks it might be safer to stay home until she gets a grip on this panic thing, though she wonders if she ever will. Nowadays she seldom leaves the house.

Don't go blaming Jane's husband or Neil's wife for making them worse—or yourself, if you've made comments like these to a fearful person in your life. Everybody does. Our protagonists' spouses learned how to help them get better, and you will too. Sometimes the learning is all trial and error.

What should you say to a fearful person about secondary gain?

Nothing.

Keep your mouth shut. At this stage of the game, you don't want to say anything that would hint of disbelief. The best way to deal with the *You think it's all in my head* explosion is to prevent it. Sometimes this can be difficult. Here are a few guidelines:

NEVER TRY TO INSTRUCT EMOTIONALLY EXPLOSIVE PEOPLE BY POINTING OUT THE ILLOGIC OF THEIR BEHAVIOR. No matter how astute, such comments will make things worse. In fact, the more astute, the bigger the problem. To understand why, you have to remember what Freud said about the most frightening things in the world being the unacceptable parts of yourself.

What Jane's husband said about bunko and baseball was absolutely on target, but unhelpful because it came at the wrong time. At this stage in treatment, Jane has no idea that she has any control over what's happening to her. Regardless of her husband's intentions, any suggestion that she does will sound to her like an accusation that she's having panic attacks on purpose to get out of doing things she doesn't want to do. At some deep, dark level, she's afraid she is.

Jane hates baseball, but she's never told her husband because she was afraid he'd get mad. When they were dating, she went to games to show him how much she loved him. Now she doesn't want to go, but feels compelled by love to do so. Panic resolves the conflict for her, at least after a fashion. She doesn't have to think about her mixed feelings until her husband inadvertently throws aside the curtain between her and what she's hiding from herself. The only possible result is more panic.

Later in treatment, after Jane gained some control over her fear, we were able to talk about her internal conflicts, but not when her husband made the remark about baseball and bunko. Insights that come too soon are worse than useless. They can only be taken as attacks that create a greater need to run away. Even if you don't talk about secondary gain, you should still do your best to prevent it.

AVOID AVOIDANCE.   Amidst the swirling doubt, confusion, and painful emotion that surrounds fear disorders, this adage is the one fixed star. The more you try to protect people from what they fear, the more they fear it. Avoidance is the hardest thing in the world to unlearn, because there's never an opportunity. That's why I make such a big deal about overmedicating and not treating panic, phobia, and PTSD as handicaps that require accommodation. Once you start down that road, it's almost impossible to get off.

Fear disorders get worse through the process of *generalization*. First you avoid what you fear, then things that remind you of what you fear become frightening, so you avoid those. Then things that remind you of things that remind you begin to seem scary. Through generalization, phobics tend to pull back further and further. Neil was once able to do yard work, until he realized that there were ground-dwelling spiders as well as the ones in bushes and trees.

Neil's wife is rewarding his phobic behavior by doing the outdoor chores herself. But what else can she do? The leaves need raking, and Neil is scared to death that spiders are lurking beneath them.

She needs to remember that the simplest solution is not a solution at all. It will make the problem worse. The problem is not that people with fear disorders can't, or even that they won't, it's that they're afraid to. Unfortunately, the minute you stop protecting, it will set off another explosion.

The *You Know I Can't* Explosion

> *"Want to come out and help me rake leaves?" Neil's wife asks innocently.*
>
> *"What are you talking about?" Neil says, already beginning to panic. "You know I can't go out where there might be you-know-whats." He can't even say "spiders," and this heartless woman is asking him to throw himself to them!*

In the fight against fear disorders, sometimes the greatest kindnesses are perceived as cruelty. Take heart and grit your teeth. This next rule is hard to follow.

NEVER AUTOMATICALLY LET PEOPLE WITH FEAR DISORDERS OUT OF DOING SCARY THINGS. MAKE THEM ASK EACH TIME. The asking sets up a small barrier that is crossed by thinking rather than feeling, a step in the right direction. Being thoughtful in this way will most likely be seen as thoughtlessness, so be ready to explain yourself.

> *"No, Neil, I'm not sure what you can and can't do," his wife says. "I'm willing to help out, but you have to tell me what you want."*
>
> *"Uh, it's not fair that I ask you to do the yard work. But ..."*
>
> *Neil's wife allows a long pause for reflection.*
>
> *"I could do something else," Neil says.*

DON'T GIVE FEARFUL PEOPLE ALTERNATE TASKS TO COMPENSATE. Fearful people are often happy to do more than their share of less frightening tasks to assuage their guilt. Don't get sucked in. Even in a very busy family, fighting fear is more important than getting the chores done.

"Sweetheart," Neil's wife says. "Come on, take a little risk. Come outside and talk to me while I rake."

"But what if there are you-know-whats out in the leaves?"

"You can stand on the porch and talk to me from there."

Neil squirms a bit. "It's just that I could be doing something productive, like cleaning the oven."

"Honey, coming outside is productive. The most important thing all of us have to do now is to help you get your life back from the spiders."

"I could wax the kitchen floor."

Neil's wife hands him his jacket. "Come on out. I need you to do this."

Tempting as the offers may be, they are not worth as much as keeping phobics focused on the main issue. Sometimes guilt is good motivation. I'm not suggesting that you try to cause it on purpose, but if a little should come your way, why not use it?

INVITE THE FEARFUL RIGHT UP TO THE CLOSEST POINT THEY CAN MANAGE. Every step forward a phobic takes is, well, a step forward.

"Look ... " Neil's wife swings her rake over an expanse of grass. "I've made a big clear spot right here on both sides of the walk. As you-know-what-free as I can get it. Why don't you come on down and talk to me."

"I can't."

The main goal of therapy is to help phobics move beyond this point. Neil has relaxation techniques and medication at his disposal. His wife may need to remind him to use them.

"Maybe if you did the relaxation thing the doctor showed you, or even took one of your pills?"

The two of them sit on the porch and go through his relaxation exercise. When they finish, Neil's wife goes back to the yard. She points at the walkway. "You've got a clear escape route

right back to the house. If you can do this, you'll get a medal for
bravery beyond the call of duty."
   Neil begins to walk hesitantly down the steps.
   His wife shoulders her rake and salutes.

Even if Neil does see a you-know-what and runs, he still earns his medal. It's important to have an easy means of escape if you try something like this. The only way it could go wrong is if the frightened person feels trapped.

Usually, therapists will advise you on specific approach strategies, and teach fearful people techniques for moving closer. You may not have to come up with the plan, but you will have to follow it, even if it's inconvenient, and you'd really like to have the oven cleaned and the floor waxed. Think of it as an investment.

SECONDARY GAIN AND **PTSD**   The fact that PTSD, by definition, is caused by somebody or something else makes secondary gain a primary concern. Regardless of who caused the disorder, it cannot improve until the fearful person takes responsibility for it, even if it is more profitable not to.

> *Trish is suing the driver of the pickup who smashed into her car*
> *for psychological damages. For weeks she would have panic*
> *attacks even at the thought of driving. When she told her lawyer*
> *that her psychological treatment involved getting back behind*
> *the wheel as quickly as possible, he asked, "What's your hurry?"*

Sometimes it can actually cost money to get over PTSD. In Trish's case there was never any question of not driving. She wanted to get better more than she wanted a big settlement.

Correctly diagnosed, PTSD is a disorder so painful that it creates strong incentives to do whatever it takes to get better. I have seen many cases of PTSD in people who have been in accidents, and in law enforcement and emergency personnel who were involved in or witnessed deadly situations. When the diagnosis is applied incorrectly, the patient must sometimes choose between the relief of healing and the benefits of staying sick.

Randy's boss put him on probation. When it happened, he was so shocked he went numb. It was so unfair, but there was nothing he could do about it. Later in the day he had a panic attack, and he had nightmares about it that night. The next day, Randy could barely get out of bed. Just waiting for the bus to work he got so nauseous that he had to go home. His doctor authorized a two-week stress leave, but Randy didn't feel any better at the end of that time. He knew he'd have to go back to the same difficult and painful situation. After a few weeks, at his doctor's suggestion, Randy went to see a therapist, who diagnosed him as having PTSD. It's been three months now, and the stress leave has turned into a long-term disability that, conveniently enough, gives Randy enough time to look for another job.

The stresses of the job search were too much for Randy as well. His disability continued, finally turning into major depression. Once you start running, it's hard to stop.

It has been my experience that stress leaves for fear disorders that last more than a couple of weeks do more harm than good. There are individual exceptions, of course, but few of them. Doctors' excuses should be for a limited duration and with a clear understanding of the criteria for going back. This is difficult advice to follow, even for doctors. It's hard to say no to a person who is clearly in distress. I'm sometimes drawn into writing notes for the third and fourth week, even though I usually regret it later.

For fear disorders at work there are more appropriate accommodations than extended leave, like allowing time off for therapy, or to use control strategies like exercise or relaxation. Eventually Randy did stop running. We'll discuss his case in the section on depression.

The issue of secondary gain with the delayed form of PTSD are so complex and tricky as to be outside the scope of this book. Sometimes the legal and political issues overwhelm the psychological. I believe that in delayed PTSD the problems that create the delay—perhaps dissociative conditions or personality disorders—often need more treatment than the PTSD itself.

The Shape, Form, and Substance of Fear

We have established that fear is real, but what is reality? Real things have properties. They take up space and have weight. Psychological entities have properties as well. They exist in space and time, with measurable intensity and duration. What makes them real is words. The larger the vocabulary we have to describe our internal experiences, the more possibilities we have for controlling them. This is why simply talking about psychological problems can improve them.

Freud used to describe the overall goal of psychoanalysis by saying, "Where *Id* was, shall *Ego* be." To him, Id was the seething, inchoate mass of unconscious, primitive urges that, though repressed, form the basis for emotion. Ego is the part of the personality that reasons, organizes, and sets priorities. Freud's metaphor still fits with some of what we know about how the brain operates. The structures deep inside mediate instinct and emotion, and the outer parts think and use language. I'm sure that both Freudian and neurological fundamentalists would cringe at the comparison, but for our purposes, it holds.

Think about what we know about PTSD—that fearful images must be translated into words before they can be stored as normal memories. Perhaps this is the neurological basis of the talking cure.

Philosophical speculations aside, an important goal of psychotherapy—for fear disorders and just about everything else—is *to redefine reality as what the mind knows rather than what the emotions feel*. This is done with words and explanations, which are a psychologist's stock in trade.

> *Trish picks up the pillows on my sofa and piles them on her lap, a soft fortress to protect her. "Since the accident," she says, "I can't get the picture of that truck out of my mind. I even dream about it." A tear runs down her cheek. She says hesitantly, "I think I'm going crazy."*
>
> *"You aren't," I say.*
>
> *"I'm not?" she asks. A glimmer of hope flickers among the tears.*
>
> *"No," I say, and spend the next half hour explaining what PTSD is and how it works. I can see Trish beginning to relax, basking in the brilliance of my exposition.*

On second thought, she might have been nodding off. Whatever the reason, she *was* feeling much calmer. I gave her hope by giving her words other than *crazy* to describe her emotional reality. Anything you can talk about, you can do something about. What Trish needs is to do some talking herself to turn her experience into her own words.

> *"Tell me about what happened on the day of the accident," I say.*
> *"Where were you going?"*
> *"I was on my way to work," she says. "I just took the 164th exit off Highway 14, and was coming up the hill to where the four-way stop sign is."*
> *I nod to show I know the place she means. "Then what?"*

This interchange may not sound particularly therapeutic, but it is. Normal memories are stories that occur at certain places and times, have beginnings, middles, and ends, and connect to the ongoing internal narrative that is life. Traumatic events and emotional explosions of all sorts are episodes that don't fit into the overall story. They loom over the mind like dark clouds, casting a pall over day-to-day experience and occasionally spewing forth lightning, thunder, and torrents of neurochemicals. To gain control over these internal storms, people need to turn them into words. Unfortunately, they have little opportunity, because they and the people close to them shy away from such topics in conversation, lest they bring on more misery.

Sometimes it takes a series of small miseries to end a big one.

If there is an explosive person in your life, you can help by speaking about the unspeakable. Ask questions that require them to put their emotional storms into words. This mundane act can be a tremendous mercy.

> *"What does a panic attack feel like?" Jane's husband asks.*
> *"I don't want to talk about it. It gets me too upset."*
> *"I know it gets you upset, but sometimes it helps to talk about things that upset you."*
> *"I just want them to go away."*

Generally, explosive people don't talk about the explosions they themselves feel, but about how badly they feel about not being able to stop them. This sort of talking goes nowhere. Sympathize, but try to get them back on the track of putting their troubling experiences into words.

> *"I know how much you want them to go away," Jane's husband says. "I do too. I think talking about them might help."*
>
> *Jane draws her knees to her chest, scrunching her body into the smallest target possible. "You just don't know what it feels like."*
>
> *"No, I don't. But I really want to."*
>
> *"When I have the attacks, I feel like I can't breathe," Jane says, and begins to sob.*
>
> *Her husband puts his arms around her. "And then what?"*

Your questions may bring on tears, but they're not hurting. Don't let your own fear of making the situation worse turn you away. You won't. Treating fear disorders means encouraging people to take one small step at a time. If you ask them to go on twice and they don't continue, it means they've gone far enough for one day. Try again tomorrow.

The overall goal is to give fearful people a place to stand outside fear where they can observe it, and to see that, rather than being an amorphous mass of awfulness, it has shape, form, content, and duration. It's helpful to have people time their attacks and rate them on the 1 to 10 Richter scale used to measure earthquakes. They can go on from there to paying attention to what they're thinking at the time and what they do.

> *Jane has that funny look on her face. Her husband takes her hand. "Attack, huh?"*
>
> *She nods. "It's about a 6 now, but it might be getting bigger." She takes a deep breath. "My chest is getting tight. I probably need to walk around a little."*
>
> *"Let's go," her husband says. "I'll race you."*
>
> *Jane manages a tiny smile. "No racing today."*
>
> *As they walk, she says, "I had an attack at the bank yesterday, but it was only a 4. I think I was just in a hurry and got uptight about waiting in line."*

Panic is like a Chinese finger puzzle. The harder you pull away, the more tightly it holds you. The only way to escape is to stop fighting and accept it. Easy to say. To actually *do* it, panicky people must have some conception of what it is they're accepting. That takes words, lots of them, enough to build a bridge between the experience of fear and knowledge about it. To help, keep the conversation going. Ask questions, give encouragement, and repeat the explanations in this book as often as necessary. Eventually the pieces will begin to fit and the words can become deeds.

Unless fear disorders take on form and substance, there's no way to tell if they're getting better. Explosions into fear occur with certain *frequency*, *duration*, and *intensity*. The way they get better is by happening less often, taking less time to abate, or being less severe. Unless fearful people perceive their fear along these dimensions, rather than as simply off or on, they can improve considerably and not even notice. Unless you point it out.

> *Janes's husband comes home to find her sobbing on the couch. "Honey, what's wrong?" he asks.*
>
> *"I thought I was getting better, but I'm not. I had an attack at the mall today. They're never going away, are they?"*
>
> *Her husband sits down next to her. "Honey, you are getting better. The attacks aren't going to just go away, you know that. But this is the first one you've had in almost a week, isn't it?"*
>
> *Jane sniffs. "I was feeling so good. Then I started having the breathing thing, and I knew it was all coming back."*
>
> *"So, how big was the attack on the Richter scale?"*
>
> *"Maybe a 7."*
>
> *"How long did it last?"*
>
> *"It always feels like forever."*
>
> *"I know it does, but how long do you think the attack went on?"*
>
> *"Not long. My friend was with me, and we did a couple of laps around the parking lot, then I went back in."*
>
> *"Honey, what you're telling me is you had your first attack in almost a week and you managed it beautifully."*
>
> *Another tear runs down Jane's cheek. "I just wish they would go away."*

Both Jane's husband and her friend have done her a lot of good, even if she doesn't acknowledge it. If there is a person with panic disorder in your life, I can guarantee that you will have many similar unsung and seemingly unheeded conversations. Even when the attacks are less frequent and intense, and shorter—signs that they're managing them better—panicky people still view them as grim reminders that the disorder is still there. This is especially true of people like Jane, who have been on medications that made the panic go away, and to whom mild euphoria is their internal standard for relief. You'll have to keep pointing out progress even if your words are ignored, at least for the moment. Be patient. If you repeat the message enough, panicky people will take it in, and one day see it as their own idea rather than yours. That's when it will begin to work. As you can see, very good therapy is sometimes very slow and very mundane.

Blame as an Obstacle

You've probably noticed that though I try to organize treatment of fear disorders into steps and stages, I seem to be jumping back and forth in my expositions and anecdotes. In every chapter, we've covered material that could fit into each of the therapeutic steps, but not in any particular order. My only defense is that life is like that too, a perpetual game of Twister, even at the physiological level. Your amygdala can be in one stage and your hippocampus in another, with your heart right in between. The steps I list indicate the direction of flow. Sometimes the process of healing is disturbed by swirls and eddies, but if things keep moving, eventually people will be all right.

Which brings me to the psychological equivalent of the Hoover Dam: *blame.*

Blaming stops forward movement. It doesn't matter whether people blame themselves or somebody else. Blame is blame. Mindlessly fighting back is no better at curing fear than running away.

Though you may feel that you're being supportive, you can do harm by siding with someone you care about against mean old spiders, idiots who run stop signs, doctors who can't find the real problem, or even sexual abusers who probably should be in jail. Blaming, at best, diverts the energy needed to get better; it diverts it toward getting someone back. At worst it can convince a person that getting someone back will get them better.

Sometimes in the course of healing, people with fear disorders go through a stage of blaming. This is especially true in PTSD as they begin to realize that what they feel is the result of something that happened, not anything they did, chose, or even permitted. The relief feels so good that it's easy to trade fear for anger and stop right there. This is why I'm wary of support groups, especially on the Internet, and therapists whose major qualification is that the same thing happened to them. Misery loves company, and judging from daytime TV, it *adores* publicity.

If a person close to you gets stuck in blaming. Here are a few ideas to help get things moving again. You'll find many more in the section on anger.

STAY OFF THE BANDWAGON.   Joining the fight will not help. Righteous indignation is more like a disease than a cure.

DON'T BLAME THE BLAMERS.   No matter how richly deserved, never make disparaging comments about the not-too-hidden agendas of friends, counselors, support groups, and other people who are "only trying to help." Don't put yourself in their league. You're only an amateur, and they're pros. Instead, try to find a reputable pro of your own, and suggest that your friend get a second opinion.

POINT OUT THAT GETTING BACK AND GETTING BETTER ARE TWO SEP-ARATE GOALS.   The recovering fearful can go toward either, but not both at the same time. Once you've made this distinction, it's helpful to ask people which goal they're pursuing if they seem to be getting confused.

Whatever you do, never encourage emotionally explosive people to go on talk shows!

Step 3: Internal Control

This is the point at which the words turn into deeds. Once people under-stand what fear is, the next step is *showing* them that through their actions they can exert some control over it. This is usually done by teaching specific techniques.

Relaxation and Exercise

Relaxation training and regular exercise work wonders on two distinct lev-els. They decrease generalized arousal, thereby raising the threshold for explosions. Using only relaxation and exercise, people can counteract perhaps half of the physiological energy that ignites explosions into fear.

This is a tremendous gain in itself, and more than enough to justify their use.

The most important effects of relaxation and exercise are psychological: They move fearful people from passively accepting their disorder to doing something about it. This shift in perception shift is crucial to healing from any psychological disorder, and it cannot be achieved through talking alone. It must be experienced.

The procedures themselves are simple. Exercise can be a brisk walk or anything else that gets the heart rate up for at least 20 minutes a day.

As for relaxation techniques, there are many. You've already learned one approach in the chapter on basic calming.

Some techniques are more mechanical. They involve active relaxation of muscle groups in a standard sequence. The key is knowing that it's easier to relax a muscle if you tense it first. Try it yourself: Tighten the muscles in your face into an exaggerated frown. Hold it to the count of five. Now let go. Do you feel the difference? The Jacobson deep muscle relaxation technique does this sort of thing with feet, calves, legs, buttocks, stomach, chest, and so forth. It's direct and specific, if a bit unimaginative, which, if you think about it, is the perfect approach for people whose imaginations run away with them.

Other techniques, like *imagery* and *self-hypnosis* are more creative. They exploit the fact that the brain can't tell reality from fantasy. Try this:

1. Imagine yourself throwing up in public, with a bunch of people pointing, laughing, and holding their noses. As you picture this alarming scene, what happens to your body? I'll bet it turns on your fight or flight response.
2. Now imagine lying on the beach in the warm sunshine without a care in the world. See the palm trees, smell the salt breeze, hear the slow steady rhythm of the surf. Try to feel yourself nestling down into the soft warmth of tropical sand. Are you feeling more relaxed?

There are countless variations on this same theme, repeated endlessly in books and recordings. All of them work. The magic is inside. It's just a matter of picking one and doing it over and over. I often suggest that fearful people sample what's available and devise a technique of their own, record it, and practice it. This enhances the sense of internal control.

In addition to the relaxation itself, imaginative techniques effortlessly present an insight that is critical to the success of cognitive therapy: What you feel is determined by the words that are playing in your mind.

There are techniques that combine mechanical and imaginative methods. Most of these involve eye movements. Hypnotists have been using eye movements to induce trance (think pocket watches) for centuries. Wilhelm Reich devised an elaborate set of eye exercises to free bound-up neurotic energy. Twenty years ago Neuro-Linguistic Programming made elaborate claims about how eye movements could stimulate various parts of the brain. Today, Eye Movement Desensitization and Reprocessing (EMDR) is often used in treating PTSD. Such approaches usually begin as miracle cures that bypass laborious verbal therapy, and later settle into their place among the many techniques for achieving relaxation while imagining uncomfortable or frightening events.

Speaking of combination techniques, yoga has been combining exercise and relaxation for millennia.

The most supportive thing you can do for people with fear disorders is exercise and practice relaxation techniques with them on a regular basis. How you do it doesn't matter so long as you do it every day. If you're serious about wanting to help, this is how. Don't just tell them to do it, do it with them.

No amount of talking by you, doctors, therapists, or anyone else can substitute for the internal change that comes from actually being able to *do* something about fear. Fearful people will often delay, procrastinate, or pass exercise and relaxation off as no big deal because it doesn't get rid of the problem. Just smile and say, "Get your coat; we're going walking."

Desensitization

The basic behavioral procedure for fear disorders involves substituting relaxation for the fight or flight response, and using the new connection to help frightened people move progressively closer to what they fear. Where sympathetic was shall parasympathetic be.

Step by step *Systematic Desensitization* was developed for phobias, but in a less structured form the technique is the basis for all successful approaches to fear disorders.

> *Neil and I repeat the relaxation technique in my office. When he is calm and comfortable, I ask him to picture himself standing on the walkway, watching his wife rake leaves. Then I ask him to imagine walking toward her until he starts feeling afraid. Then we stop and relax until he's calm enough to take another step. Eventually, Neil can imagine touching an actual spider.*

As you can imagine, this process is slow and requires many repetitions before it has the desired effect. There are lots of ways to do desensitization. Most therapists begin with imaginary spiders and move forward to the real thing. Specialists have menageries of frightening animals in their offices for what they call *in vivo training*.

Sometimes these therapists will expose phobics to spiders, snakes, heights, or whatever in huge immediate doses designed to cause the fight or flight response to burn itself out and extinguish. This is *never* done as a surprise.

I refer some phobias to specialists, but treat many in my office with imaginative techniques, which I teach them and their friends and family members, who are the ones who actually take phobics out on in vivo assignments.

> *Neil's mission was no walk in the park. Well, actually it was. After imagery training in my office, he and his wife were able to go out and walk through a city park and even on trails in the mountains. When they saw webs, or in one case an actual you-know-what, he and his wife would back off to a safe distance, relax, and move forward.*
>
> *The end came about a month later when Neil stood poised, ready to squash a hapless spider with his hiking boot, and decided to let it live.*

Not all phobias are so easily treated as Neil's. Some require medication, elaborate strategies, and extensive work by skilled specialists. In many cases, however, especially when the other steps have been accomplished in sequence, when the insights are attained, the working through becomes little more than a walk in the park.

Desensitization is at the heart of all treatments for fear. With panic disorder, the places and situations in which attacks might occur are approached first, and finally the panic itself.

Throughout this narrative, we have been moving in circles around the details of Jane's treatment. Her biggest breakthrough came when she was able to enter a panic attack knowing that she would come out alive. That actually happened fairly early in her disorder, but the learning was obscured by her frantic attempts to escape.

Cognitive Therapy

The basic idea of this approach is: What you feel is determined by what you say to yourself inside your head. To feel better, you have to talk yourself out of overly negative interpretations of your experience by substituting internal phrases that more accurately describe reality.

> *When Jane finally recognized that panic wouldn't kill her, she still had to convince her body. Her therapist had her repeat the phrase "I'm going to be fine" hundreds of times. Eventually it worked. The physical components of fear began to decrease.*

Cognitive therapy is simple, though not quite so simple as I have portrayed it. We will explore its intricacies in later chapters. For now, realize that almost every sentence in this book is meant to be used as an internal phrase that more accurately describes reality.

Step 4: Creating a New Balance

Whatever else they are, psychological symptoms are like lights on the dashboard warning that something is wrong under the hood. Therapists must first be mind mechanics, able to fix the symptoms. Consider the chapter thus far as the shop manual for the repair of fear disorders.

We aren't just mechanics, though; we're creatures of art and intuition.

When therapists look at an explosive person, they don't see a collection of symptoms, but rather a whole personality, often clearly out of balance, with too much of one trait and not enough of another. A therapist's art is in helping people create a new balance that leaves them stronger and more resilient than ever before.

Much of what we know about this aspect of therapy comes from early psychoanalysts, who were always popping open hoods and poking around, sometimes trying simultaneously to make repairs and discover how engines work.

Freud discovered that people actively hide parts of their personalities from themselves. *Repression,* he called it. We already know that people try to avoid what they're afraid of; Freud found out that this happens on the inside as well as the outside. What frightens people most are parts of themselves that don't fit with their beliefs about who and how they ought to be.

Jane is a nice person. She has always prided herself on putting other people's needs ahead of her own. Her life is dedicated to making other people happy.

Admirable though Jane's goals may be, they don't allow enough room in her awareness for an entire personality. What's missing is *aggression.* Like everything else in psychology, aggression is on a continuum. At one end is hitting people over the head; at the other is knowing what you want and asking for it. Jane has trouble with the whole continuum because aggression means putting your needs ahead of someone else's. Once you start doing something like *that,* who knows where it will end? People will be upset, and perhaps they won't like you.

Repression doesn't make unacceptable thoughts go away. There *is* no away. You can't get rid of parts of yourself. Whether you recognize them or not, they're still there, lurking just outside awareness, often determining your life choices. All repression actually does is set up internal alarms to scare you when you step out of bounds. We've heard about alarms already, having characterized fear disorders as alarms that go off for no reason. Sometimes there is a reason.

Please don't make the mistake of expecting one-to-one correspondence. Jane's panic attacks are not merely suppressed urges to hit someone over the head. Her internal conflicts about putting her own needs first do, however, add energy to an already overloaded system.

Many people with panic and anxiety disorders, like Jane, have trouble with the expression of aggression. Not just with getting angry at people, but with asking for what they want, and saying no to what they don't want. Sometimes they let their symptoms do it for them. Remember the debacle about baseball and bunco?

After the symptoms of fear disorders are under control, it's often helpful to poke around under the hood a bit, looking at how formerly fearful people handle their aggressive urges.

> *"I'm just a people pleaser," Jane says, shrugging her shoulders. "I guess I do have a hard time saying no once in a while. It's not a big deal or anything."*
>
> *"What do you have a hard time saying no to?" I ask, making a bigger deal of it than she says it is.*

As we talked, I discovered that Jane was much more attuned to everybody else's needs than her own. This is not unusual for people who develop fear disorders, but not universal. Phobics are less likely to have conflicts about aggression. People with PTSD often avoid retelling, both because of the horror of the incident itself, and their equally frightening feelings of guilt for somehow having caused the incident, complied with it, not prevented it, or for merely having survived it. Occasionally, scattered among the disjointed pictures are normal but troubling feelings that the person defines as unworthy.

People with fear disorders need to feel comfortable doing things they have previously seen as selfish, like saying no. One way to accomplish this goal is by going back into their history to see where they got the idea that they were never supposed to put their own needs first, and then have them rethink their conclusions.

> *"Is there anyone in your family who has a harder time saying no than you do?" I ask.*
>
> *"My mother,"Jane says. Then she starts to laugh.*
>
> *"What's so funny?"*
>
> *"Omigod, I'm just like her. She used to have panic attacks too."*
>
> *"Hmm," I say. "When did you decide you wanted to be just like Mom?"*
>
> *"I didn't," Jane answers quickly. "She's miserable."*

The purpose of analyzing the past is to get people to try something new in the present. With Jane, we were able to use her mother as a negative role model. Whatever her mother would do in a situation, Jane would try to do the opposite. This worked beautifully because Jane, like most people, was willing to invest a good deal of effort in not acting like her mother. Unresolved adolescent rebellion is one of the most potent energy sources in the universe. By tapping into it, I can help people find the power to change.

Each time Jane said no, it made her a little stronger.

"I'm really sorry, but I don't have time to be president of the PTA," Jane says, a bit tremulously perhaps, but the important thing is she actually says it.

* * *

Jane looks her boss in the eye. "I worked late Tuesday and Wednesday. It's my turn to go home on time." Her voice doesn't shake at all.

* * *

"Mom, I , uh, already have plans for Saturday."

People close to the formally fearful applaud the newfound ability to say no. Until it's said to them.

"No, I don't want to go to the game; I don't particularly like baseball. Why don't you go with one of your friends?"

This lights the fuse for one final blast.

The *Why Aren't You as Nice as You Used to Be?* Explosion

This outburst won't be from *them,* it will be from *you.*

When it happens, here's a little cognitive therapy that may help: Overly nice people tend to turn their aggressive impulses inward, in the form of panic attacks, phobias, depression, and other disorders we have yet to discuss. If you want them to get better, they're going to have to tell *everybody* no once in a while. Even you. Deal with it.

Chapter 7

Generalized Anxiety Disorder

Explosions into Worry

ACCORDING TO DSM-IV, generalized anxiety disorder is:

1. Excessive anxiety and worry (apprehensive expectation), occurring more days than not for at least 6 months, about a number of events or activities (such as work or school performance).
2. The person finds it difficult to control the worry.
3. The anxiety and worry are associated with three (or more) of the following six symptoms (with at least some symptoms present for more days than not for the past 6 months).
   a. Restlessness or feeling keyed up or on edge
   b. Being easily fatigued
   c. Difficulty concentrating or mind going blank
   d. Irritability
   e. Muscle tension
   f. Sleep disturbance (difficulty falling or staying asleep, or restless unsatisfying sleep.)

We've seen such symptoms before; they're signs of an overactive sympathetic nervous system. All of us experience symptoms like these occasionally when we're under stress. People with generalized anxiety disorder experience them constantly, because they are constantly generating stress for themselves.

The self-generation is what defines the disorder psychologically. People with generalized anxiety disorder continuously imagine potential dangers, often as a means of protecting themselves. Their internal world features continuous replays of remotely possible disasters, shown in gruesome closeup, with every hideous detail—both real and imaginary—blown completely out of proportion. Their poor brains can't tell the difference between reality and fantasy, so every replay switches on the fight or flight response. This continual arousal in the face of imaginary threat wears them down in ways reality can never hope to match. In PTSD, people are haunted by a single terrifying and all too real memory. With generalized anxiety disorder, people are pecked to death by their own fantasies.

Anxious people believe that if they know about problems in advance, they can at least be prepared. They always expect the worst, just to be on the safe side. What they do to be safe is usually more perilous than actual danger.

There are two basic strategies people use to protect themselves: passive avoidance of supposedly dangerous situations, and active attempts to control possible dangers by worrying about them. Both strategies create more anxiety than they dissipate.

Medications can't cure generalized anxiety disorder, but they can sometimes provide a short-term solution. Though serotonin reuptake inhibitors are sometimes prescribed for generalized anxiety, they don't work nearly so well as they do for panic disorder. Effexor, an SNRI, seems to work a little better. Anticonvulsants like Neurontin are prescribed also, with mixed results. They sometimes relieve anxiety, but often at the expense of feeling bleary and disconnected.

Benzodiazepines, as you might imagine, do work, but since the anxiety is constant, they have to be taken constantly. The danger of addiction is considerable. Often, doctors will prescribe Valium, Xanax, or Klonopin, or a similar drug in limited doses to be used when the anxiety is particularly acute. Benzodiazepine sleeping medications like Ambien and Halcion are used in a limited fashion too.

BuSpar, a newer serotonergic drug, was developed to control generalized anxiety without addictive potential. In some cases, it works well, but it doesn't make much of a dent in the levels of anxiety I see in clinical practice.

For anxiety about a specific performance, beta blockers—drugs usually used to calm the circulatory system and lower blood pressure—are sometimes effective.

Medications can calm people enough so they can begin learning to calm themselves, or at least begin to recognize that the source of their pain is their own imagination.

The Passive Strategy: Being Stressed Out

Stress, like many other concepts from psychology that have drifted into popular culture, has lost its specificity and now has vastly different meanings, depending on who is using it. *Stress* can be a verb or a noun, a cause or effect, internal or external, friend or foe.

Before we talk more about strategies to control stress, we have to come to some agreement about what it is. Is stress dangerous, a hidden killer to be eliminated on sight? Is it just a part of life, to be endured as best we can? Or could it actually be good for us?

The answer is: All of the above.

Stress is merely a load on the system—anything that gets our hearts going and our breathing rate up. Sex, walking up stairs, or making a presentation to a group of shareholders are all forms of stress. Any of them can wear us out or build us up, depending on how we handle them. Stress, like exercise, can make us stronger if we take it in regular, increasing doses. Actually, exercise is a form of stress that everyone agrees is beneficial.

So why does stress have such a bad connotation?

Back in the 1950s the idea that psychological turmoil could influence physical disease was fairly radical in medicine. Psychiatrists and psychologists had been saying as much for years, but the "real" doctors were not convinced. Many thought that there were as yet undiscovered physical causes for psychological symptoms, rather than the other way around.

In 1950, Hans Selye, an endocrinologist, was the first to use the word *stress* as we think of it today, meaning a physical or emotional factor that causes internal tension and psychological damage. He hypothesized a *generalized adaptation syndrome* in which the body mobilizes to deal with stress. At first, physiological resistance holds the stressors at bay, but eventually the system becomes exhausted, opening the door for mental and physical disease. Selye thought that the modern world was just too stressful for healthy living. This simple idea spread into the popular consciousness like wildfire. Stress was a hidden killer, and there was just too much of it. Selye also said that too little stress was just as bad as too much, but that part was largely ignored in the rush to blame modern life for the ills of modern life.

Some of the earliest research on the effects of stress involved assigning common environmental stressors, such as *Death of a spouse* or *Christmas*, a numerical value. Then the numbers in a person's life were added up, and the higher the total, the greater the likelihood that person would get sick within the year. You have undoubtedly seen the checklist in a magazine or Sunday supplement. How high was your score? Danger zone, right? So why aren't you in the hospital?

For one thing, the test is rather crude, and many people come out as false positives.

For another, later studies showed that there were a number of people who carried huge stress loads and still managed quite well. These stress-hardy individuals seem to share three characteristics: (1) They believe that what they do affects what happens to them, (2) they're connected and committed to something larger than themselves, and (3) they go out of their way to take on challenges and to learn new things. If you want a definition of psychological health, this is the best one I know. As you've seen in the previous chapters, the overall purpose of psychotherapy is to foster these very attitudes and behaviors.

Stress is most dangerous to people who think stress is dangerous and try to avoid it. One of the reasons the stress checklist is so popular, despite its relative inaccuracy, is that it offers proof—to those who seek it—that an external force is causing their pain, and suggests by implication that to get better you ought to get rid of stress. These views fly in the face of everything we know about fear disorders, but they're seductive nonetheless.

Remember Randy from the last chapter, who became anxious after a disciplinary action at work and was misdiagnosed as having PTSD? When I saw him, almost a year after he went out on disability, he was still worked up about the stresses of his job.

"The pressure was incredible," Randy says. "The pace was impossible, nobody could keep up. Everything was top priority. They'd assign you one project, then change it the next day, and then act like that's what they wanted you to do all along. Like maybe you were a mind reader or something. To make things worse, once a month you'd have to give an oral report in front of the management team, where they'd ream you out for everything you didn't get done because they told you to do something else."

The job from hell, right? That's the way Randy saw it, but to other people who labored away in those same fiery pits, it was business as usual. Randy was devastated by the stress that his coworkers took in stride because he saw it as devastating. There's no question that Randy's job stressed him out. What was questionable was how much of the stress came from the job and how much Randy was creating for himself. The stress in his job wasn't all in his head, but what he imagined stress to be made it much harder for him to cope with it effectively.

First, he believed that stress was the result of somebody or something messing up. Every new crisis would provoke an internal tirade about whose fault it was and how damaging their incompetence was to him. Sometimes the tirades were external.

The *I'm So Stressed* Explosion

Actually, this explosion is more like a perpetually sputtering fuse.

In the break room at about 10 a.m., Randy pours his fourth cup of coffee. He smiles weakly. "The doctor says I ought to cut back on this stuff," he says, "but I don't know how I can get by without it. I swear, you've got to be a mind reader around here to know what they want. When I came in this morning, Jim asked me to check on what was happening with the EnCom account. No sooner had I gotten started on that than he e-mails me that headquarters wants my monthly contact figures right now. Then, ten minutes later, he pops in saying he's having a project managers meeting in an hour.

"So, which one does he want me to do? Who knows?

*"Anyway, by the time I get back to my office, there'll prob-
ably be something else."*

*He finishes his coffee and refills his mug. "The doctor says
I need to cut down on stress. My blood pressure is through the
roof." Randy shrugs. "I told him to talk to Jim."*

There are a lot of things you *could* say to a person like Randy. You could start by asking him why, if he has so much to do, he's sitting around in the break room drinking coffee. Don't bother. He'll just say that his doctor told him to take it easy to keep down his stress level. Generally, the only people who actually follow this kind of recommendation are the ones who shouldn't.

In an effort to help Randy, you could point out that caffeine, being a generalized stimulant, is increasing, rather than decreasing, his sympathetic arousal. Actually, there's quite a bit of good advice you could give him, but don't waste your breath. He won't listen.

Randy would rather you'd pull up a chair and commiserate with him, and afterward go out and tell the world about his suffering. Maybe you could even take on a few tasks to help him out. You know better, of course, but you're a kind person and you can see that his pain is real.

The best way to help is by asking: What are you going to do about it?

This is another one of those tiny interventions that can make a huge difference. With one question you step outside the expected pattern, suggest that the problem is Randy's to solve, and propose, gently, that he reflect on the ineffective strategies he's already using. Not that he'll do all these things, but he will at least have to think about them.

Explosive people believe things *should* be different, that jobs should be reasonable, that panics should go away, or that people should do what they're supposed to do. Emotional explosions are often futile demands that the world fix itself. Normal people recognize that if they don't like the way the world is, they either have to change it or change themselves. Griping only makes it worse.

Randy thinks his job is too stressful because there's a lot of it he's scared to do. He uses the popular conception of stress as danger to justify avoiding what he fears. All of us do this to a certain extent. We call enjoyable stress *excitement* and actively pursue it. Dating, skiing down a slope, or waiting in delicious anticipation for a bingo number to be called are all more stressful than writing a monthly report, but few people would consider avoiding these activities because of the physiological strain.

The kinds of things that Randy has to do to get by in his job—staying with boring tasks, figuring out ambiguous situations, speaking in front of groups, and saying no to people who make unreasonable demands—are less pleasant. The physiological sensations they elicit are similar to excitement, but the thoughts we have about them are different. These are the stresses we wish we could avoid. We don't, because we consider them necessary to succeeding at our jobs, to our developing as human beings, or maybe we just think other people are counting on us. Frightening as these tasks are, we do them, and by doing them we develop the strength to do more. We see ourselves as having a choice in the matter. We're committed to our work, so we take on the things we fear and make them into challenges. Most often, we make these choices automatically, never thinking that they keep us from getting stress-related disorders or developing mental illness. We just do what we need to do, regardless of how we feel about it.

On the other side of this vast psychological gulf are emotionally explosive people who, by attempting to avoid negative emotion, invariably experience more of it. Randy doesn't do the difficult parts of his job because he sees them as reflections of his boss's incompetence. If Jim would just do his job correctly, Randy would have no problem with his. The logic here is a bit thin, so Randy plays it over and over both inside and outside of his head, in a vain attempt to convince himself and everyone else that his pain is someone else's responsibility.

Sometimes people who see their stress as someone else's fault will explode directly at that person. We'll deal with them in the section on anger, but I'll tell you now that they're rarer than you might think. Most angry people pick safer targets, like people who love them.

Though Randy's thought patterns might lead to anger in someone else, he—like most people with fear disorders—prefers the passive approach to aggression: *Run away* rather than *fight back*.

Not that it makes much difference. Other people don't distinguish between active and passive aggression. They recognize and respond to attacks, whether they take the form of directly complaining about what they tell you to do or just forgetting to do it.

The Active Strategies: Worrying and Controlling

DSM-IV says that worrying means *apprehensive expectation*. It's more than that, as any worrier can tell you. Worrying is an almost magical attempt to prevent bad things from happening by thinking of them in advance. The idea is that whatever you think of is somehow less likely to occur. It's not just planning. That's part of it, but there's more, something almost spiritual, as if heartfelt worry taps into the mysterious force that keeps cars on the road and planes in the air.

Worrying is a full-time job. If anxious people let down their guard for a minute, who knows what will come crawling in?

The *Danger Is Everywhere* Explosion

"Do you know anybody with a microscope?" Catherine asks, clearly upset about something.

"A microscope?" her friend asks. "What do you want a microscope for?"

"I read this article about dust mites," Catherine says. "They live in rugs and sheets and sofas and pillows and all over the place. You actually breathe their droppings!"

"Come on, Catherine," her friend says, almost laughing but knowing better than to do so. "I've seen those articles. They magnify these tiny little bugs and make them look like monsters. They're just trying to get you to buy some kind of expensive vacuum cleaner."

"But you breathe their droppings! You can be allergic. It's a major cause of asthma! You know how Adam was wheezing last week."

"He had a cold, Catherine! He's not wheezing now, is he?"

"I thought I heard him last night. When he was asleep."

Catherine's friend works hard to keep from rolling her eyes.
"Did you ever think he might have been snoring?"

"Do you know where I can get a microscope?"

Generalized anxiety is a mental disorder that can drive other people crazy.

Today, Catherine is freaking out over bug poop. Yesterday, it was pesticides on fruit. The day before it was lead in drinking water. All of them are low level threats compared to the stress of someone you love torturing herself in front of your eyes, and you not knowing what to do about it.

The secret for handling explosions into worry is to remember that *it's the worry itself that is the problem, not what the person is worrying about.* Hold this in your mind and you'll be less likely to get caught, as Catherine's friend did, trying to reassure. If you focus on content, the reassuring never ends. As soon as you talk an anxious person out of worrying about one thing, another takes its place.

Here are some specific suggestions that might help:

AVOID CONTENT AT FIRST; FOCUS ON ANXIETY. The most supportive thing you can do for a person like Catherine is point out that she's working herself up, then help her to calm down.

> *"I can see you're really upset, Catherine. Take a deep breath,*
> *then let's go for a walk and talk about it."*
> *"But I need to find out if there are dust mites in Adam's*
> *room."*
> *"Forget the dust mites, The best way to take care of Adam*
> *is to take care of yourself. Get your coat."*

Don't worry about being insensitive, you're doing a kindness. As we've seen before, people in the midst of an emotional explosion have energy to burn. Help them do it in a constructive way. You'll be surprised how much more clearly you both can think when you're moving. You can accomplish more on the move. If they're very upset, feel free to use other basic calming techniques as well.

In dealing with a panic attack, it's important to demonstrate understanding that the person's fear is real. This is less necessary in generalized anxiety. You can safely brush aside the content of worry if your actions show concern. Simply ignoring the person will not work. Worrying is an internal process, and it doesn't require your participation to continue.

Needless to say, you should try to keep from getting worked up yourself. The last thing either of you need is to drop everything to dash around trying to make the world safe from bug poop.

PUT THE SITUATION INTO PERSPECTIVE.   We have seen that one aspect of the fight or flight response is shutting out everything but the present peril. Anxious people lose their sense of proportion. You can help them regain it by asking questions that get them back in touch with the relative nature of experience. The questions are similar to what you'd ask people with other fear disorders. Scales of 1 to 10 are always useful.

> *After a few minutes of brisk walking, Catherine's friend asks, "On a 1 to 10 scale, how important is this dust mite thing?"*
> *"Eleven," Catherine says.*
> *Her friend laughs, "How can it be an 11?"*
> *Catherine draws herself up tall. "My son's safety is the most important thing in the world to me."*

The first answer is usually 11. Each new danger becomes preeminent as soon as anxious people think of it. Most often they do this by connecting it, as Catherine did, to a real top priority. To worriers, *anything* can hurt their children, destroy their marriage, or cause them to lose their jobs. Ask them to rank order, then point out that they've left out one more very real risk.

> *"Which do you think is a bigger threat to Adam's health, dust mite, or the pesticides you were upset about the other day?"*
> *"They're both dangerous."*
> *"Are either of them more dangerous than having a mom who's always upset and worried that something's going to kill him?"*

This technique is a little like jujitsu, using anxious people's own psychological momentum to get them going in the direction you want. It's also a little like a guilt trip, which, when applied judiciously, can be quite therapeutic.

Another strategy is suggesting that they do something about their top priority rather than worry about it. In fact, worry is sometimes used as a substitute for more productive actions that require more effort, or are scary.

> *"If you think Adam has asthma, forget the dust mites." Catherine's friend says. "Take him to the doctor!"*
> *"I don't want to bother the doctor with this," Catherine says.*
> *"You just want to bother yourself, huh?*

"It's not really a bother."
"Yeah, right."

POINT OUT THAT WORRY IS THE PROBLEM. If you follow most any line of questioning outward from a *danger is everywhere* explosion, you'll eventually get to a place where the anxious person has to agree that the worry is a bigger problem than whatever she was worrying about. The more you employ this sort of reasoning, the quicker it will go next time.

ASK FOR ACTION TO DEAL WITH THE WORRY. The way to get over fear disorders is by taking small steps in the right direction. Each one counts.

"Catherine, have you been listening to that relaxation tape the doctor gave you?"
"Well, no. Not lately; I've been too busy."
"Too busy worrying about everybody else's health to take care of your own?"
"I guess so."
"You know what you need to do, don't you?"

If Catherine is in treatment, then in addition to relaxation tapes and exercise, she'll also probably be working on cognitive techniques that help her place her worries in perspective, assess their actual danger, and then to take more constructive action. You already know something about cognitive techniques; you've just done one with her.

SUGGEST SCHEDULED WORRYING. Worry, because of its magical properties, is hard to give up. If Catherine stopped worrying about her son's health, she'd feel that she wasn't doing her job as a parent. Her worrying, destructive though it may be, is still an act of love. Don't tell her to stop. Instead, propose that she worry on schedule.

The difference between constructive worrying and anxiety involves time as well as content. Thirty minutes of worrying a day can prevent people from making stupid mistakes; more than that can distract from useful problem solving by making problems bigger than they actually are.

Schedule worrying in two 15-minute periods a day. One should be about an hour before bedtime. It may help prevent the next explosion.

The *I Can't Sleep* Explosion

Catherine looks haggard at seven o'clock as she sets a half grape-
fruit in front of her husband.
   "Another bad night?" he asks.
   She nods sadly as she pours herself another cup of coffee.
"I was up until almost five just looking at the clock." She yawns.
"It's been just as bad all week. I can't even remember when I last
had a decent night's sleep. I just don't know how I'm going to
get by at work."

Anxious people have trouble sleeping, but not nearly so much trouble as they think. The problem is as much worrying about not getting enough sleep as it is not sleeping itself. Studies of sleep disorders show that anxious people actually get far more sleep than they say they do. There is evidence of real sleep deprivation in depression, but we'll discuss that in the next section.

Despite the research, never try to convince anxious people that they're not really awake all night, even if you've heard them snoring. They won't believe you, and they'll think you're insensitive for saying so. However, it is useful for you to know that the problem may not be as serious as they think.

If there's an anxious person in your life, you'll probably be called upon to give advice about sleeping. Here are some guidelines that are supported by research. Anxious people seldom follow any of them:

YOU CAN'T FORCE YOURSELF TO SLEEP.   Sleep comes unbidden when its rhythm overtakes the brain. You let it happen; you can't make it happen. The more you worry about sleeping, the more you keep yourself awake. Like all the automatic functions in the body, sleep has a slow, steady cadence. Worry has no rhythm at all, it is an endless series of fits and starts, twists and turns that cancel out the slow, natural rhythms of life. You can't pursue sleep, you have to slow down enough for it to catch up with you.

GO TO BED AT THE SAME TIME EVERY NIGHT.   The sleep cycle is part of the circadian rhythm, which is regulated by lower brain centers that are extremely repetitive and ritualistic. Court them with your own repetitious rituals.

Anxious people usually go to bed when they're done with whatever they're doing. Bedtime can vary tremendously from one day to the next. Like almost everything else anxious people do, this disrupts the natural rhythm.

Set a bedtime and stick to it, even on weekends. The actual time you get in bed should be preceded by about 45 minutes of winding down.

DEVELOP A BEDTIME RITUAL. Winding down should be the same every night: reading, watching TV, taking a hot bath, doing relaxation exercises or whatever else calms you down. Before you relax, however, you should do something to get your worries out of the way. Start your bedtime ritual by sitting down with pencil and paper, and make your to-do list for the next day. Write notes to yourself about what you have to do, and even what you have to worry about. The idea is to impose an artificial end point on the day's tasks so you don't have to stay up reminding yourself of what still has to be done. By making this list, you're counteracting the *Ziegarnik effect*, which is the brain's tickle file for unfinished tasks. Things that aren't finished are automatically brought up into memory so you won't forget. You don't want this to happen at one A.M.

DON'T TAKE NAPS. Speaking of unfinished tasks, if you didn't get enough sleep last night, you want to catch up tonight. Your brain and body will help you do this by making you really tired—if you don't take away the momentum by sleeping during the day.

USE IMAGERY. Telling someone not to worry is like telling them not to think of a white horse. Instead of not thinking about something that keeps you awake, think of something that relaxes you, such as a safe and comfortable place, or a situation in which you were so sleepy you could barely keep your eyes open. Ninth grade geometry class works for me.

IF YOU CAN'T GO TO SLEEP IN 20 MINUTES, GET UP. The idea here is to keep your bed a conditioned stimulus (remember Pavlov?) for sleep rather than lying awake and worrying about how long it will take you to get to sleep and how drowsy you're going to be the next day.

If sleep eludes you for 20 minutes, get up and read a boring book for another 20, then try again. You can also listen to music or a relaxation tape, but TV usually doesn't work as well if the program is even slightly interesting. You could try watching infomercials.

Avoid caffeine and alcohol. People with sleep problems sometimes drink a lot of coffee (or tea or cola) to stay awake during the day. The caffeine keeps you awake at night, perpetuating the cycle. A good rule is to avoid caffeine after noon. Watch out for decongestants as well. Cold pills with pseudoephedrine can be as stimulating as caffeine. If the label says it won't make you drowsy, it may well keep you awake.

Alcohol can put you to sleep, but it disrupts brain rhythms, so you're likely to wake up again in short order, possibly with a headache. One drink in the evening may be beneficial, but more than that can create more problems than it solves.

Use medication, but sparingly. Everybody knows how easily you can become dependent on sleeping pills. This assumption is at least partly a relic of the days when sleeping pills were highly addictive barbiturates to which people quickly built up a tolerance, so that it took more and more to do less and less. Benzodiazepines, like Ambien and Halcion, have the same problem, but create tolerance more slowly. These medications are very useful however in breaking a pattern of insomnia, giving the sleepless hope and enough will to try other methods.

One of the most effective sleep medications is Trazadone, a sedating antidepressant that metabolizes quickly and does not create a tolerance.

Cold medications containing antihistamines but no decongestants may also help you to sleep. Antihistamines are the active ingredient in most over-the-counter sleeping medications. They don't build a physical tolerance, but people can become dependent on them.

Health food stores offer a number of sleep-inducing herbs and nutrients. Tryptophan and melatonin have some research support behind them and are safe and nonaddictive. My clients typically don't find them to be particularly effective, but they're probably worth a try.

Warm milk and herbal teas work for some people. The mechanism may be as much the ritual as the chemistry, but do you really care?

Anxious people feel out of control, and will do almost anything to regain their sense of mastery over their own lives. Usually they pick the wrong thing, thereby creating more anxiety for themselves. Developing and following programs to limit worry in order to get to sleep is a form of positive control that may divert anxious people from more negative and damaging pursuits, like trying to control you.

Dealing with Control Freaks

It's no secret that some anxious people try to protect themselves by controlling other people. You know who they are. They run your company, they taught you in school, and they probably even live in your house. Come to think of it, control freaks are everywhere. They've been on your case since you were a kid, trying to run your life, always telling you what you did wrong, never what you did right, like the time your dad ...

I did tell you about the power of unresolved adolescent authority issues, didn't I?

The first and most important thing you have to know to deal effectively with control freaks is that the perception of control is in the eye of the beholder. What you see is what you expect, regardless of what's there. If you're the sort who doesn't like to be told what to do, *everybody* is a control freak. A word to the wise is sufficient.

The *I Can't Believe You'd Forget* Explosion

Here's a catastrophic thought: What if Catherine were *your* boss? Now who would have the job from hell?

> *"Did you fill out the pink form that goes to the state?" Catherine asks.*
>
> *"Uh," you say, playing for time. "I was busy, and I wasn't really sure when you were supposed to fill them out except when—"*
>
> *" Do you mean to tell me that you sent off everything else, without filling out the state form? Omigod, do you know what kind of trouble we can get in for not sending those in at the same time? There are fines, penalties, and even criminal charges."*

Control freaks see themselves as overburdened with the task of protecting an ungrateful world from mistakes. Fear is, of course, at the heart of their neurotic need.

Imagine a dog inside an electric fence. After he touches it once or twice, you can turn off the power, because he won't go near it again. This is the way people with control problems deal with their fear of doing something wrong. Somewhere in the dim past they were stung; now they never get close enough to see whether the power is still on. They avoid the challenge of facing their fears, but cover it over with piles of work.

The strategy is self-defeating. Unconfronted fears mutate in the darkness beyond the fence like alien fungi. Gradually they take over more and more of the person's daylight world. The safe area becomes narrower, and the only way to keep back the creatures of the night is with more control and more distance from the awful possibility of error.

If you ask them about it, they'll just say they're doing their job.

So, what do you do if you are attacked by one of these poor, frightened people?

Make no attempt to defend yourself. Even if you're right — especially then — never try to explain your point of view. There's no way you can do it without sounding defensive. Don't start a fight you can't possibly win.

Getting mad and calling them controlling will make the situation worse. They will see your behavior as clear evidence that they must watch you even more closely. You'll be the one with the problem, not them.

Forget trying to talk them out of their need for control. Even seasoned therapists have trouble with that. (Remember what I said about the difficulty of treating someone for something you have.)

Ask, "What would you like me to do?" Dealing effectively with control freaks is a matter of negotiation, not recrimination. Most control freaks prefer lecturing about the dangers of what you've already done rather than thinking about what to do next. This sort of pointless catastrophizing is what they say in their own heads to scare themselves into good performance. It may be scary, but it does little to improve performance — theirs or yours.

Explosions are often merely the externalization of the internal process that is fanning the flames. Explosive people are talking to themselves, not you; you can hear them convincing themselves that the situation is bad, dangerous, hopeless, or all three. These internal monologues are the evil twin of cognitive therapy. You can actually hear people making themselves feel worse. By asking simple questions, such as, What would you like me to do? or What are you going to do? you press the stop button and get explosive people to focus outward. There is no greater service you can do for them. It will also make your life considerably easier.

Once control freaks—or any other explosive people, for that matter—tell you what they want you to do, you're on the road to negotiation. They are using the part of their brain that thinks rather than emotes, and a solution is possible.

ASK THAT THEY CLEARLY DEFINE THE PRODUCT. Every task has an end product—whatever needs to be done—and a process—the actual behaviors through which the end product is achieved. Controlling people will act as if you should already know what you're supposed to do. Usually this is because they haven't thought through the situation well enough to explain it in terms of actions. This is an appropriate time to be persistent.

> *Catherine sighs. "Do I have to tell you everything?"*
>
> *"I guess so," you say with an even tone and a completely straight face. "What, exactly do you want me to do?"*

Negotiate to deliver a very specific product at a very specific time. If you hand over the goods, there is less motivation to quibble about how you got them.

REQUEST PRIORITIES. We have also seen that anxious people will let everything sneak up to top priority if you let them. Don't let them. If they're managing you, make them do their job by telling you the relative order of importance of the tasks they assign.

Needless to say, you need to have some history of delivering the goods for strategies like these to protect you from control freaks. If you do what you say, when you say you'll do it, they'll probably go away and bother somebody less reliable.

Treatment for Generalized Anxiety Disorder

Treatment for generalized anxiety follows the same general pattern as treatment for other fear disorders. The focus is mostly on disrupting the internal dialogues that create and maintain anxiety.

> *Catherine and I worked for several months on getting her anxiety under control. She was referred to me through her work, but in treatment I brought in her husband, her son, and even her best friend. We worked out programs for exercise, relaxation, and cognitive strategies for dealing with her self-defeating explosions into worry.*
>
> *I won't say that Catherine isn't anxious anymore. But her worry—which she tries to limit to 30 minutes a day—is far more constructive. When she catches herself thinking about possible disasters, she's able to stop herself before she blows things too far out of proportion and asks, quietly in her own mind, what she calls "Dr. Bernstein's question": What are you going to do about it?*

I can't ask for more than that.

Part Three

Explosions into Sadness

Chapter 8

Explosions into Sadness

Facing Depression, the Great, Gray Beast

Rachel cries herself into deep, dreamless sleep that lasts 12 hours most nights. She also naps on weekends. "Sleep is my escape," she says. Her voice sounds dull and gray as dishwater. "What's the point of getting out of bed? Some days, I don't even get up to eat. Not that you could tell. There are other times when I just can't stop eating."

* * *

Alonzo eats almost nothing, and hardly sleeps at all since his wife asked him to leave. A couple of stiff drinks knock him out, but after three hours or so he's up again, remembering. "I keep trying to figure, I mean, why would she do it? I get up and try to read, but I can't concentrate. I end up just sitting there, staring at the boob tube."

Alonzo shakes his head. "Guess I wasn't man enough for her. Probably not man enough for anybody." He sighs, deflating like a poorly tied balloon. "I don't know if I can live without her."

* * *

Randy watches TV too, constantly. At least since he went on stress leave. "Guess I'm kind of a couch potato," he says. "I watch a lot of cable. Mostly educational stuff, like the History Channel, or those animal shows, or the ones about Egypt. And Jeopardy. I always watch that. People say I should try out, since I usually know the answers." He snorts. "Yeah, right. As if I could handle that kind of pressure."

* * *

Carol would rather move the couch than sit on it. She's always busy. "You know how it is," she says, shrugging her shoulders. "Always something to do. Everybody needs something." Between phrases she forces her face into smiles that are too big, too bright, and show too many teeth. "There's my family, of course, and my job. I do a little volunteer work at the church, and the PTA, and then there's Scouts." As she enumerates the demands on her time, Carol seems to be scanning the room to see if anything needs straightening or dusting.

* * *

Kinesha awoke from troubled dreams to find herself transformed. "One day everything was pretty much okay, and the next it was like I was empty inside. I don't feel anything. I'm just kind of going through the motions. I get up, get the kids off to school, and go to work, but it's like nothing matters. I can't think; most of the time I don't even know what I'm doing. It's like I'm not really there."

WHAT'S WRONG WITH THESE PEOPLE? Any clinician will tell you without a moment's hesitation. They're *depressed*. But what's that? How can the same disorder cause people to smile or cry, sleep too much or hardly sleep at all, pig out or starve themselves, work all the time or stay glued to the couch?

Concerning *Major Depression*, DSM-IV says that "five (or more) of the following symptoms have been present during the same two-week period and represent a change from previous functioning; at least one of the symptoms is either (1) depressed mood or (2) loss of interest or pleasure.

1. Depressed mood most of the day, nearly every day, as indicated by either subjective report (e.g., feels sad or empty) or observation made by others (e.g., appears tearful). In children and adolescents, can be irritable mood.
2. Markedly diminished interest or pleasure in all, or almost all, activities most of the day, nearly every day (as indicated by either subjective account or observation made by others).
3. Significant weight loss when not dieting, or weight gain (e.g., a change of more than five percent of body weight in a month), or decrease or increase in appetite nearly every day.
4. Insomnia or hypersomnia nearly every day.
5. Psychomotor agitation or retardation nearly every day (observable by others, not merely subjective feelings of restlessness or being slowed down).
6. Fatigue or loss of energy nearly every day.
7. Feelings of worthlessness or excessive or inappropriate guilt (which may be delusional) nearly every day, not merely self-reproach or guilt about being sick.
8. Diminished ability to think or concentrate, or indecisiveness, nearly every day (either by subjective account or as observed by others).
9. Recurrent thoughts of death (not just fear of dying), recurrent suicidal ideation without a specific plan, or a suicide attempt or a specific plan for committing suicide.

There are other, more minor depressions, but the list covers the usual symptoms of this most commonly diagnosed mental disorder. It is difficult to see an underlying disease process in a disorder that can be so many different things. I call this section *Explosions into Sadness*, but not all depressed people are sad. *All* depressed people aren't anything. They're just, well, depressed.

Depression is not a single disorder, but each different type grades so subtly into the next that there is no clear dividing line between them. So, what is depression? We could take the medical approach and say that depression is whatever responds to antidepressant treatment. But that doesn't work anymore. As we've seen, almost *everything* responds to antidepressants.

Sometimes depressions are classified according to whether or not people have a reason to be depressed. Alonzo lost his wife, so his depression is *reactive*. Reactive depressions are usually intense and relatively short-lived, though they can last for years.

Kinesha is depressed for no reason that we can see. Her depression is *endogenous*, which means "from the inside." Endogenous depressions arise from internal chemical imbalances with no external cause and are thought to have a hereditary component. Kinesha's mother had bouts of depression as well. Many depressions, like Kinesha's and her mother's, are episodic, having periods of greater severity that last for several months and then get better.

Some depressions are interspersed with periods of high energy and an artificially cheerful mood called *manias*. Carol's is like that. Disorders that have both components are called *bipolar*. Mood swings in bipolar disorder usually last several weeks to several months. Mood swings measured in minutes or hours do not constitute bipolar disorder. They are usually overreactions to immediate external circumstances, often related to hormonal excess in adolescence and to adolescent thinking in adulthood. There are also some rapid hormonal mood swings associated with menopause and premenstrual syndrome.

Some depressions are *acute*: short, sharp, and sometimes dangerous. Others are *chronic*: dull, blurry, and lasting for years. If you have experience with depressed people, you know that these distinctions are never as clear face-to-face as they are on paper. People with acute depressions have histories of chronic depressive tendencies. People who say they have no reason to be depressed are clearly starving from a lack of emotional stimulation, and manics laugh to keep from crying.

So, what is depression?

What follows are some patterns of thoughts, feelings, and actions that are common, but by no means constant.

Melancholia

Often, depression is not so much sadness as the diminished capacity to be happy. The extreme version is a black mood that settles like a pall before dawn, waking people in darkness to show them only more darkness, another dreary, colorless day. Melancholic people feel that life is empty, that they always have been depressed and always will be. The mood lifts a bit later in the day, but not much.

Goethe, who had melancholic tendencies, said, "Despair knows itself not," which is a profound psychological observation. Depression is a distortion in perception that is invisible to the people who have it. They think it's the world that's dismal rather than their own mood.

Depressed people will say they're not overly negative, only realistic. Sadly, they're right. In many studies, depressed people are more accurate observers and predictors of events than their more "normal" peers. Mental health at least partly consists of unwarranted optimism. As Alexander Pope said, "Hope springs eternal ... "

Most "normal" people remember only the first part of Pope's couplet, and take it for grudging praise of a positive attitude. They don't get it. The whole thing is:

> *Hope springs eternal in the human breast:*
> *Man never is but always to be blest."*

Pope, like Goethe, was clinically depressed.

Though depression tends to diminish motivation, there is something about melancholia that makes people want to write. Without depression, there wouldn't be much need for literature. Movies would suffice. Depression lends depth to human experience. When people are happy, they seldom look inside themselves to find out why. When they're unhappy, they seldom do anything else.

DISTURBANCE OF VEGETATIVE PROCESSES. Depressions often involve physiological slowing, with disruption of basic survival functions like eating and sleeping. Thinking and movement may also slow down.

The gauge of a depression's severity is the extent to which vegetative functions are impaired. Disturbance of eating and sleeping are very common in the first week or so following a loss like a death or divorce, when the body shuts down in response to shock. That part of the condition usually resolves fairly quickly. If it doesn't, or if people who have not suffered a loss are not eating or sleeping for more than three days, the condition is serious, and requires immediate professional care.

Depressed people are notorious for not taking care of themselves. They may eat and sleep, but not well. Their grooming suffers: Sometimes they skip showers and wear the same clothes for several days. Here we find the first of many examples of how depression blurs cause and effect. Think of how you'd feel not having showered and wearing the same clothes for three days. Pretty depressing, isn't it?

The symptoms of depression often become the cause for more depression. Depressed people typically want to wait until they feel better to do the things that will make them feel better. As a consequence, they get worse. It is in this aspect of the disorder that friends and family can have the greatest positive effect. If there is a depressed person in your life, you can help by coercing them into taking care of themselves, even though they don't feel like it. Encourage grooming, exercise, healthy eating, doing things for fun, seeing the doctor, or whatever. They will resist, but keep pushing. It's the best thing you can do for them.

HELPLESSNESS AND HOPELESSNESS.   Depressed people don't believe they can do anything to improve their situation. Whatever you suggest, they can't do it, or it won't work. Often this turns into a self-fulfilling prophecy.

What you would usually think of as a remedy for this sort of thinking—pointing out things they've done that have worked—doesn't help much at all. If you've tried it, you know it's like banging your head against a wall. You may make a dent, but the gain is hardly worth the pain.

Instead of turning away in frustration, look more closely at this phenomenon. It is a window into the very heart of the disorder.

Depressed people are helpless as long as they let what they feel determine what they do. Depressed people are helpless because they're hopeless, and hopeless because they're helpless. It's one of the vicious circles that are the very essence of depression.

The cure for depression is not feeling better, but learning to do what you need to do, regardless of how you feel. We usually think of our feelings as motivators that pull our actions along. If we think this way about depression, everything comes to a halt and the situation is indeed hopeless.

ANOMIE.   Depressed people feel helpless and hopeless, disconnected from purpose, from other people, and from anything larger than the emptiness of their own being—existentialists afraid to take even the smallest leap of faith because they're certain there is no one out there to catch them.

To get better, they must leap, and you must not catch them.

Philosophical considerations aside, remember, in the last chapter, the characteristics of people who did not succumb to stress: They believed they were in control of their own lives, they felt connected to something larger than themselves, and they actively sought out challenges. All three of these crucial attitudes are damaged by depression. Or perhaps the damage causes depression, who knows? Regardless of whether it is cause or effect, this is the damage that must be repaired to cure depression. Feeling better is merely a side effect.

The Physiology of Depression

Hippocrates thought that depression was caused by too little phlegm and too much black bile. In the intervening years, the names for what is deficient and overabundant have changed but the theory has stayed pretty much the same.

Nowadays you can't talk about depression without mentioning brain chemistry. This is a relatively modern development. Before the late 1950s everybody thought depression was merely a psychological disorder. Today, the psychological part of depression is in danger of being washed away by tiny droplets of neurotransmitters.

The first modern physiological theories of depression derived from the stress research of Hans Selye, whom we encountered in an earlier chapter. Selye said that when exposed to too much environmental stress, the organism goes into a state of exhaustion, or physiological shutdown. This model explains the disruption of vegetative functions and the general lassitude characteristic of many depressions. Stress, the theory said, depletes the body of something important that is needed for ongoing activity.

ADRENALINE DEFICIT THEORY. One of the earliest suspects was adrenaline, the hormone that facilitates the fight or flight response by speeding everything up. The theory said that when you have too much stress, you run out of adrenaline, slow down, and become depressed. It was not a bad theory, except if you actually look at depressed people, they're often quite anxious as well, and there is no evidence of an adrenaline shortage. At least not in the way they were thinking about it when the theory was first proposed.

In those days, the late 1950s, the idea that chemicals transmitted electrical nerve impulses through the brain was quite radical and not widely accepted. Several things happened to change this. Partly, it was actual rocket science.

THE DAWN OF ANTIDEPRESSANTS, HYDRAZINE. After World War II there was a surplus of *hydrazine*, which the Germans had made in huge quantities to fuel their V-2 rockets. Nobody knew what to do with all that hydrazine, but lots of people were trying to find uses for the complex, expensive organic chemical that could be had for almost nothing. Drug companies discovered that hydrazine could kill tuberculosis bacilli, and soon developed several hydrazine-based drugs for treating tuberculosis.

Doctors noted that one of these drugs, *ipronaizid*, seemed to make depressed patients feel better. Ipronaizid became the first antidepressant.

MONOAMINE OXIDASE INHIBITORS. Researchers thought that iproniazid inhibited the action of *monoamine oxidase* (MAO), an enzyme that breaks down epinephrine and norepinephrine in the brain. Epinephrine is another, newer name for adrenaline. To avoid confusion, I call the hormone *adrenaline* when it's in the body and *epinephrine* when it's in the brain. Colloquially, we think of adrenaline as a substance that speeds things up. It is, but for years nobody knew exactly how it worked. It is actually a transmitter substance. In the body, it works within various kinds of muscles. In the brain, it works all over the place, just like serotonin.

MAO breaks down epinephrine and norepinephrine—a related hormone that is more important than epinephrine as a transmitter substance in the brain. Anything that inhibits monoamine oxidase creates more available norepinephrine. It may create more dopamine and serotonin as well. Soon, a class of drugs called monoamine oxidase inhibitors was developed specifically for treating depression. They are still in use today, but not widely, because of a troubling side effect: In combination with tyramine, a chemical found in foods, mainly in cheese and aged meat, MAO inhibitors can cause death. In fact, this does not pose a problem today, since the only people for whom these drugs are prescribed are those who can manage their diets.

The action of MAO inhibitors led researchers to believe that depression was caused by a norepinephrine deficit, which they assumed disrupted activity in the reward centers of the brain. In the 1960s, as new neurotransmitters were being discovered, each one was in its day seen as implicated in depression. Norepinephrine, acetylcholine, dopamine, and serotonin have all had their advocates.

THE AGE OF SEROTONIN. Tricyclic antidepressants were originally developed to increase available norepinephrine, but they also increased serotonin, which in the 1980s became the odds-on favorite as the neurotransmitter whose depletion caused depression. Then came Prozac and the selective serotonin reuptake inhibitors, and depression came to be understood, or at least advertised, as a serotonin deficiency that can easily be treated in any doctor's office.

There are several problems with this theory:

First, not all depressions respond to serotonin-enhancing drugs. This one is so easy to fix, it needs little explanation. Newer products like Serzone, Effexor, and Remeron have been developed that increase available norepinephrine as well as serotonin. Each new antidepressant is formulated to bind with either very specific serotonin and/or norepinephrine receptors, or as many different kinds of receptors as possible.

The second problem, more difficult to explain, is that most of the drugs that increase available serotonin or norepinephrine do so within a day or two, but take at least two weeks to have an effect on depression. It seems apparent that increasing serotonin has other, slower repercussions, or that something else besides increasing serotonin is actually responsible for the antidepressant effect.

THE SUPERSENSITIVITY HYPOTHESIS. There are, of course, theories to explain the delay. One suggests that serotonin receptors are "supersensitive" in depressed people, that they overreact to small amounts of serotonin, essentially telling the cell that there is already too much serotonin when there is really not enough. Strange as this sounds, there are several disorders—notably Type II diabetes—that operate similarly. According to supersensitivity theory, serotonergic drugs affect the response to serotonin as well as to the amount. The change in sensitivity takes several weeks.

THE HIPPOCAMPUS NEUROGENESIS THEORY.   Another theory has to do with the manufacture of new cells in the hippocampus, which as you'll remember is the little seahorse in the brain that seems to be involved in modulating many emotional processes. Based on the research of Selye and others, we know that stress creates chemicals called *glucocorticoids* that kill nerve cells in the hippocampus and elsewhere. A few studies have found that the depressed have smaller hippocampi than other people. Normally, the hippocampus grows its own new cells. But according to the theory, *neurogenesis* is stopped or reversed by stress and started again by serotonergics. The time lag is equal to the time it takes new cells to mature.

But intriguing as neurogenesis theory is, it's mainly speculation based on animal studies. Also, it requires an initial period of undefined "stress" to explain why cells start dying in the first place, which brings everybody's favorite vague psychological concept into play in explaining the physiology of depression. There's also the question as to whether a medication that stimulates the growth of new brain cells is a treatment or a form of disease.

Even more difficult to explain than the time lag from serotonin increase to depression decrease is the fact that sometimes serotonergics simply stop working. Medications that at one time controlled depression quite well can cease doing so after about a year of treatment. Switching to another, chemically similar drug can restart the antidepressant effect. As you would imagine, there are theories to explain this phenomenon as well, but at this point there is little research to back them up.

Though medications that increase the amount of available serotonin and/or norepinephrine can do wonders for alleviating the symptoms of depression, it seems that the disorder is something more complex than the neurotransmitter deficiency you see advertised in magazines.

But What Is Depression?

To a clinician, depression consists of four related symptom complexes that may have different neurophysiological correlates. Really, there isn't much of a dividing line between the complexes. One grades seamlessly into the next, and to make matters more confusing, it is possible that any one complex could influence all the others. Nevertheless, it helps to think of the symptom complexes as separate because depressions generally tend toward one set of symptoms more than others, and treatment is most often based on which sort of symptoms seem most prominent. The four are:

- Sadness or unhappiness
- Lack of motivation
- Rumination
- Sleep disturbance

SADNESS OR UNHAPPINESS.   Depressed people are either sad or have a diminished capacity to be happy. The distinction may seem irrelevant if you have to spend time with them, but if you're trying to help them, it is extremely important. Sad people are experiencing too much negative emotion and are actively miserable. They cry out in pain and loss. People with diminished capacity to be happy don't cry, or feel much of anything other than the existential emptiness of melancholia.

There is some evidence that sad people have too much activity in the *thalamus* and *hypothalamus*, parts of the *limbic system* responsible for raw emotion. Unhappy people may have too little activity in the hippocampus, the *nucleus accumbens*, and other areas associated with pleasure and reward, some of which are also parts of the limbic system. Whatever systems are involved, sad people need to have their emotions toned down, and unhappy people need to have theirs stimulated. Though both groups may be called *depressed*, they often respond to different medications and different psychotherapeutic approaches.

LACK OF MOTIVATION.   Some depressed people can't seem to get themselves going, and others seem to be perpetually moving, but with little focus or direction. Again, there is some speculation as to differing amounts of activity in different areas of the brain, perhaps the basal ganglia and the limbic system, but nobody is really sure. What we do know is that depressed or not, agitated people are often anxious and irritable and need some basic calming.

RUMINATION.   Some depressed people have negative thoughts that just won't stop. It's as if their brains have faulty brakes. Thoughts move around in circles, expanding and becoming more negative with each lap. It's like worry, but slower and less interesting. Rumination could be the result of too much activity around the cingulate gyrus, and may improve with medications and therapeutic techniques that reinforce control.

SLEEP DISTURBANCE. Depressed people have all kinds of problems with sleep—too much, too little, or not the right kind. They have trouble getting to sleep, staying asleep, and their nights are haunted by nightmares, or worse, dreams that are exactly like their day-to-day existence, making them feel as if they never sleep at all. Sleep is supposedly regulated by the *Raphe nucleus*, the nexus of a number of serotonin pathways. The same medications can put some people to sleep and keep others awake, just like depression.

Current theories suggest that different pathways of the same neurotransmitter may have different functions. Some newer medications are supposed to stimulate one serotonin or norepinephrine pathway and block others.

Depression clearly involves some changes in neurochemistry, but it's uncertain whether this change is cause or effect. It's likely that there are different biochemical explanations for depression's varied symptoms, or it may be that the same physiological process manifests itself differently because of different underlying personalities. Or both. Or all of the above.

And, despite the phenomenal success of antidepressant medications, we still cannot remove psychology from the equation. Studies comparing the effects of therapy and medication regularly show that the two together work better than either alone, and that over the long run therapy works better than medication in preventing the recurrence of depression. Though there are difficulties with these sorts of studies, such as the impossibility of defining therapy with anything like the specificity of drug dosage, the evidence does point to the necessity for some sort of psychological intervention.

Medications for Depression

Antidepressant medications make people feel better, generally by delivering more of some transmitter substance to the synapses of the brain—serotonin, norepinephrine, dopamine, or all of the above. What happens after that is open to question. Nevertheless, each kind of medication has predictable main and side effects, though there is tremendous variability across individuals.

When I think about medications for depression, I first look at symptom complexes, then confer with the prescribing physician about which medication might be most effective in treating those aspects of depression.

Each of the five people I described at the beginning of the chapter had some experiences, both positive and negative, with antidepressant medication. Let's use them as case studies on how various antidepressant medications might be prescribed.

Alonzo is actively sad, preoccupied with the loss of his wife. He has lost his appetite and is having a hard time sleeping. Following in a grand tradition of abandoned lovers, he begins treatment by medicating himself with alcohol.

Alcohol

The oldest psychoactive substance is absolutely the worst possible medication for depression, yet it is the most widely used. The main reason for its popularity is that it immediately treats all the symptom complexes that make up depression, though badly.

As discussed in an earlier chapter, alcohol can cross the blood-brain barrier. It's absorbed directly from the stomach into the bloodstream, and goes from there right into the brain. Alcohol works fast; it causes an immediate, stimulating dump of dopamine followed by a relaxing flow of GABA. Unlike reuptake inhibitors, which make transmitter substances available for a longer time in the synaptic area, alcohol and most other addictive substances weaken the walls of the *vesicles* that carry transmitter substances, causing them to spill out into the synapse. Dopamine pathways lead right to the nucleus accumbens, the so-called pleasure center of the brain. This feels good, but it uses up the dopamine quickly, so there is less of it later on. The brain is designed to feel good a little bit at a time, so that anything that makes it feel good all at once is bound to create the opposite effect when the chemical is all used up.

Other substances are even better at causing transmitter dumps than alcohol. Cocaine and amphetamine are at the top of the list. They cause brain cells to pour out dopamine, serotonin, GABA, norepinephrine, and whatever else they may be holding in their vesicles. In the past, both have been widely prescribed as antidepressants.

Freud and many of his contemporaries thought that cocaine was a miracle drug that alleviated depression, improved the personality, and stimulated the creative process. Their writings about its marvels might embarrass Timothy Leary. Sherlock Holmes took cocaine to improve his detection skills, and many Victorian writers used it as well. Robert Lewis Stevenson's *Dr. Jekyll and Mr. Hyde* might be considered the "Lucy in the Sky with Diamonds" of its day.

Until about 1915 you could buy cocaine almost anywhere. At soda fountains there was coca in the cola and countless other concoctions designed to pep people up and make them happy. Cocaine was considered a respectable, higher class alternative to demon rum. You could also buy it mixed with alcohol and morphine as nerve tonic. Cocaine was wonderful stuff—until it began to wear off, leaving a synthetic melancholia caused by drug-induced depletion of transmitter substances, and sometimes tactile hallucinations of worms crawling under the skin. A typical remedy was more cocaine.

Amphetamine works similarly to cocaine, but it has a bit less effect on the central nervous system and more on neuromuscular synapses, making it more physically stimulating. Caffeine operates similarly, with even more muscular involvement. Until the early 1960s the antidepressant of choice was amphetamine mixed with phenobarbital to take off the physical edge.

Phenobarbital and alcohol release GABA, which serves as an inhibitory function throughout the brain. After the initial dumping of dopamine, which feels like stimulation, GABA slows things down, and generally decreases activity in the central nervous system starting with the newer, higher level thinking equipment. In one fell swoop it eases the pain of guilt and rumination, and if you take enough, it will put you to sleep.

Alcohol feels like the perfect short-term antidepressant. It works well until the middle of the night, when it disturbs sleeping patterns, and the next morning, when all the GABA from the night before stimulates the release of glutamate, yet another transmitter substance that leads to feelings of pain and irritability. A common treatment is more alcohol.

Alcohol, cocaine, amphetamine, and phenobarbital are all lousy antidepressants. They make people feel better in the short run, but over a longer term they actually create some of the same chemical depletions that may cause depression in the first place.

With alcohol, there are even greater dangers.

Alonzo goes out drinking with his buddies after work. For a while he feels better, but when he gets home, he feels much worse. At first alcohol eased his pain, making him forget about his wife. Now, the thoughts are back, and the alcohol has removed his inhibitions. Tears wash over him and deep currents of sadness seem to sweep away everything he's ever hoped or dreamed. He takes out his pistol and stares at it, thinking that death might be a relief. Before he can load it, he passes out.

People with a reactive depression are the highest risk for suicide, and people with reactive depressions who drink are even higher. We think of alcohol as removing inhibitions, but it actually works by inhibiting the higher, more rational parts of the brain that worry about consequences. People think and do things when they're drinking that they never would while sober. The same chemical action that gets uptight people out on the dance floor can make a depressed person like Alonzo forget that there's more to life than pain, and think about death as a permanent solution to an immediate problem.

Medications for Reactive Depression

Painful as it is, a reactive depression is a normal response to loss. People usually go through it and come out the other side within a month. During the acute phase, the best treatment is social support and enforced healthy living—eating, sleeping, exercise, doing things for fun, etc. Antidepressants that take two to four weeks to work are often superfluous, but just as often are prescribed anyway, because doctors see the symptoms of depression, have the technology to alleviate them, and want to make their patients feel better.

Though serotonin reuptake inhibitors are the usual treatment for most depressions these days, they are not a good choice for someone recovering from a loss, especially a marital separation. Agitation is a common side effect when starting SSRIs. Though it generally abates in a few days, the damage may already be done. People in the throes of reactive depression are often agitated already. Their minds are working overtime to try and make sense of their loss, which is not altogether a bad thing. Often they can't sleep, and that symptom is the most disturbing and dangerous. Tricyclics tend to be more sedating than SSRIs and, in a reactive depression, may be more useful for that quality than for their antidepressant effect. Amitriptyline, a tricyclic that is quite sedating, is used for sleep. Trazodone, a sedating SARI that has a relatively short half-life, is a better choice as a safe sleeping medication since it causes less grogginess the next day.

Sometimes people get stuck in a reactive depression. Not only can't they stop ruminating about who or what they've lost, but the thoughts seem to become more frequent and more morbid. If a reactive depression does not appear to be abating over the course of a month or so, medications make more sense. Meanwhile, the best thing you can do for people suffering a loss is to stay close and encourage them to talk. They often want a lot of alone time, but it is not a good idea to give it to them.

Serotonergics

> *Kinesha's depression came out of nowhere, for no discernible reason, changing her from a well-adjusted, outgoing person into a zombie. She can't think clearly, has no energy, and feels as if she's dragging herself through her daily activities. Her mother had a history of depressive episodes as well.*

As discussed in the chapter on fear, this group includes SNRIs, SSRIs, SARIs, NDRIs, and NASAs. By far the most widely used medications for depression are SSRIs.

Kinesha is the sort of person for whom serotonergics—especially SSRIs—are nothing short of wonder drugs. It's likely that her endogenous depressive episode arose from a change in her brain chemistry, perhaps that very serotonin deficiency that gets so much publicity in magazines. Kinesha's doctor wanted to prescribe Prozac. She knew that its activating properties work particularly well for the kind of glum, unmotivated depression that Kinesha was experiencing.

> *"Prozac? You want to put me on Prozac?" Kinesha's tone makes it sound like her doctor is suggesting heroin. "No thank you. I don't need any of that stuff. I've read all about it, and I'd rather just work things through on my own."*

Type *Prozac* into your Internet search engine and see what Kinesha is talking about. Most of the listings are about the dangers of Prozac rather than its beneficial effects. Extreme agitation, suicidal impulses, weight gain—the horror stories abound.

Prozac and the SSRIs *are* dangerous drugs if they're misprescribed, which they sometimes are. When Prozac first came out, it was heralded not only as a drug for depression, but one that could improve normal personalities as well. It was even supposed to make people lose weight! Books were written about how wonderful it was, and people beat a path to their doctors' doors to get prescriptions, whether they needed them or not. This is nothing new. It happens every time a new type of psychoactive medication comes out. Cocaine and Valium were also touted as personality enhancers until a lot of people started taking them and the extent of their side effects became known.

Prozac got great publicity from a number of sources. In addition to the misguided prophets, many physicians and drug companies touted the first SSRI as evidence of what they knew all along: that mental disorders were physical problems better treated with medication than with the vagaries of psychotherapy. There are some doctors who believe that depressions are now in the same class of disorders as sinus infections, and that no special expertise is required to treat them. .

Prozac could not live up to its hype, but what can? Selective serotonin reuptake inhibitors, as we have seen, are useful in treating a number of disorders, but they are not panaceas, nor, for that matter, are they particularly selective. SSRIs are machetes that are sometimes sold as scalpels. They can chop away mental underbrush, but not without collateral damage. Now that they've been around for a while, we have a clearer idea of what that damage is and what we can do about it:

AGITATION. People starting out on SSRIs often feel agitated, as if they've had way too much coffee. They feel nervous, jumpy, and can have difficulty sleeping. This side effect seems to come from the same chemical action that increases energy and motivation, which is a very desirable main effect in cases like Kinesha's

Usually, the unpleasant agitation only lasts a couple of days. It's often controlled by starting people on a very low dose and working up. Though this can delay the antidepressant effect several weeks longer, the wait may be worth it.

Psychologically, agitation is the most dangerous side effect. It can be like adding an anxiety disorder. People should be warned about agitation in advance, and if it persists for more than four days, they should probably try a different medication. There are plenty more to choose from. Agitation seems most prevalent in the first-generation SSRIs, Prozac, Zoloft, and Paxil, but it is totally unpredictable. It may occur with one and not the others, though they're chemically quite similar. Newer serotonergics have been formulated to affect one serotonin pathway and block others so as to be less agitating and to have less side effects in general, but sometimes they're also less generally effective. The effects of all antidepressant medications vary more widely from person to person than from drug to drug.

SEDATION. SSRIs agitate some people and put others to sleep. Serotonin pathways go almost everywhere in the brain, so you never know what you're going to get. Usually, serious sedation occurs for only a few days, then abates. If it persists, the medication should probably be changed.

SEXUAL IMPAIRMENT. About half the people taking SSRIs and newer, similar compounds experience sexual side effects. Lack of libido and delayed orgasm are the most common. Some serotonin pathways go places you'd rather not have them.

There is some speculation that adding BuSpar helps with this side effect, but the most common tactic is switching to Wellbutrin, which is a dopamine and norepinephrine reuptake inhibitor, and is chemically different from both tricyclics and SSRIs. It usually helps with the side effect, but in my experience it doesn't always work as well as an antidepressant.

WEIGHT GAIN. Virtually every seretonergic can cause weight gain if people are on it long enough. Some, like Prozac, can cause an initial loss followed by gain. Wellbutrin and Serzone are supposedly less likely to put weight on, but the evidence is not conclusive. Wellbutrin also has its own side effects, which are potentially more dangerous than those of the SSRIs. It was taken off the market briefly because of the danger of seizures.

APATHY. SSRIs can cause people to move from feeling too much to feeling nothing at all. This effect is particularly disturbing to artistic people, who sometimes feel that antidepressants sap their creative energy.

WITHDRAWAL EFFECTS.   People should never stop any antidepressant abruptly, as almost all have withdrawal effects in some people. Effexor and Paxil seem to be the worst in this regard, though the others are right behind. The most common withdrawal effects are extreme agitation and exacerbation of depression.

When antidepressants are working correctly, people usually don't feel them, they just feel better. Sometimes they'll stop taking the medication because they don't think it's doing anything. Bad idea. Sudden cessation can bring on a dramatic increase in symptoms.

The usual course of antidepressant treatment is six to eight months for a single depressive episode. At the end of that time, tapering off should be done with a doctor's supervision. Generally, people who have had repeated episodes or chronic depression stay on the medication longer, perhaps even for life.

DIMINISHED EFFECTIVENESS.   Sometimes SSRIs simply stxop working for no apparent reason. Usually this happens after about a year of treatment, but it can be sooner. The diminished effectiveness is often less apparent to the person taking the medication than to family and friends. Switching medications can usually restore the antidepressant effect.

There are horror stories in addition to these. Most have occurred when the prescriber did not follow the course of treatment closely enough, and especially when the agitation persisted beyond several days.

> *After checking out the Websites on Prozac, Kinesha decides to go with something safer and more organic. She begins taking St. John's wort with valerian and kava kava.*

St. John's Wort

I'll cut right to the chase here. I have never known St. John's wort or any other herbal preparation sold over the counter to be an effective treatment for clinical depression. I know that St. John's wort is popular in Germany, but even there it is used primarily for milder depressions. Many of the equivalency studies that compare St. John's wort to other antidepressants tend to stack the deck by using a lower than recommended dose of the prescription medications.

Since St. John's wort is an herb and not a medicine, there are no out-side checks for purity and dosage size, so you never know exactly what you're getting, especially if you buy it off a shelf at the grocery store. And just because it's an herb rather than a prescription medication, there is absolutely no reason to believe that it's safer. The only safety in St. John's wort is its weakness.

In larger dosages St. John's wort seems to operate as an MAO inhibitor, though this is not by any means certain.

There are certainly cases of depression I see in which I think medi-cation is not necessary or is optional. Even then I haven't known St. John's wort to make a difference. If medication is necessary, so is a competent professional to prescribe it and to monitor its effects.

> At my urging, Kinesha finally decides to take Prozac. For her, it works just like the magazine ads say it will. She feels better and has no side effects to speak of.
>
> Kinesha's depression was a single episode with a family history. Her adjustment before the episode was excellent, with strong relationships and a responsible job. Three weeks after she began taking Prozac, she and I agree that we have nothing more to talk about.
>
> Six months later, after conferring with her doctor, she tapers off. She and her husband know they have to watch her sleeping and energy level as early indicators of relapse. Kinesha agrees that if she goes a whole week without laughing, it's time to call the doctor.

Medications for People Who Don't Think They're Depressed

I'm sure there are hundreds of cases like Kinesha's—people for whom medication is enough and no psychotherapy is necessary. Generally, these people don't contact therapists in the first place, but many such people do need therapists and don't contact them either. They're pushed into it by friends, family members, or physicians.

> "Really, I'm just fine," Carol says. She tries to smile, but her eyes are already brimming with tears. She dabs at them with a tissue.

"I don't know why I do this." I don't have anything to be sad about. I just get upset sometimes for no reason. My daughter thinks I'm depressed, but I don't think it's that bad. I do have a lot of nervous energy, and sometimes I don't sleep too well."

Carol is what we in the trade call a "smiling depressive." Her cheerfulness is maintained by sheer nervous energy. She must always swim to keep from sinking beneath the weight of her sorrow. Carol is fidgety and flustered, but doesn't fit the pattern of an anxiety disorder because sadness rather than fear is her dominant emotion. Her sleeping problems—early waking rather than difficulty falling asleep—suggest depression as well. Carol gets up around three A.M. and does housework.

It's hard to know in advance what kind of medication might work best for an agitated depressive like Carol. Obviously, one that might increase her arousal would be less suitable, so a tricyclic, which is more sedating, seems a better choice than an SSRI. Her doctor prescribed Amitriptyline, an older tricyclic that is *very* sedating. For a few days it knocked her out. She slept most of the time. When she was awake, she'd cry easily and often, as if the medication had slowed her down enough for her depression to catch up. The antidepressant effect was still about a week away when Carol stopped taking the Amitriptyline. She didn't mention it because she didn't want anybody to worry.

A day later, Carol woke up cured, or so it seemed. She had energy again, and she was cheerful and talkative. She'd make little jokes, and sometimes would laugh at nothing. She became interested in genealogy, and began spending hours on the phone with distant relatives. For a couple of nights she was so wrapped up in her family tree project that she never even went to bed.

In people whose depression is a manifestation of bipolar disorder, antidepressant medication can sometimes precipitate a hypomanic episode, like Carol's. In her case, there was no predicting this effect because nothing similar had ever happened to her before. Her genealogic research did seem to show that there were a lot of alcoholics in her family tree, and a few suicides. Both are more common in bipolar families.

Carol's husband brought her to see a psychiatrist, who at first calmed her with lithium, and eventually stabilized her on Serzone and a low dose of Neurontin, an anticonvulsant sometimes used to prevent manic episodes. He arrived at this combination by working closely with Carol and her family, getting almost daily information about her mood, activity, and sleeping patterns.

Agitated depressions are difficult to medicate. Some medications can increase agitation, and the initial slowing by more sedating medications may make the depressed person feel worse,even if they're getting better. Either side effect may cause them to stop taking the medication before it does them any good. There's also a remote possibility of precipitating a hypo-manic episode if the underlying disorder is bipolar.

If you're the friend or family member of an agitated depressed person, you should make sure that the doctor has an accurate picture of what's going on. Often, agitated depressed people like Carol tend to minimize their problems. It will also be important for the doctor to follow the person closely to see how he or she responds to the medication.

Carol's situation is not like Kinesha's. For her, finding the appropriate medication is the beginning of the road, not the end.

How Medication Can Make Depression Worse

Physical side effects are often less of a problem than philosophical ones. Sometimes the *idea* that medication that can cure depression actually makes it worse.

> *"I don't think there's anything that will help me," Rachel sobs into the phone during one of her late night calls. "I've tried medication and therapy, but nothing works."*

For Rachel, the road winds constantly and never seems to get any-where. Over several years, she's tried any number of treatments that were supposed to cure her depression but didn't. In Chapter 2 we followed her through several different antidepressant medications. Zoloft made her feel better, but it caused her to put on weight. And Wellbutrin didn't do much to relieve her symptoms. Therapy with Dr. Judy focused mostly on her dysfunctional relationship with her mother rather than her depression. Rachel's experiences have reinforced the feeling of helplessness that is the essence of depression. In her heart, she believes that nothing works for her because she's just too crazy. The cheerful magazine ads about depression being a chemical imbalance easily cured with medication only make her feel like more of a freak.

If there is someone like Rachel in your life, you probably know the whole long, sad story by heart, because you've heard it so many times. She's convinced that she's hopeless, and though she calls her friends for help, she seems more interested in telling them how awful her situation is than in getting any advice about how to change it. She's sure that nothing will help because nothing has.

Actually, there are a number of approaches that will help, but none by itself will cure her. Rachel's case is typical in that respect. Her depression is not a single thing, and no single treatment can fix it. Medication, psychotherapy, her own efforts, and support from her friends can each help a little. Over time, the small positives accumulate and slowly come together to make a meaningful life.

Rachel is also typical in that she's gone in so many different directions trying to escape her depression that she's lost her way. The paths she chooses are just as apt to lead her deeper into her disorder as out of it.

If there is a person like Rachel in your life, you may have to be a guide, pointing her in the right direction, encouraging her to do better, to stay with the small actions that help a little, rather than thrashing about in search of the magical cure that will make her feel well enough to do the things that will make her feel better.

In Rachel's case, the idea that depression is a physical disease to be cured with medication merely drives her around in circles. For other people, attempted cures can be more debilitating than the disease.

Randy continues to get worse. He now spends most of the day lying on the couch watching TV, waiting for something to make him feel better. He's followed doctor's orders by cutting down on the stress in his life, but that hasn't helped. He's been off work a few months, and his anxiety is worse than it's ever been.

Now he has depression too. The doctor says it's a chemical imbalance and has prescribed several different medications, which haven't worked. His doctor finally sends him to a psychiatrist in hopes that an expert can come up with the right combination of medications to cure Randy's mental illness.

Augmentation

Psychiatrists these days usually see people who are more seriously disturbed, or who haven't responded to antidepressants that other doctors have prescribed. Often, psychiatrists will try to achieve a better effect by combining two antidepressants with different properties, or combining antidepressants with other kinds of medications like lithium, BuSpar, or anticonvulsants. The general idea is to try and strike the exact chemical chord that will resonate with a particular depression. Augmentation techniques, when used carefully by skillful psychiatrists, can work wonders. The technique can be disastrous in the hands of psychiatrists who are less skilled.

The very best psychiatrists and the very worst rely on augmentation. The way to know which kind you're dealing with is by the amount of time spent in appointments, the number of questions asked, how well previous sessions are remembered, and the level of insistence that people under medical treatment be involved in psychotherapy and other activities as well. The best psychiatrists are the first to admit that medication can't do it all.

Professional rivalries aside, the evidence is clear that depression is a complex disorder that requires complex and coordinated treatment, not just throwing a lot of drugs at the problem.

Sometimes augmentation works, but at other times it results in difficulty determining whether the problems come from the disease or all the medications used to treat it.

Electrotherapy

What used to be called shock treatments still have a place in the treatment of depression, though in a more sophisticated and gentle form. Electrical jolts applied to various areas of the brain, sometimes in voltages strong enough to cause convulsions, can actually improve some kinds of depressions, especially those in which the patient is practically bedridden and hasn't responded to medication.

Needless to say, this sort of treatment is a last resort because of all the possible side effects. There was a time however, from the 1940s to the mid-1970s, before the advent of SSRIs, that shock was used in private psychiatric hospitals as a treatment for almost everything. Many people who were hospitalized back then don't remember much about it. This is not repression, but a side effect of shock treatment. Many people had their memories permanently damaged. Today, the use of electrical treatments in hospitals requires extensive consultation, but some doctors still use milder forms in their offices. Such treatments have their place, but probably not with people who can function outside a hospital.

The Blind Men's Elephant

Depression has as many different aspects as the blind men's elephant. It could be several disorders, lumped together in the diagnostic manual because they respond to the same medications, or it could be a single entity that manifests itself differently according to the underlying personality of the individual who has it. Or both.

To those of us trying to help depressed people, the issue of what depression really *is* may be irrelevant. We need to focus on what depression *does*, and somehow try to undo it with whatever tools we have. Depression affects sleep, mood, activity level, the nature of relationships, and the quality of thought. In most cases, we have to deal with each element separately. Medication can help, maybe even cure the whole thing for some lucky people. It can also make the situation worse, with side effects, or by reinforcing the central belief that people with depression are helpless in the face of the great, gray beast.

Chapter 9

The Psychology of Depression

IN THE PREVIOUS CHAPTER WE LEARNED that depressed people don't get much pleasure out of life because of a deficiency of transmitter substances, an excess of black bile, or other factors. Their feel gooders are somehow broken. At first, your heart will go out to them and you'll try to make them feel better—until you discover that there is no more futile role than attempting to be somebody else's feel gooder.

> *"I just don't see the point in going on," Rachel says, in her typical monotone.*
>
> *"Come on, Rachel," you say, a bit less enthusiastically than you'd hoped. "Don't think that way. You have a good job, friends who care about you, and it's a beautiful day for a walk in the park."*
>
> *"I know I should want to," Rachel says. "I know I have no reason to be sad. There are lots of people who are worse off than me ... but when I walk in the park, I see lovers hand in hand, and I wonder what's wrong with me that I can't find a relationship. It's probably the way I look."*

"That's ridiculous. You look fine."
"If you like fat."
"You're not fat."

You can't talk depressed people into feeling better. Don't even try. It will only wear you out, and it won't do them a bit of good. What both of you need to do is pay less attention to what they feel and more to what they do. This is the secret to helping depressed people without becoming enmeshed. Everything else is commentary.

Steps in the Treatment of Depression

The point of psychological treatment is not to make depressed persons feel better, but to make how they feel less of a factor in their day-to-day choices. If depressed people start thinking better and doing better, they'll usually feel better as well, but it's merely a positive side effect.

Step 1: External Control

As we saw in the last chapter, antidepressant medications can work wonders. For some lucky folks, they can even make the whole disorder disappear. All depressed people should at least discuss the possibility of medication with a physician or therapist, especially if they're not eating, thinking about suicide, or they're sleeping less than five or six hours most nights.

Medication may not cure, but it makes many people feel well enough to do the things that *will* cure. Your job is to help them keep doing those things.

Step 2: Increasing Pleasant Activity

Behaviorists conceive of depression simply as a lack of positive reinforcement. Depressed people don't get much out of doing what they used to enjoy, so they stop. The problem is, if depressed people do only what they feel like doing, they'll become even more depressed. The second step in treating depression is to disrupt the downward spiral by getting people up and moving. They will see any activity as absolutely pointless, so don't try to explain; make them do it to humor you.

A frequent comment to depressed people is: "Do it for yourself, not for me." This is not useful advice. Depressed people don't do anything positive for themselves. It's you or nobody. They'll hear the sentence as an indication that you're giving up on them too.

If you hear yourself saying, "Do it for yourself," it usually means you're trying too hard. Chill out, and explain to yourself once again that you can't make them feel better. Let go of responsibility for their feelings, and focus on keeping them active, which is difficult enough, but at least not impossible.

They won't like it, but so what? They don't like anything. Their software for liking has crashed and they need you to help them reboot. Let them mumble and mutter just so long as they're moving. Even when depressed people start feeling better it will take them a long time to realize it, and even longer to admit it to you. Helping the depressed is a thankless task. Literally. If they thank you, you're probably not helping. Better they should be slightly annoyed with you for pushing them.

> *"Seems like you have a choice," you say to Rachel. "You can sit in here and feel lousy or you can go out and feel lousy in the fresh air. I don't know about you, but I'm going to the park. Want to come with me?"*
>
> *"I guess one waste of time is as good as another," Rachel says, reaching for her jacket.*

The depressed usually feel tired and listless, so they rest, which makes them more tired. If people are getting fairly adequate sleep at night, rest during the day only saps their energy and motivation. Vigor follows the prime directive of biology: Use it or lose it.

Though inactive, most depressed people are still experiencing considerable anxiety. They can profit more from 15 minutes of relaxation exercises from the section on fear disorders than they can from hours of sitting around.

As with fear disorders, exercising regularly with depressed people is the most helpful thing you can do, but it is far harder. Fearful people often have energy to burn, and are eager for the chance to work it off. Depressed people have to be dragged. Even a little walk in the park can be quite a workout.

But first you have to get them on their feet.

When the psychiatrist suggests that Randy should go into the hospital for electrotherapy, his wife hits bottom. From his first complaints of job stress, through his disability, and on into his depression, Randy's wife has always tried to stand by him, but often it feels like standing idly by. At some intuitive level, she knows that Randy's attempts to make himself feel better by doing less were making him worse, but she doesn't know what to do about it.

Randy, meanwhile, just stares at the TV.

Television is poisonous to depressed people because it keeps them from noticing that they're really doing nothing.

Randy, his wife, and I agreed that his situation was serious enough to warrant drastic action. At my suggestion, they moved the television and the couch to their son's garage, and every day before she left for work, Randy's wife would pile things on the bed so he would have to have to move them if he wanted to lie down.

We enrolled Randy in a day treatment program that met twice a week. He hated it, but he went. Every day, we set him a series of tasks. Every afternoon, he had to call my office and report on his progress.

In the evening he and his wife would go for a walk, then fix dinner together.

Behavioral therapy involves similar task assignments as well as the charting of activity and mood over time to demonstrate, with scientific precision, that what you do determines how you feel. The problem with this approach is the doing.

For behavioral therapy to work, there has to be enough emotional connection with the therapist to provide motivation. Irritation works just fine.

At first Randy thought I was picking on him. I agreed, and pointed out that he was also paying me to do it. For an instant I saw the ghost of a long dead smile cross his face. In our sessions I'd drag his mind out into the fresh air. We'd discuss current events, for which he'd have to prepare by reading the newspaper, something he once enjoyed but had stopped doing months before. Sometimes we'd try to stump each other with trivia questions.

Devious doctors can only take it so far. The emotional connection that makes behavioral therapy work is with loved ones. Recruit all you can. Think about the things depressed people used to do for fun, then don't give them any peace until they start doing them again. Don't just send them; go along.

> *"Yo, Dad," Randy's son says over the phone. " I hear some of the big guys are biting out at the lake. I'm going tomorrow. You in?"*
>
> *"Oh, I don't think so," Randy says. "I'd have to oil my reel and put on new line, then I'd have to get all my tackle ready and—"*
>
> *"Good try, Dad, But I'm on my way over to help you with that right now."*

Step 3: Figuring Out Which Kind of Depression You're Dealing With

Discrimination is critical, because depression is really two or three disorders that share a few symptoms but are different enough in their basic nature to warrant almost opposite approaches to treatment.

So we're back again to the old *What is depression?* question

There are number of theories, of course, each of which describes one aspect of the great gray beast. But as we already know, if you pay too much attention to one part of the elephant, you may miss others.

Depression Is Loss

Long before there were psychoanalysts, there was a recognized connection between depression and loss. People who lose something they cherish are sad. They cry, they don't eat, they don't sleep, and they don't want to do much of anything. It seems logical that the converse would also be true—that people who are sad have lost something. Not necessarily. The issue is important because what helps people recover from loss makes other kinds of depression worse.

Grieving a loss is hard work. You have to load up all the memories and haul them from one part of your brain to the other, from *is* to *was*, crying all the way, tired from not sleeping, and feeling like you just can't go on. After that you have to figure out who you are now that a big part of who you were is gone. No wonder the analysts called it *mourning labor*. Obviously, there's a great deal of emotion involved in this task, but expressing the emotion, while necessary, is not the same as doing the work.

In the late 1960s, Elizabeth Kübler-Ross popularized the notion that people go through stages in relating to death—denial, anger, bargaining, sadness, and finally acceptance. Her stages became the model for understanding what people experience emotionally as they learn to accept any kind of loss.

The Strong, Silent Explosion

> When Carol's mother died, she felt like an orphan, even though she was a grown woman and had a loving husband and family of her own. Her mother was the only person on earth with whom Carol could act like a little girl, which was how she defined any sort of dependency, asking for help, or expressing less than cheerful emotion.
>
> Carol was astounded and repelled by the anger she felt toward her mother for leaving her. She thought she was some kind of awful, selfish person, and hid her unseemly emotion beneath piles of work. She arranged the funeral, sorted through her mother's belongings, had an estate sale, and sold the house, all within three months of her mother's passing. "Somebody needed to do it," she says bravely. Through it all, Carol was a pillar of strength for everyone.
>
> Late at night she would go down to the basement and cry like a baby.

Carol had never heard of Elizabeth Kubler-Ross, so she didn't know that the anger she felt toward her mother was a normal part of the grieving process. Perhaps if someone had told her, she would have listened. That's the premise behind support groups for the bereaved. Maybe Carol could have gone to one, but she probably would have said she was too busy.

People like Carol use busy work to distract themselves from feelings they consider inappropriate and from work that needs doing. What she needs is to sort out are her mixed memories of her mother, but that hurts too much. She feels so badly about herself every time she turns up an emotion that she thinks should not to be there. She avoids her real task by frantically putting her mother's house in order.

Inside Carol, the pressure continues to build. The way to help her is by setting off an emotional explosion. As with most psychological techniques, the theory is more complicated than the practice. All you have to do is encourage her to talk and be there to listen.

> *"What was your mother like?" Carol's friend asks as she helps sort a lifetime worth of bric-a-brac into cardboard boxes.*
>
> *"She was a very kind and loving person," Carol says. Then she throws a handful of cooking implements into the yard sale pile and begins yanking pans out of a cupboard.*
>
> *"That's all? Just kind and loving?" Carol's friend opens a drawer full of string, rubber bands, and twist ties. "She was also a bit of a pack rat. What else was she?"*
>
> *"Why are you asking all these questions?" Carol's voice quavers and her eyes begin to well with tears. Pans thump, clang, and rattle, then grow still.*
>
> *"I think you need to talk about her," her friend says.*

Small questions like these can breach internal dams and release a torrent of tears. If you're going to try this technique, be sure you know how to swim. Here are some ideas that will help keep you both afloat during an explosion into sadness:

BE THERE.   All you really have to do to help bereaved people is listen, nothing else. Never worry about what to say, because you don't have to say anything. You'll never go wrong by laying a hand on their shoulder and encouraging them to go on. The idea is to keep them talking as long as they need to, so don't start if you have to pick up the kids in 20 minutes.

ALLOW WHATEVER HAPPENS.   Opening yourself to another person's sadness is a profoundly disturbing experience. Our reactions to grief are hard-wired into the motherboards of our brains. We want to respond to cries of pain with something, anything, that will make them stop and help the person feel better. If there's nothing we can do to make the situation better, we feel like crying ourselves. Which is also a perfectly adequate response.

It's hard to sit quietly while someone else cries. You will feel this uneasiness in many ways, most commonly the urge to talk, or to get up and *do something* for the sad person. Fetch a Kleenex if you need to, but forget the tea, pillow, blankets, or the picture you took of their mother last year. The best thing you can possibly give bereaved people is staying with your discomfort long enough to accept theirs.

Validate their experience. People in the midst of an emotional explosion feel crazy. Tell them that they aren't. Let them know by your actions, quietly listening and not freaking out, that you consider what they're doing appropriate and reasonable. You may also want to remind them of Kubler-Ross's stages as the standard for normal mourning.

Share carefully. A typical way of showing emotional support is by sharing your own similar experiences. If you feel the impulse to do this, be careful, because what is meant as heartfelt solidarity may be misinterpreted.

First, make sure the experience you're sharing is really similar. Carol is struggling not only with sadness over her mother's death, but with feelings she considers shameful. If you can share a comparable disappointment with yourself, go ahead; it will help. If what you're willing to share is merely sadness over a loss of your own, it's best to keep silent. The person may take your lack of mixed feelings as a rebuke, or evidence that her feelings are indeed out of the ordinary.

Second, if the person you're trying to support is male, be even more careful about bringing up your own experience. Men rarely understand this kind of sharing as support; it's just not the way guys do it. Men may see you as vying for the center of attention, and will probably give it to you by simply clamming up.

Politely decline reciprocity. Bear in mind that many strong, silent people like Carol are uncomfortable with taking, so they may try to turn the situation around so they're the one who's giving to you. This is much more likely to happen if you start sharing your own experiences. They'll be only too happy to give you support. The relief will be palpable.

At first, you may not notice that the wrong person is talking. When you do notice, shift the attention back immediately; say: "This is about you, not me."

If you look back at Chapter 1 and the approach I described for dealing with Rachel's explosion into sadness when criticized at work by her manager, you'll notice that most of it is the opposite of what I'm suggesting for bereaved people like Carol. The discrepancy represents what I consider to be the biggest problem with people's conception of what psychotherapy is and how to do it.

For almost 100 years our ideas about the talking cure have been based on the rather simple hydraulic model that works well for treating grief but little else. To help people who are grieving, all you have to do is sit quietly and listen while they express what they feel. This relieves internal pressure, and eventually people get better on their own. This technique works so well for grief, and is so easy—all you have to do is keep enough distance to avoid being swept away—that it's become most people's unconscious model for how psychotherapy is supposed to work.

But though this approach helps people who are grieving, for most other disorders, particularly the emotionally explosive kind, sitting passively while people talk about how badly they feel makes them worse. People work themselves up to emotional explosions by *ruminating*, repeating their fears, sadnesses, and angers over and over inside their heads, making them larger with each retelling. There is no evidence that duplicating this process in a doctor's office or in a support group does anything to make explosions less likely. Still, almost everybody who isn't a therapist—and far too many people who are or would like to be—believe that the purpose of psychotherapy is to get your feelings out.

If you want to help the people in your life who explode into the sadness, emptiness, or whatever that is classified as depression, you have to look beyond the diagnosis and the popular misconceptions about the nature of therapy, and see not so much the source of people's pain but what they're doing about it. Are they facing it or running away? If they're facing their pain, by all means listen and validate their struggle. If they're running away, you need to gently turn them around so they're pointing in the right direction, or, at the very least, avoid encouraging them.

Unfortunately, recognizing whether a depressed person is facing or running away from pain is difficult, because the only thing they have to run to is more pain. This time you have two stars to guide you. First, that *feeling good is ultimately based not on what happens to people, but what they do about it.* And second, that *moving away from depression generally involves moving toward fear.*

To see what I mean, let's look at another case of loss. Instead of facing the pain of his separation, Alonzo tries to escape it.

The *False Hope* Explosion

> "I brought the papers to her yesterday," Alonzo says. "She smiled and asked me how I was doing. Like, you know, she really cared." A tear of joy glistens in his eye. "I told her I loved her. She said she knew. And she put her hand right here on my shoulder."

Alonzo is clearly grasping at straws. His attempt to create hope for rekindled love out of basic decency will just make him feel worse because it diverts him from the mourning labor that is the only thing, short of a miracle, that will make him feel better. You'll do him no good by encouraging his misperception, even if it does calm him temporarily. To really help him, you must gently turn him back to face his pain.

> "Alonzo," you say. "She's filed for divorce. Just because she patted you on the shoulder doesn't mean she's changed her mind."
> "I know," Alonzo says. "It's just that it hurts too much to imagine living without her." He collapses into sobbing.

There are several lessons here. The first is practical. After the breakup of a relationship, the people involved shouldn't see each other, because painful misinterpretation is almost inevitable. Getting over a breakup involves moving the lost love from the heart into the memory. It can't happen if the people involved are still making regular contact, so they shouldn't.

I have been giving this advice to divorcing people for close to 30 years. No one takes it, and everyone says later that they wish they had. Rejection hurts, whichever side of it you're on, but as we've seen, the only way out of psychological pain is through it. It doesn't matter whether the pain is caused by loss or guilt over inflicting a loss on someone you once loved.

The next lesson is more subtle. Sometimes it hurts too much to do what it takes to get better, but that's not the only reason that depressed people don't do it. They can't even *imagine* doing it. Depression, at one level, is a disorder of imagination. Depressed people are so certain of the worst that they can't even conceive of anything else. For Alonzo, the worst is not that his wife will leave him, since that's already happened. The worst is his fear of being overwhelmed by pain if he admits that she won't come back.

In Alonzo's case, the expression of suffering isn't a side effect of doing his mourning labor; it's an explanation of why he *can't* do it. The more he repeats it to himself, the more certain he becomes.

The third lesson is totally pragmatic. Freud reputedly said, "If they want to talk about sex, ask about aggression," meaning that therapists should push people in the direction of whatever they're avoiding.

Learn from the master; the art of therapy lies in simple comments that disrupt the mindless repetition of self-defeating behavior. Again, the theory is more complicated than the practice. If people are avoiding emotion as Carol did, encourage them to express it. If they are expressing it, stop them when they start to repeat themselves, because then they're no longer talking to you—they're talking to themselves.

Depression Is Guilt and Anger-Turned-Inward

Doing therapy is more like plumbing than most people realize. A lot of it involves removing clogs and getting things flowing again. The main difference is that in therapy, everything always flows in both directions at once.

The psychoanalysts saw all human thoughts and actions as having *manifest content*—what people say—and *latent content*—what it really means. Often, latent content is the exact opposite of manifest content; thus, many emotions can be expressed directly as themselves, or indirectly as their opposites.

This idea is not as weird as it sounds. We see examples of it every day. Little boys show their affection by teasing girls; ex-smokers express their repressed cravings by being nasty to those who still indulge. People who say they blame themselves are also quite likely to blame others. Depressed people talk about feeling guilty.

"I should have spent more time with my mother," Carol says.

* * *

"And I should have been a better husband," Alonzo chimes in.

* * *

"My depression is my own damn fault," Rachel says.

* * *

"I'm not even worth that much of a damn," Randy says.

These people talk about guilt, but what do they *really* mean? For a minute, think like an analyst. Who brought up the issue of anything being anybody's fault in the first place?

The analysts also noticed that sometimes depressed people use their suffering as an emotional bludgeon.

The *I Don't Mean to Be a Burden* Explosion

The phone rings just as you're going out the door. It's Rachel, crying.

"I'm really sorry, Rachel," you say, "but I don't have time to talk now, I've got to get to the bank before it closes."

"It's okay," Rachel says. "I don't mean to be a burden."

You don't have to be an analyst to realize that your unavailability is *not* okay with Rachel, and, for that matter, that you're not particularly sorry you can't talk with her. Each of you is too worried about the other's feelings to say what you really mean. You may not even know what you really mean. One minute you're irritated at Rachel for being manipulative, the next, you're beating yourself up for having uncharitable thoughts about someone who is obviously in pain.

Rachel herself is undoubtedly doing something similar. Back and forth your emotions go, between guilt and resentment. Just two short sentences spoken, but this explosion can reverberate inside both your heads for days. The fact that it's all in your imagination, and you know it, does nothing to decrease its power to depress.

If you've ever experienced a situation like this, you can understand what the analysts meant about emotions being expressed as their opposites.

They're both there, always. Guilt and resentment are not separate — they're two sides of the same feeling. One cannot exist without the other. You can't blame yourself without blaming someone else, or vice versa.

Mixed feelings are normal, especially when they have to do with sex or aggression, both of which have very strong moral overlays. There's often an internal struggle between what you actually feel and what you think you should feel. Sometimes people use repression to make the less acceptable part go away, but there is no *away* to go to.

Often, depressed people have strong compunctions about aggressive impulses, so they push them out of their awareness. As we've seen with fear disorders, just because people can't see aggression in themselves doesn't mean it isn't there.

Analysts theorized that depression was anger turned inward, and the appropriate therapy involved turning it outward again by having depressed people talk about who they were *really* angry at. Sometimes it works, but sometimes it just taps into the endless spiral of blame and guilt that is depressive rumination.

> *Rachel stares out Dr. Judy's window at the world that seems to be passing her by. "Even if someone did want to go out with me, I couldn't fall in love," she says. "I have no way of knowing what love is, because I've never had any."*

Today, the idea that depression is anger turned inward is often cited as evidence of how silly psychoanalytic theory is. But is it? If you've ever had a midnight call from a depressed person, you know how mixed and confused their feelings are, and how easily they can elicit the same mixed and confused feelings from you. It's enough to make you wish that depression was just a serotonin deficiency.

Regardless of your opinion about psychoanalytic theory, you'll still have to deal with explosions into contagious guilt that may or may not be anger turned inward. Here are some ideas that may help:

DEAL ONLY WITH MANIFEST CONTENT. By definition, latent emotions are unconscious, which means that *people are not aware of them.* Remember that always.

It's pretty clear that Rachel is a bit miffed that you won't abandon your needs and minister to hers. She's not aware of her hostile feelings, she's just acting upon them. She feels too unworthy to come out and ask for your time, so she unconsciously relies on a threat to your perception of yourself as a caring person to extort you into giving her what she wants: If she were aware of what she was doing, it would count as asking you as much.

As she cringes at your rejection, Rachel actually believes that you're treating her like a burden because she *is* one, that you're only giving her what she deserves. She feels hostility toward herself, but not toward you; at least not consciously toward you. Never in a million years would Rachel accuse you of being the sort of person who'd let a friend down. You have to do that to yourself.

There's only one way to keep from being sucked into this neurotic morass. *Take her absolutely literally.* Let the analysts worry about the unconscious meanings. What you want is a relationship with Rachel in which she asks for what she wants and you're free to say yes or no. Sanity lies in playing by those rules yourself, even if you suspect she isn't.

Think like a behaviorist: Giving Rachel what she asks for is the best way to teach her to ask for what she wants.

Forget the word *manipulative.* The concept of manipulation as we use it today is a relic of the human potential movement, when an adolescent view of healthy functioning was confused with morality. In that simpler world in which we were not put to live up to other people's expectations, manipulation was a sin. It broke both the prohibitions on caring what other people think and withholding your own authentic feelings. The encounter groups may be gone, but the stigma is still there.

Manipulation used to be a more neutral term that described a convoluted interpersonal process. It is now merely a crime against mental health. Manipulation is something *parents* do to us, not something we do to others. If you think about it in the psychoanalytic sense, there can be no first person form of the verb *to manipulate.* What then is the point in accusing people of doing something that, by definition, they cannot be aware of doing? It's about as useless as telling them they're in denial.

All they'll hear is that you're irritated with them, which you aren't really, since you're only stating a fact.

To avoid this sort of senseless argument, erase the word *manipulation* from your vocabulary. The way to be effective in the situation formerly known as *being manipulated* is to respond to what people are doing without trying to explain to them what they're doing.

BE CLEAR ABOUT WHAT YOU FEEL, WHAT YOU WANT, AND WHAT YOU'RE WILLING TO DO. There is no way another person can deny *your* feelings. If you have to talk about the emotional bind people like Rachel put you in, do it something like this:

> *"Rachel, when you say you're a burden, I feel stuck. If I go do what I need to do, it's almost as if I'm admitting that you are a burden. If I stay and try to convince you that you're not a burden, then I have to cancel my own plans, and then I get upset.*
>
> *"I know that none of this is your intention, because you did tell me to go ahead. Still, I end up feeling like the kind of person who lets down a friend in need. But I guess that's my problem, isn't it?"*

There are times that addressing the issue in this way can clear the air between people who are close. Rachel has a face saving out, and you get to leave without feeling selfish.

Generally, it works better to skirt the issue altogether. Just tell Rachel what you're willing to do, and let the guilt fall where it may.

> *"Rache, I have some errands to run, but I'll be free at 7:30. Call me and we can talk then."*

SCHEDULE APPOINTMENTS. Take a tip from your friendly neighborhood therapist. We have regularly scheduled times to talk with our clients, and we discourage emergency calls when there is no immediate danger. This is mostly for our own benefit, of course, but it's also the most helpful thing we can do for explosive people like Rachel.

Step back and look at the larger picture. Rachel's emergencies are usually overreactions to day-to-day frustrations. She replays events in her mind, expanding their implications and making herself more depressed with each retelling. Eventually she feels she can't take it anymore, so she picks up the phone and calls you, since I'm not in.

If you're always available, you become an emotional landfill where she can go to dump her loads of distress. If you're not there, she must at least figure out how to manage her feelings until you get back. Often, she'll do that by having an imaginary conversation with you.

I don't know what your conversations with depressed people are like, but mine are not strikingly new and different each time. Mostly, I say the same things over and over, hoping they'll sink in.

The way they sink in is through those imaginary conversations.

Most of my clients already know what I'm going to say. In my absence, they can say it to themselves. At times they actually create their own instructions and follow them because they think they're coming from me. If that's not manipulative enough, I often schedule appointments at irregular intervals to capitalize on this effect. Clients are sometimes upset by my inscrutable schedule; they tell me how hard it is to wait for the next appointment. It's flattering to be so desperately needed, but I know that the waiting can do them more good than the appointment.

If you have a friend or family member like Rachel, it will help both of you to put limits on your availability for discussing emotional issues. I'm not suggesting that you avoid them, but that you set specific times for the beginning and end of your talks about how she feels. At other times do something else, like going for a walk in the park.

The I Absolutely Refuse to Be a Burden Explosion

In Carol's case, the idea of depression being anger turned inward makes more sense, as does treatment that involves expressing her aggressive impulses. Remember, however, that aggression means imposing your will on the world. It is a continuum that begins with asking for what you want and saying no to things you don't want. (selfishism).

Carol never asks for anything for herself, and she never says no to anybody else. Her life is a flurry of forced cheerfulness and selfless activity, punctuated by episodes of vague illness that last about a week, during which she mostly stays in bed and feels guilty about not working.

The latent meaning of Carol's periods of lethargy is No! But it has other meanings as well. We also know that she has bipolar disorder, that there's a strong biochemical component to her variations in energy and mood. During the *external control* step of treatment, it took careful balancing of medications to help her stabilize.

Stabilized, however, is not cured. While taking medication, Carol still followed her old patterns of cheerful selflessness. She was less frantic about it, but the medication did not enable her to stand up for herself. The pressure inside her continued to build, and she had to find some other way to express it. Often it would be by stopping her medication and precipitating a hypomanic or depressed episode. Eventually her psychiatrist referred her to me for therapy to find out why she wouldn't stay with treatment that was obviously effective.

Carol's treatment had been effective for one part of her disorder. On the medication, she no longer had drastic mood swings, but she was still suppressing her own feelings to avoid conflict with other people, letting the latent content of her actions express what she was afraid to say directly.

Carol's story illustrates once more the difficulty of trying to specify what depression *really* is. Her disorder is a clear case of *all of the above*. She's plagued by chemical imbalance, loss, anger turned inward, internal conflicts, external stress, and just about everything else that depression can be. Carol is not particularly unusual. Depression is a disorder of many levels, physical and psychological; somehow, we have to deal with all of them. The ones we leave out come back to haunt us.

Being a therapist in the age of serotonin is not easy. In the early days of my training, professors would laugh at the crackpots who thought mental disorders were caused by brain chemicals. Now they laugh at crackpots who don't. Fashions change, yet at any given moment, we act as if history were nothing but prologue for the age of enlightenment in which we now live. The pronouncements of the old order seem dated and a bit silly.

Before we knew much about the brain, therapists speculated about the mind. Every disorder was supposedly caused by unconscious, psychodynamic processes in which everything represented something else. To make matters worse, different disorders can have the same dynamics. You've probably recognized that, though Carol's symptoms are not like Jane's panic attacks, they both seem to arise from the same internal conflicts over expressing aggression.

You might ask: If therapists are so smart, why can't we figure out which conflicts cause which disorder?

The reason we can't, and never could, is it doesn't work that way. Conflicts don't cause disorders—they are the fuel that runs them, and sometimes causes them to explode. If you throw a match into gasoline, everyone knows there will be an explosion, but who can say whether the match or the gasoline causes the blast? Disorders erupt at points of physiological or psychological weakness. Faulty brains and faulty minds both play a part, but neither can be called the ultimate cause.

Step 4: Separating Thinking, Feeling, and Acting

Whatever else it may be, depression is a distortion in thinking that causes negative feelings, which lead to self-defeating actions, which cause more negative feelings, which further distort thinking, and so on. There are no straight lines in depression, only downward-twisting spirals. Depressed people believe that thoughts, feelings, and actions are inextricably connected, trunk to tail, with feelings always in the lead. The goal of psychotherapy is to stop the parade, or at least change the order of the elephants.

The *I Just Don't Feel Up to It* Explosion

Depressed people let their feelings determine their choices. They always seem to be waiting to feel better before they do what it takes to feel better. Ask any of them why they didn't go for their walk today:

> "I just didn't feel up to it," Randy says, looking longingly at the place where his couch used to be.

> * * *

> Carol zips by, carrying an armload of laundry. "The house is such a mess; I'd feel guilty if I didn't clean it first."

> * * *

> "Seeing the lovers in the park makes me more depressed," Rachel says.

The flaws in their logic are easy to see, but try explaining them. It's like rolling a huge rock up a mountain only to see it roll back down again each time. The trick is to get depressed people to see the pattern, to somehow get their despair to recognize itself.

Medications often make people feel better, but as an unintended side effect, they enhance the perception that feelings lead the parade. Behavioral treatment drags action to the front of the line, then demonstrates with indisputable numbers how much better you feel if you have a little fun.

COGNITIVE THERAPY. Behavioral treatment works if depressed people try it, but as we've seen, it can require heroic efforts to get them up and going. You can't just talk them into action, because they're sure it won't do any good. *Cognitive therapy* attacks that negative certainty by pointing out how irrational thoughts lead to false conclusions. It works, but it still requires a good deal of convincing to get depressed people to believe that examining their thinking could possibly make them feel better.

Before any of the techniques can work, we somehow have to convince depressed people to doubt their own perceptions. I've discovered that tricks work far better than earnest explanations. Here's one I've used. You actually can try it at home.

> *Rachel slouches in the chair across from me, droning on about how hopeless her life is. Unless you're relentlessly optimistic, working with depressed people can get very depressing. I turn away from Rachel and start fumbling around in my desk drawer.*
>
> *"Am I boring you?" she asks.*
>
> *"No more than usual," I say. Then I hold out a pair of glasses with brown and smeary lenses. "Here, put these on."*
>
> *"Why?"*
>
> *"To humor your crazy therapist,"*
>
> *Rachel puts on the glasses because she knows I'll hound her unmercifully until she does. "Yuck," she says, as she reaches up to take them off.*
>
> *"Keep them on for a minute," I say. "I want you to see what it's like looking at the world through [expletive deleted]-colored glasses."*
>
> *Rachel snatches off the glasses as if burned. "That's what you think I'm doing, right?"*
>
> *"What do you think you're doing?" I say, stroking my beard.*

I'd love to say that in a moment of blinding insight Rachel recognized the true nature of her depression, threw off her own metaphorical glasses, and lived happily ever after. Unfortunately, therapy doesn't work that way. Not even on television.

Rachel and I still had piles of [expletive deleted] to slog through. The glasses gave us a way to talk about it. And joke about it. I believe so strongly that depressed people need to learn to laugh at themselves, that I'm not above laughing at them. I am not unusual among therapists in this respect. Humor is one of our most important tools. You can use it too. Don't be afraid to joke with depressed people about their depression. Be gentle and loving, but most of all, be funny. If they get offended, tell them it was my idea.

Randy's wife hands him a small stuffed donkey. "What is this?" he asks.

"It's Eeyore," she says. "From Winnie the Pooh."

Randy looks at her blankly. She beckons him into the room where the grandkids watch videos on the only working television left in the house. She starts a tape, and together, sitting in bean-bag chairs on the floor, they watch the depressed donkey ward off all attempts at good cheer.

Randy's wife holds up the stuffed animal again. "You're my Eeyore," she says, hoping she hasn't pushed it too far.

Randy takes a deep breath. "Thanks for noticing me," he says in a deep donkey-voice.

Talk about manifest and latent content! Freud himself wrote a treatise attempting to analyze humor. I guess he didn't realize that jokes aren't funny when you have to explain them. Humor, nevertheless, is the best argument that human experience exists on a number of levels at the same time.

Affectionate joking is the best answer to the *I just don't feel up to it* explosion, but if you don't feel affectionate, don't use humor to disguise irritation.

Jokes, whether Eeyore, expletive-deleted-colored glasses, or whatever else you come up with, provide a useful means of externalizing the perceptual distortions inherent in depression. Not only does despair get to know itself, but, if your timing is good, it may laugh at itself as well.

If you don't get a laugh, immediately take responsibility for whatever aggression you're feeling. You'll still provoke a useful conversation. Even ill-received humor will work out fine if you remember this rule: Never try to explain aggression away by saying you were only joking. There is no such thing as *only joking*.

Joking aside, cognitive therapy is a more exhaustive attempt to categorize, explain, and offer arguments against distorted thinking in depression. Depressed people engage in typical and recognizable patterns of self-defeating thought. Based on very little evidence, they quickly conclude that situations are hopeless, that they are helpless to change them and therefore worthless.

Cognitive therapists ask depressed people to go back and take a closer look at the evidence on which they base these negative conclusions. Like the behaviorists, cognitive therapists often have clients chart the relationship between their thoughts, actions, and mood. The two approaches are usually combined, and turn out to be extremely effective at helping depressed people get better and stay better.

INTERPERSONAL THERAPY. Another approach widely used in the treatment of depression is interpersonal therapy. It involves teaching depressed people more effective strategies for dealing with human problems, like disputes, role transitions, and social skill deficits using standard procedures, manuals, and lesson plans. The approaches for dealing with loss described earlier are similar to what an interpersonal therapist might do.

Recent studies show that both cognitive-behavioral therapy and interpersonal therapy can change the brain scans of depressed people in a manner quite similar to that achieved by antidepressant medication. Other studies have shown that these approaches are more effective than medication in preventing relapses into depression over time.

This is all well and good, but before you tell the depressed people in your life to throw away their Prozac and get in to see cognitive or interpersonal therapists, wait. The research is valuable, but the results are not as simple as they seem.

Most research on the treatment of mental illness involves pitting one treatment against another and against a control group that gets no treatment at all to see which one works best. But what is *best*?

Considering all you've learned about the idiosyncracies of the great gray beast, think of the difficulty of devising a study to measure the effectiveness of a treatment for depression. First you have to define the disorder, and then decide how recovering from it might be measured. Then you have to specify what you mean by treatment. Drug dosage is easy, but how would you define psychotherapy? The treatments that fare best in research will obviously be those most clearly delineated by lesson plans, exercises, and the like. This is why cognitive-behavioral and interpersonal therapies looks so good.

In the real world, there is no clear separation between techniques, unless the therapist is particularly anal-retentive. Most of us have a whole bag of tricks; if one doesn't work, we reach in and try another. Every patient and practitioner combination is different, but not so much so that we can't make a few generalizations. The inescapable conclusion from the research is that *structured approaches aimed at teaching people new skills and getting them to do things differently are most effective with depression.* Skilled therapists, regardless of theoretical approach, try to accomplish similar goals in treating depression. What they say about what they do varies considerably more than what they actually do. It's the sequence of goals that is important, not the particular tricks we use to help people accomplish them.

Less skillful therapists are likely to focus more on the technique than what the technique is supposed to accomplish. In the last chapter of this book, I'll share my ideas about how to find a capable therapist. For now, remember that there's more than one way to skin an elephant.

Step 5: Living at the Crossroads

According to the cognitive therapists, depressed people think in characteristic, self-defeating ways. They expect the worst and usually get it, or at least think they do because they pay more attention to negative aspects of situations than to the positive ones. At the heart of their distorted view of the world is *global thinking*, the tendency to see life as a series of impossibly distant end points rather than a process that must be taken a step at a time.

That first step is the hardest. Sometimes dying seems easier.

How to Handle Suicide Threats

There are approximately 30,000 *successful suicides* per year in the United States. More than half of these are done with firearms. Hanging is the next most common method. There are about 300,000 *suicide attempts* every year, so one in ten is successful. Most unsuccessful attempts are by overdose. Men are about five times as likely to kill themselves as women, but women make three times as many suicide attempts as men. It's difficult to say how many *suicide threats* happen in a year, a threat being defined as an immanent plan for self-destruction with the means readily available. If the one in ten factor holds, it would be about 3 million threats. There's no way to tell how many people experience *suicidal ideation*, which means considering the possibility and, usually, talking about it. The National Institute of Mental Health estimates that there are almost 40 million cases of depression and PTSD, the disorders most closely associated with suicidal thinking. You do the math.

The people most likely to kill themselves are, in rough order, those who have made previous attempts, people who have been hospitalized for major depression, men—the older, the more likely—substance abusers, and those who have experienced a recent loss. The suicide rates for teenagers have increased over the past 50 years, but despite the publicity, they are no more likely to kill themselves than anybody else. The percentage of suicides is about equal to the percentage of teenagers in the entire population.

There are two important points to be made from these statistics. First, that very few of the people who talk about suicide, perhaps one in 1000, actually do it. The second is that aside from very general statistical trends, we have no way of telling *which* ones will commit suicide.

Talk of suicide has to be taken seriously. In my opinion, the more seriously, the better. Suicidal people should be in active treatment with a mental health professional, and should probably be taking medication. These are the goals to shoot for when people in your life talk about exploding into death. No matter how much you care about them, you cannot keep them alive by your own efforts, nor figure out how much effort it would take if you could.

"I almost did it last night," Alonzo says.

"Did what?" you say, feeling a prickle at the back of your neck.

"You know, man. I sat there for two hours with that .357 in my hand, just sipping beer and staring at it. Finally, I fell asleep."

What next? Fueled by fear for your friend's life, everything you've heard about suicide comes scrolling through your head. A suicide threat is a cry for help; you should listen, but not too much, because it might just be a device for getting attention. The people who talk about it don't do it;

the people who talk about it do it. You feel confused, torn by conflicting urges. You ache for Alonzo's pain and want to help him, but you also feel irritated at him for putting his life in your unqualified hands. Mostly, you're scared, afraid to speak lest the wrong thing push him closer to the edge. Eventually you have to say something. Here are a few ideas:

Take action, not responsibility. *There is absolutely nothing you can do to prevent a person who really wants to die from killing himself.* At best, you may be able to delay the inevitable, but in the end the decision will be his, not yours.

Your actions should be directed at clearly communicating that you're dead set against suicide, decreasing the opportunities for harm, and getting him professional help as quickly as possible. By his responses, you may begin to draw some conclusions about the purpose and seriousness of the threat, but your assessment should make little difference. *The most helpful thing you can do is to treat even small hints about suicide formally and seriously.* The message you want to send, start to finish, is that thoughts of suicide are nothing to play around with.

With divorce, a pistol, and beer in the picture, you should have no problem taking Alonzo's threat seriously. But what about Rachel's? A few years ago she went through a period of making suicide threats that were, by all the standards a professional would apply, far less serious than Alonzo's.

The phone rings a little after midnight. Again. You fumble for it in the dark.

"I just can't take it anymore," Rachel sobs. "There's just no hope. This time I'm afraid I'm really going to do it. I've got the pills in my hand."

If there is a dependent depressed person like Rachel in your life, chances are you've heard statements like this before. Probably more than once. You're pretty sure she isn't actually going to do anything to herself, but that should not make a difference.

If a suicide threat is serious, you want to do whatever you can to stop Rachel from harming herself. If the threat is less serious, you want to stop her from threatening. The same approach is most likely to accomplish either goal.

SEPARATE THE PERSON FROM THE WEAPON. Your first move should be to get Alonzo's guns or Rachel's pills. Ask for them immediately.

> *"Buddy, you're scaring me," you say. "I know we can get through this, but I want that gun for safekeeping right now. That one, and whatever other guns you have in the house."*

The reason for this is obvious. It takes less than a second to pull a trigger.

If you're not comfortable with having guns in your home, arrange for Alonzo to give them to someone else, perhaps the police. Make sure you ask for all his firearms. Many gun owners have more than one.

If Alonzo does give you his guns, he will at least be safe from them. It won't stop him from using other means to do himself in, but everything else is slower and requires more thought and effort.

If he won't give you his guns, you need to involve someone else more qualified. If he's seeing a mental health professional, call that person. Say, "This is a suicidal emergency regarding Alonzo ____," or it will take all day to get a return call. If Alonzo isn't seeing a professional, call the crisis hotline. Most cities have them; they're usually listed on the inside front cover of the phone book. If there isn't one where you are, call the police business number—not 911 at this point.

Obviously, if you don't feel you know Alonzo well enough to ask for his guns or to contact the authorities if he doesn't hand them over, you need to enlist the aid of someone closer to him, perhaps a relative. If separation is involved, don't call the ex-spouse! There's no point in pouring gasoline on the fire.

Before I say more, and raise your anxiety level even further, I should point out that Alonzo's life is probably not at stake. Remember, actual suicides are rare—far less frequent than heart attacks and fatal car accidents. You might regard what I'm saying here in much the same way you would information from a CPR class. It's nice to know, but you'll probably never need it.

The nightmare scenario is if someone like Alonzo calls you in the middle of the night, drunk and suicidal. This will probably never happen to you. It seldom does, even to mental health professionals, but it has happened to me many times in my years as a crisis worker. *This situation is a police emergency; call 911.* You don't want an intoxicated person driving somewhere to give up his gun, nor do you yourself want to enter the house of a person who is armed and intoxicated. The chance for accidents is too high for amateurs. If possible, keep Alonzo on the phone while someone else calls 911 at a neighbor's or on a cell phone. You'll need his address or phone number so the police can find him.

You don't have to hide what you're doing. Make it clear that you're calling the police because of *your* need to know he's safe, rather than his need to be protected.

> *"Alonzo, I'm really afraid for you, and I'm not qualified to deal with this. I'm going to call 911 to get you some help right now."*
> *"You don't have to do that, man. I'll be okay. I'm just going to go to sleep."*
> *"Alonzo, you're not okay. You wouldn't have called if you were okay. Now I need to know that you're safe. I couldn't live with myself if I didn't call 911. When they tell me you're okay, I'll believe it."*

Alonzo is calling because his pain has exceeded his ability to deal with it. He's giving the situation to you to handle because he doesn't know how to handle it himself. Chances are good that he will do exactly what you tell him to do. Don't be afraid of overreacting! It is the most therapeutic thing you can do.

Often, when you mention 911, suicidal people will minimize the danger as Alonzo did. They are probably being honest, but it isn't your decision. The police have experience with such situations, you don't. Laws and procedures differ from state to state, but what will probably happen as a result of your call is a mandatory evaluation with a mental health professional. For years I did such evaluations, and I can tell you that there is no more effective time for a therapeutic intervention, because at that moment you have people's undivided attention.

I must also tell you that on extremely rare occasions suicidal people tell police, friends, or mental health professionals what it takes to get released, then just go home and kill themselves anyway. This has happened to me twice during a 30-year career of dealing regularly with suicidal people. Do not hesitate to make the call. The odds of helping are slanted overwhelmingly in your favor.

With Rachel, even though you know that she isn't in a great deal of danger, you should still treat the situation as a life and death emergency. If she isn't intoxicated, demand that she bring her pills to you, or somebody, right then. She will definitely back down and begin to minimize, but you shouldn't. Handling Rachel's threat this way may cost you the rest of your night's sleep, but it's a good investment. If you back down, she'll likely call again another night.

You want Rachel to feel that the situation has gone too far, and that people are taking her more seriously than she ever intended. This is actually far more validating than it is punishing. Even if she says that next time she'll think about killing herself and just not tell you, she probably won't. After Rachel hands over her pills, take her to the emergency room. They usually have a mental health worker on duty. That person should make the final ruling on her safety.

In Rachel's case, I'd be less likely to call 911, and might even settle for the sound of her flushing her pills down the toilet, followed by a promise to see a mental health professional in the morning. My judgment is based on years of experience. Unless you're certain that she's safe, don't take chances. Remember, if in doubt, overreact.

DO NOT LEAVE A SUICIDAL PERSON ALONE UNTIL A QUALIFIED PERSON TELLS YOU IT'S SAFE TO DO SO.   Think of it this way: When people threaten suicide, they lose their right to privacy until they are actively dealing with the issues that brought them to the point of considering death. Inconvenient as it may be to both of you, you shouldn't leave them alone. This is a safety consideration, of course, but it's also therapy. Your inconvenience provides a strong incentive for them to get into treatment. Hound them unmercifully until they do.

My rather draconian approach to suicide threats is designed both to scare people and make them feel safer. Rigid though my advice may seem, it's based on years of experience with suicidal people and what I consider to be a sympathetic understanding of their suffering, and a sincere desire to alleviate it.

Suicidal thinking is not an involuntary handicap. People are not beset by it, they *do* it. Their best bet, and yours, is making them take responsibility for what they're doing—not by scolding or punishing them, but by exposing them to the natural consequences of their actions. Tell the professionals who regularly deal with suicide threats about them. The worst thing you can do is keep suicidal thinking a secret between the two of you because you think that calling the police or the guys in white coats will be so embarrassing as to make suicide more likely. Take it from one of the guys in white coats—it won't. Regardless of what suicidal people may threaten, they will not kill themselves to punish you for trying to get them help.

Suicide, suicide threats, and even suicidal ideation are attempts at solving life problems by running away into death. As we have seen countless times before, running away creates more problems than it solves. If you're dead, you don't even get to experience the relief.

Sometimes depression forces people to choose between life and death. More often, the choice is between doing and waiting for something to happen.

The *What's the Point?* Explosion

> *"Rachel," you say, "you're always talking about wanting a relationship, but you never do anything to meet men. Why don't you try one of those on-line singles chat rooms?*
>
> *"You mean with all the creeps and weirdos?"*
>
> *"Well, they're not all creeps and weirdos. Ellen met Chris on line, and he's really nice."*
>
> *"Yeah, like somebody normal would be interested in me."*
>
> *"Come on, Rache, you've got to kiss a lot of frogs before you find a prince."*
>
> *"What's the point?"*

Before you answer, wait. You're about to be sucked into a philosophical black hole. There is no answer to Rachel's question, because it ultimately boils down to the great human dilemma: Why live if you're just going to die? There is no way you can answer this for another person. You can only offer a sermon about whatever beliefs keep you going, and depressed people do not respond to sermons. There's no way you can talk them into believing in their ultimate prospects for happiness.

To make matters worse, depressed people are usually right. Many studies have shown that the depressed are better at predicting the future than people who have no discernible mental disorder. Normality, as I said earlier, is actually a state of unreasonable optimism. Most of us shiny, happy people move toward the joys that life offers, blithely ignoring the inevitability of pain. Hope *does* spring eternal in the human breast. This may make us shallow, but it also makes us brave.

In order to deal effectively with the *What's the point?* Explosion, you have to understand what you're actually hearing. You've heard it before in a slightly different form. Underneath many depressions are our old nemeses—fear and avoidance.

Ask Carol why she doesn't tell people no:

"Well, they might get angry."

Ask Alonzo why he doesn't find someone new to love:

"I couldn't bear the pain if she were to leave me."

Ask Randy why he doesn't look for work:

"I don't think I could handle the stress."

You can't say that these fears are unrealistic, so don't try. Instead, you need to understand how these depressed people came to be where they are.

If you run away from fear, you end up in depression. It is a simple fact: There is no avoiding pain, but you do have a choice about what sort of pain you experience. The ultimate cure for depression is recognizing that we stand at the crossroads between fear and despair at every moment, and the choice is ours. Why then should we go forward?

Why not?

The kind of existential philosophy I've been spouting is an example of how great depressed minds of the past have reasoned their way out of depression. Talk about rolling a rock up a hill! Luckily, normal, unreasonably optimistic people never have to come to grips with such questions.

Or is it lucky? I told you that depression adds depth to human experience. Where else can you get the realization that life is only rock and roll?

What *is* lucky is that you don't have to explain the meaning of life to help depressed people get better. When you encounter the *What's the point?* explosion, respond to the fear beneath it. You already know how to deal with fear disorders.

"Rachel, I just realized how frightened you are."

"Who wouldn't be frightened? There's so much to be afraid of."

"I know, but the only way to deal with fear is to turn around and move toward it one little step at a time. Let's start with a walk in the park. While we're there, we can decide what the next step might be."

The ultimate cure for depression is recognizing that there is no ultimate cure. There are many things that help—medication, psychotherapy, and the support of friends and family—but nothing by itself will make depressed people well except their own moment to moment choices. They must see themselves as living perpetually at a choice point. The path that looks easiest usually leads deeper into despair. The way out is to take the road that is less certain and more frightening, and travel it one step at a time. The only thing that makes the choice easier is that depressed people have seen what lies at the other end.

Rachel, Carol, and Randy all got up and started moving away from depression. Carol is working to manage her agitation with enforced relaxation and setting limits on what she does for others.

Randy is dealing with stress a little at a time rather than running away from it. He's been doing volunteer work and is now looking for a real paying job.

Rachel is back on medication, exercising her buns off to keep from gaining weight. She hasn't found a long-term relationship yet, but she has kissed a few frogs. xShe's also working on a more adult relationship with her mother. And her friends. There are no more middle of the night calls.

If there are depressed people in your life, remember that you can't make them feel better. The way to help them is to be there at the crossroads as a guide, pointing them in the right direction, encouraging them to stay with small actions that help a little, rather than thrashing about in search of the magical cure that will make them feel well enough to do the things that will make them feel better. Happiness is not the end of the road, it is the journey.

Part Four

Explosions into Anger

Chapter 10

Explosions into Anger

Bad Chemicals or Bad People?

The traffic is even slower than usual tonight. The exit is backed up all the way onto the freeway. You take your place in line and wait through six cycles of red to green. Finally, it looks like you're going to make it. But no. The car in front of you stops on yellow. Well, next time for sure.

In your rear view you see a pickup squeezing by on the shoulder, pushing his way to the head of the line. He stops with his nose just in front of your bumper. You studiously avoid eye contact and let up on your brake, closing the space between you and the car ahead.

Green. The truck barges in front of you. You honk. The driver raises a one-finger salute, guns his engine, and zooms ahead. At the next intersection he pulls in behind you and leans on his horn.

* * *

After a horrendous day of rushing around, you turn into the restaurant parking lot at about 7:05, relieved that you weren't considerably later. You get out and rush in.

David is standing by the door, looking at his watch. "Do you know what time it is?" he asks. His voice is soft, but cold and pointed as an icicle.

"About five after," you say. "And it looks like your customer isn't here yet. Guess I lucked out."

"But what if he was?"

"But he isn't," you say.

"That's not the issue," David says. "You know how important this meeting is to me. If my feelings made any difference, you would have been here early instead of bopping in almost 10 minutes late."

"But David—"

"How many times do I have to tell you how important punctuality is to me? I guess it doesn't matter to you."

"Of course it matters to me, but—"

"Not now," David says. "He's here. We'll talk about this later."

You sigh, knowing you won't get much sleep tonight.

* * *

Jenna is race-walking down the hall. Behind her back they call her the wicked witch, or something that rhymes with it. Luckily, since she's a senior partner, most peons don't have to endure more than the occasional glare as she strides by the bullpen. This time she stops and looks around. She's holding a binder in her hand. "Which of you is responsible for this literary masterpiece?" she asks, holding up the offending document gingerly, as if it were a dead animal.

It's yours.

* * *

"There's something wrong with this stupid toaster," Zack say, as he yanks the plug from wall, and begins fumbling with the lever. "This thing is stuck."

"Maybe you should work on it later when you have more time," you say hopefully, knowing he won't listen.

Zack's movements become more rapid and jerky. His conversation turns to four-letter words muttered under his breath.

You clear out of the kitchen, knowing what's coming next. Just as you close the door, you hear the crash of the toaster hitting the floor.

✳ ✳ ✳

You call your team together for the Monday meeting. As usual, Brittany strolls in late and disrupts everything by loudly sliding a chair so she can sit next to her friends. You wait until she's situated and go on.

"There have been some changes in the security regulations," you say. "If you look at your handout, you'll see that the ones I've marked have a direct effect on procedures in this department."

Amid the shuffle of papers, Brittany snorts.

"Do you have a comment?" you ask.

"No-uh." Brittany says, stretching the word out to two syllables like your daughter used to do when she was 12.

You go back to your discourse. When you next look up, Brittany is rolling her eyes.

WHAT'S WRONG WITH THESE PEOPLE?   That's easy. They all have *anger control problems*, which are unique among psychiatric disorders in that they are regularly treated but do not officially exist.

Though irritability and angry outbursts can be symptoms of virtually all the disorders we've discussed, there is no DSM diagnosis for "anger control disorder." The only thing close is *intermittent explosive disorder*, a rare disease characterized by sudden episodes of unprovoked physical assault in an otherwise normal personality. IED is probably more neurological than psychological. The people I've described wouldn't come close to qualifying.

What *Are* Anger Control Problems?

Anger control problems are like pornography: Nobody can define them, but everybody knows them when they see them. In public, everyone is against excessive anger, but a surprising number of people indulge in it in the privacy of their own minds.

To understand what anger control problems are and how to deal with them, more instructive than a list of symptoms is a discussion of why there is no official list of symptoms to discuss.

In many ways, anger control problems are the mirror image of other psychiatric disorders. Those afflicted usually don't think there's anything wrong with them. This is quite different from fear and depression. Unlike other disorders, anger control problems are defined less by what the people who have them are experiencing, and more by the effect their experience has on us.

Look back at the examples. Though the words and actions I've described are disparate, the one thing all these people have in common is the negative emotional response their behaviors elicit. Angry people make us angry at them. *Anger, unlike other mental disorders, is highly contagious, and one of its most salient symptoms is not realizing that you have it.*

If you think the people in the examples make you afraid rather than angry, you know what I mean about not realizing, or are about to find out. We've already seen that the differences between anger and fear are more semantic than psychological. Choosing one state over the other means that to you, the distinction between anger and fear is clearer than it actually is in reality. This is a polite way of saying you're in denial.

You are not alone. The words we use to describe our own experience are different, more varied, and often more positive than those we use to describe that of other people. *They* may be *angry,* but we are *afraid.* Or *hurt, upset, irritated, out of sorts,* or perhaps *premenstrual.* We can almost fool ourselves into believing that we're talking about different emotional states entirely. But why do we need to do this?

We need to do it because anger is inseparable from morality. People get angry because other people are not doing what they're supposed to do.

Brandon, who you probably guessed was driving the pickup truck, believes that *you* insulted *him* by making a big stink over his perfectly reasonable request to be allowed into the line of traffic.

David believes that punctuality is one of the many ultimate measures of love. If you're late, he feels abandoned.

Jenna is adamant that anything short of a perfect product—meaning that something is done exactly the way she would—constitutes lack of proper respect to the firm and to her. She takes every deviation personally.

Zack would say that toasters should work correctly or suffer the consequences. Brittany would say that nobody has the right to tell her what to do.

Of course they're wrong. But before you try and convince them, wait. You're about to step into their world, where everything is clearer and in sharper contrast than in ours. Over there, it's so much easier to tell the difference between right and wrong.

Anger involves an almost hopeless intertwining of morality and psychology, yet our only hope for communicating effectively with angry people lies in being able to separate the two. The reason there is no diagnostic category for anger control problems is that mental health people can't decide whether angry people are sick or just bad. Sick people are entitled to sympathy and treatment. Bad people deserve punishment. Grudgingly, we insert *not guilty by reason of insanity* between the two, but that's for people who are *really* crazy. Where do we put people who are convinced they're fine but whose actions drive everybody else crazy?

Enter the *personality disorder*, which today is diagnosed along a separate axis from more genteel problems like anxiety and depression. According to the DSM-IV, a personality disorder is "an enduring pattern of inner experience and behavior that deviates markedly from the expectations of the individual's culture." The pattern is manifested in two (or more) of the following areas:

1. Ways of perceiving and interpreting self, other people, and events
2. Range, intensity, lability, and appropriateness of emotional response
3. Interpersonal functioning
4. Impulse control

Isn't this a remarkably civilized way of saying *bad?* The trait that supposedly distinguishes people with personality disorders from those who are normal is *disturbed object relations*, which means treating people not as people, but as objects to supply one's own needs. I've never met anyone who doesn't do this to some degree, but most of us are not exploitative enough to meet the criteria for full-fledged personality disorder.

A good way to think about these disorders is as the unbridled pursuit of a single psychological goal—excitement, attention, affection, adulation, and control are the usual suspects—that feels as necessary as air and water. Personality disorders are like addiction, another mental disorder with moral overtones. Actually, they may be variations on a single theme. People with personality disorders are often addicted to various substances, and treatment for addiction usually involves the structured force-feeding of morality, which is similar to current treatments for personality disorders.

Personality disorders wound up in their own separate category because many psychiatrists believed that they weren't really medical disorders, meaning they couldn't be treated with drugs, and wouldn't improve much, even with years of expensive psychotherapy. Such attitudes are changing, but slowly. To this day, your medical insurance will not cover the treatment of personality disorders.

You may be wondering why we bother with these morally and chemically impaired people at all. There are, however, two problems with ridding ourselves of those exhibiting personality disorders. First, the symptoms of these disorders are pervasive if not universal. Everybody has them to a certain extent. Second, and more fiendishly ironic, is the fact that much of what makes people attractive and interesting bubbles up from the same dark source as personality disorders. People who don't want anything are dull. But our desires distort our perceptions, make us do things that aren't good for us, and mess up our relationships with other people. The question is: Does this make us mentally ill or human?

All of the above.

The elements of personality disorders—yours, mine, and theirs—keep life interesting, sometimes too interesting. They also keep me employed. If personality disorders didn't get in the way, anybody could treat mental illness. Everybody would get along, and you could just tell people what to do to get better, and they would do it gratefully. A computer program could then handle my job.

Villains and Victims

Before we begin a discussion of the disorders that make people angry, there are several points I believe are essential to understand regarding the entanglement of medicine and morality as it relates to anger.

First and foremost, we're talking about *you* as well as *them*. It is not possible to see anger from only one side of the looking glass. Anger, unlike the other disorders we have discussed, is *always* interactive. What it is, and what it will become, may be as much a function of how you react to it as a function of the internal workings of the angry person.

The most destructive and dangerous thing you can add to an explosion into anger is further provocation. Expressing your own anger, whether you're aware of it or not, is like pouring gasoline on a fire. The less aware you are of your own emotional state, the more destructive it is likely to be.

Second, though anger in some degree is universal, most people define it as negative, and so do not recognize it in themselves until it becomes an undeniable explosion. For this reason, awareness of the thoughts and feelings that signal rising indignation is a critical element in the treatment of anger control disorders. It is likewise crucial in learning how to deal effectively with angry people.

Third, anger is inextricable from morality. What we get angry at defines us as surely as what we believe in, and often far more clearly than what we say about our beliefs.

We are accustomed to defining angry people as villains, and ourselves, or other affected people, as victims. Whether this is true or not, it's usually also an attempt to counterattack by seizing the moral high ground. People who see themselves as victims or the defenders of victims are claiming the right to victimize others. In 30 years of doing therapy with angry people, I have never met a bully who did not consider himself or herself a victim. To me, it makes no sense to try to deal with angry people by distorting reality in exactly the same way they do.

Angry people hurl invectives, and sometimes toasters. We throw diagnoses back at them. It's not that the diagnoses don't fit; they all describe patterns of thoughts and behaviors that actually exist. It's just that there are diagnoses to fit everyone, and, even if you're a mental health professional, your own diagnosis always influences how you diagnose others.

Though it may be of some importance to recognize the disorders that lead people to explode into anger, it is far less so than with other explosive disorders. Anger, regardless of its source, must be managed carefully to avoid escalation. The easiest way to make angry people angrier is tell them they're bad or wrong. Most of the diagnoses we use for them are polite ways of saying just that. Many people who know a little about diagnosing people are tempted to use that skill to win arguments. This tactic *always* fails. Can you imagine how you would feel if you were upset, and instead of listening to you, people told you that you were messed up in the head?

Anger is different from the other disorders we've discussed. When people are depressed or anxious, we want to help them and make them feel better. Our feelings toward angry people are considerably less charitable. Their anger evokes our anger, which brings out more anger in them. Our concern with them has far more to do with what they make us feel than what they're feeling, as I alluded to above. This lack of empathy is reflected at almost every level. It confounds our attempts to diagnose and treat angry people, and often leads us to choose strategies for dealing with them that just make them angrier.

However, it is far more difficult to empathize with anger than with other sorts of emotional explosions, especially if that anger is directed at you. Empathy is critical in keeping all kinds of emotional outbursts from escalating. To deal effectively with explosive people, you have to approach them based on what *they* are feeling, rather than what you're feeling about them. This is far easier to do when people are anxious or depressed than when they're angry.

Empathy for the irritable is possible only if you clearly separate it from sympathy. Empathy requires only understanding; sympathy requires understanding *and* agreement. At its heart, dealing effectively with anger is a matter of semantics. Even if you strongly disagree with an angry person's perception of a situation, you must still be sensitive enough to recognize the danger of sharing that opinion. Now that you've been warned of the dangers, we may safely step over to the other side of the looking glass.

Disorders Associated with Anger

Personality disorders are the mental illnesses most often diagnosed in people who explode into anger. Since such diagnoses relegate a person to a place slightly beyond the pale, they are most often awarded to people of whom therapists disapprove. Personality disorders are fascinating enough to warrant their own book. For those who wish to delve more deeply, I have expressed my views in a previous work, *Emotional Vampires* (New York: McGraw-Hill, 2002). For the present discussion, I'll attempt a brief summary.

ANTISOCIAL PERSONALITY DISORDER.   Antisocials are hooked on stimulation. They aren't called antisocial because they don't like parties, but because they're heedless of social rules. They love parties, also sex, drugs, rock 'n' roll, and anything else exciting, like maybe a good fight. Anything is better than boredom. All they want out of life is a good time, a little action, and immediate gratification of their every desire. If they don't get it, they get angry. Their anger is an attempt to engage you, either to get you to give them what they want or simply for the joy of fighting. Brandon, with his drinking and shameless aggression-turned-outward, is a fairly typical example of an antisocial.

Brittany is also an example. Like teenagers, antisocials get huffy when you tell them what to do. That's a good way to understand them—as perpetual adolescents. Rebellion is the nearly inexhaustible power source that drives them into one brick wall after another. There is an up side, however. Without antisocial personalities, there would be no country and western music.

HISTRIONIC PERSONALITY DISORDER.   Histrionics are addicted to attention and approval. Some want to look good, others are satisfied with just making you look. Histrionic means dramatic, so scenes of all sorts are a specialty. Their emotions run a mile wide and an inch deep. What you see is mostly for show, and definitely not what you get.

Histrionics are experts at hiding their own motivation from themselves. They believe that they never do anything unacceptable, like making mistakes, having bad thoughts about anyone, or ever getting angry. They're just nice people who only want to help. If you question that, you're likely to suffer their disguised wrath.

The important thing to understand about histrionics is that their behavior is directed more toward fooling themselves than toward fooling you. Zack, for instance, the toaster terminator, sees himself as an easygoing, happy-go-lucky guy.

OBSESSIVE-COMPULSIVE PERSONALITY DISORDER.   Obsessive-compulsives want the world to be perfect. They believe they can achieve that goal through rigid rules, scrupulous attention to detail, and swift correction of the tiniest infractions. To obsessive-compulsives, punishment is good for the soul, and even the slightest word of praise will lead to terminal indolence. Jenna, the wicked witch, uses her perfectionism the way overseers use whips. And with the same relish.

Like most obsessive-compulsives, she doesn't consider herself an angry person because she never yells. She prefers more civilized punishments, like flaying you alive with constructive criticism. If you asked, she would point out with pride that she is *much* harder on herself than she is on you.

NARCISSISTIC PERSONALITY DISORDER.   Have you ever noticed that people with huge egos tend to be really tiny everywhere else? All narcissists want is to live out their grandiose fantasies of being treated as the smartest, most talented, and all-around best people in the world. It's not so much that they think they're better than other people, but rather that they don't think of other people at all.

Narcissists are legends in their own minds. They'll explode into anger if you get in their way, make them look bad, or expect them to live by the rules of mere mortals. They belive they're entitled to far more. Though Brandon is mostly antisocial, his belief that the shoulder of the road was built to be his personal lane is pure narcissism.

Though there is plenty of narcissism without greatness, there is no greatness without narcissism. It will be easy to see narcissistic tendencies in your boss, and just as easy for your subordinates to see them in you. It will be almost impossible for you to see them in yourself.

Narcissists never laugh at their own foibles. Teasing one is like juggling bottles of nitroglycerine.

PARANOID PERSONALITY DISORDER.   In common parlance, *paranoid* means thinking people are after you. Paranoia is really an almost preternatural sensitivity that enables people to see things that others can't, coupled with the naive belief that the world is either black or white. Paranoids want to banish all ambiguity from their lives by discovering the Truth, using torture if necessary. Paranoids live by concrete rules, like David's about punctuality. Their idea of disloyalty is forgetting one of the 1001 preferences they mistake for natural law; their idea of infidelity is speaking the name of a former lover. Paranoids believe you should live by the letter of their laws also. If you don't, may God have mercy on your soul. Paranoids see even less humor in their actions than do narcissists.

BORDERLINE PERSONALITY DISORDER.   Borderlines feel everything more intensely than other people. They can be loving and caring, but are so terrified of abandonment that they will lash out at you, themselves, and anyone else in range with the barest hint of rejection.

A Few Cautions

Just because people act in the ways I've described, it doesn't mean they have personality disorders. Even if you strongly suspect that an angry person in your life meets the diagnostic criteria, their inflammatory names should never pass your lips, even at a relatively calm time. This is a matter of self-preservation. Should the person look up the disorder, he or she will find a great deal of unflattering material, and it will be as if you had written it all. Your best bet is to suggest anger control treatment and let the therapist handle the diagnosing.

There are other, somewhat more acceptable conditions that are also associated with anger. Most have already been mentioned. Since personality disorders are diagnosed on a separate axis, it's possible to have one along with any of the other disorders we've discussed. Again, when anger is a symptom, it should be your focus, rather than the differential diagnosis.

Most Frequent Anger Disorders

The disorders most frequently associated with anger are substance abuse, generalized anxiety disorder, depression, bipolar disorder, and post-traumatic stress disorder.

SUBSTANCE ABUSE.   By far the most frequent cause for explosions into anger is substance abuse. Alcohol, of course, is at the top of the list. Its generalized numbing of the central nervous system beginning with the inhibitory prefrontal lobes removes inhibitions and makes emotional over-reactions much more likely. Even people who are relaxed and friendly when inebriated will still have a lower threshold for anger. It also seems that the longer people abuse alcohol, the more angry they become.

The metabolic by-products of alcohol—acetylaldehyde, among others—and the depletions of dopamine often cause as much irritability as the alcohol itself. Substance abusers who were relaxed and happy the night before can become holy terrors the morning after. This sort of rebound effect is characteristic of substances that work primarily as depressants, such as cannabis, barbiturates, and benzodiazepines. Marijuana intoxication can also cause acute paranoid states that can easily lead to explosions into anger.

Stimulants of all kinds, including caffeine, cocaine, and amphetamine, lead to increased arousal and agitation. Anger is seldom far behind. The most important thing to remember about the relationship of substance abuse and anger is that the substance abuse must be treated first. *No treatment for anger control, neither therapy nor medication, will work on people who are actively abusing substances.*

Most of the strategies for dealing with explosions into anger that I present here won't work either. It is not possible to reason with someone who is intoxicated. Don't even try, especially if you've been indulging yourself. The most effective approach for intoxicated anger is to get away as quickly as possible and deal with the situation at a later time.

GENERALIZED ANXIETY DISORDER.   We've seen how anxiety brings out the desire to control. When anything or anybody refuses to be controlled, anxious people get upset. Generalized anxiety can lead to irritability and carping, but seldom to full-blown explosions. On the receiving end, it feels more like being pecked to death than having your head bitten off. I include the disorder here because of its prevalence rather than its severity.

People differ widely in their perception of the intensity of anger directed at them. What one defines as irritability, another may call rage. Regardless of how you label the emotional state, the approaches for dealing with explosions into anger vary only slightly.

DEPRESSION.   Depressed people don't like much of anything, and sometimes they express that dislike with outbursts of anger. Usually, the anger doesn't have much energy behind it, but occasionally, especially in agitated phases, the depressed can work up a good head of steam. People who are turning anger inward can sometimes turn it outward as well.

Also, since antidepressants are the medication of choice for anger problems, there are those who maintain that all anger is really depression.

This may be more semantics than biology, but as we have seen repeatedly, there is a great deal of physiological overlap among all the conditions we have discussed.

BIPOLAR DISORDER.   People in the hypomanic phase of this illness may be extremely irritable and even assaultive. There will be other symptoms as well. Most common are several nights of sleeplessness and pressured speech. Hypomanic people can seldom stop talking for more than a few seconds at a time. These same symptoms are also characteristic of stimulant intoxication. Either way, this condition can be quite dangerous. If you see it, do what you can to get away, or arrange immediate treatment. Chapter 13 will give you some ideas about whom to call and how to go about it.

POST-TRAUMATIC STRESS DISORDER.   Displaced anger is a characteristic symptom of PTSD. Here's how it works: People who have suffered traumatic abuse in their past, sexual or physical, may be triggered into that same emotional state by events in the present. A look, a touch, or certain words can all elicit intense anger in people with a history of trauma.

Such overreactions are a more severe version of what Freud considered a universal phenomenon called *transference,* in which people in the present are regularly confused emotionally with people in the past. Transference, to the analysts, is the force behind all neuroses. Everybody does it, but people with PTSD do it with more vehemence.

Such angry outbursts should be treated as a hang-up and not a handicap. Controlling them is usually a primary focus of treatment for PTSD. Regardless of what past horrors may have been endured, if you are not presently abusing the person with PTSD yourself, you have a right not to be treated as if you were.

People in treatment for abuse may go through periods of confusion in which outbursts are very hard to control. You may have to forgive them quite a bit as they wrestle with integrating the past and present. The approaches to anger described in the next chapter will help you get through difficult times.

Difficult times should not be permanent. If treatment for PTSD seems to focus less on the person gaining control over outbursts and more on you having to learn how not to act like the abuser, chances are that the wrong person is being treated, or doing the treatment.

Type A personality.   This is not a disorder at all. It actually started out as a public relations device. In the early 1970s the notion that stress could affect serious medical disorders like heart disease was still radical. Hans Selye and others had talked about the relationship, but there was little actual research because government agencies weren't interested enough to fund it. Type A personality was invented to catch the attention of funding sources. Driven, competitive, and obsessed with cramming as much activity as possible into the shortest amount of time, Type A's were presented as heart attacks waiting to happen. Type B's, who were more laid back and less achievement-oriented, were supposedly the pictures of health. Don't forget that this was in the 1970s.

The distinction caught on big-time with the public, but it didn't really bear out in the research, which did indeed get funded. Both groups seemed to have the same number of heart attacks, and Type A's were actually more likely to survive them.

By the mid 1980s, Type B slackers had become the unhealthy group. Some suggested that Type A led to success and Type B caused cancer. This didn't turn out to be the case either. Hostility, whether in Type A or B, turned out to be a better predictor of heart disease, but there were even problems with that. Nevertheless, the Type A personality has become an archetype. Everybody knows what it is. We just can't figure out whether it's good or bad.

What You Can and Can't Do

Now that you know the disorders associated with anger, forget them. Well, that's not completely true, but if at this point you clutter your mind with diagnostic niceties, you may miss something more important: Your job with angry people, whether loved ones or strangers, is to protect yourself, not try to cure them. Actually, the very best thing you can do for both of you is to keep from becoming caught up in their anger and responding to it with words or actions that make it worse. This is difficult, because it involves ignoring most of what your brain and body are telling you to do. Luckily, you've spent the last chapters learning how to help other people make intelligent choices about their internal programming. It's now time to try these same lessons on yourself. As you'll see Chapter 12, the steps to follow in treating anger are identical to the steps for dealing effectively with angry people.

Consider this: There are only two situations when angry people are likely to accept your assertion that there is something wrong with them that requires treatment. One is if you're completely engaged with their anger and have enough power to force them into treatment against their will by threatening to leave them, fire them, jail them, or beat them up. The other is being so totally disengaged from their antics that they can believe that your suggestion of treatment is in fact what's best for them and not a way of winning an argument by labeling them as mentally ill. *These strategies are mutually exclusive.* The most damaging and dangerous thing you can do is attempt them both at the same time, which is what everybody tries until they finally realize it doesn't work.

The Physiology of Anger

As nearly as we can tell, the physiology of anger is identical to that of fear. The fight or flight response is the same; the only difference is the choice of which to do. Try though they might, scientists have not been able to discover solid evidence of a physiological basis for that choice.

It's not as if they haven't tried. There have been many theories, none of which has borne out. Hormones were suspected of causing aggression almost from the moment they were discovered. Early research suggested that fear was caused by adrenaline by itself and that anger was provoked by a mixture of adrenaline and noradrenaline, a similar hormone. The idea was neat, simple, and incorrect.

Testosterone, a male hormone, is persistently cited as a cause for anger. Everybody knows that men are more aggressive. What could be more natural than blaming one of the bodily fluids that makes them men?

Violent criminals have higher testosterone levels than other men, and testosterone shots tend to make people, well, testy. Unfortunately, that's about the only proof there is. Almost any hormonal imbalance can cause irritability, but that doesn't mean the converse is true.

There are also theories that implicate various areas of the brain. The amygdala is a typical suspect, because lesions there cause uncontrollable rage in laboratory animals. Brain scans, however, show very few differences that can distinguish one form of agitation from another.

Even if we don't have much in the way of biochemical explanations as to why one person would choose to fight and another to fly, recognizing activation of the sympathetic system is even more important in anger than in fear. With fear disorders, the goal is to be able to tolerate excessive arousal; with anger, the goal is to prevent it. This is only possible if you can recognize arousal almost as soon as it begins.

Unlike people with fear disorders, angry people are not afraid of their sympathetic systems. Sometimes they like them very much. Bubbling anger makes them feel focused, invigorated, and right. Instead of worrying about the strange sensations in their bodies, angry people pay more attention to external events, which they convince themselves are the source of their arousal. When they finally explode, they believe they're driven to it. They are seldom aware of the effort they've invested in fanning the sparks of irritation into bright, cleansing flames of anger.

Unlike fear, anger is a cathartic process. People explode, and their agitation dissipates, leaving them relaxed and calmer. Often, they pride themselves on how clean and straightforward their anger is: Something happens, they blow up, and then it's all over. To them it's a natural, healthy activity, much like passing digestive gas. If other people are offended, well, that's their problem.

Actually, the *possibility* of cathartic release is the real problem. Working themselves up and then blowing out all the tension in one orgasmic blast is a powerful positive reinforcer. It makes the whole chain of thoughts and actions that lead up to it more likely to happen again, whether the people doing it are aware of it or not. The fact that the cathartic outbursts don't always occur actually makes the effect stronger, because behaviors automatically increase when their rewards are unpredictable. Slot machines exploit this same principle. It is also behind what's often called *psychological addiction*. Only rarely does a subsequent dose of any substance have the same pleasant effect as the first sip, snort, or toke of the evening, but the chance that it might is what keeps addicts sipping, snorting, and toking. The *possibility* of reward has a much stronger effect on behavior than does the reward itself. Hope springs eternal.

Angry people are often psychologically addicted to the process of getting angry. Despite the fact that their anger can feel bad, and may have very unpleasant consequences, the early stages are exciting and sometimes pleasant. Nobody intends to lose all their money in a slot machine, or drink enough to throw up; it just happens. Likewise, nobody intends to get angry enough to bring on negative consequences. They just want to recreate the feeling of sweet relief on those few occasions that anger has cleared the air or gotten them what they wanted.

AVOIDING PAIN. The only motivational force strong enough to beat the excitement of random rewards is avoidance of pain, which is as real in the imagination as the sound of quarters rattling into a metal bin. No form of anger control treatment will ever work until angry people see their anger as dangerous *to them.* The essence of therapy is turning the sometimes pleasant arousal of the fight part of the fight or flight response into a cue for fear, so that angry people will be tempted to run away by calming down, rather than working themselves up to a cathartic fight.

Most angry people are not aware of the addictive potential of anger, or even that they do anything to bring it on. Once they consider anger dangerous enough to avoid, they must begin to realize that it isn't something that just falls on them from out of the blue. Like most other human maladies, anger starts small and grows, and is easier to control if you catch it early. In the next chapter we'll look more closely at how people use their thoughts to fan the flames of anger, but for now lets concentrate on the signs and symptoms that indicate that anger is beginning to smolder.

Noticing the Signs

The physical sensations that accompany sympathetic activity differ widely across individuals, but usually there are some common elements in a given person's experience of arousal from one instance to the next. The trick is getting them to notice the signs, and to use them as cues to do something to avert an explosion—like relaxation, physical exercise, or simply getting out of the situation. As a review, some of the signs of sympathetic activity are:

INCREASED HEART RATE AND BREATHING. Blood and oxygen have to get to the muscles in order to make them ready to fight back or run away, so the heart and lungs have to speed up. Everyone becomes aware of these changes when they reach the level of pounding and panting, but most people don't register smaller changes unless they're actually counting. The usual rule I use with my clients is: If you're aware of your heart and breathing, keep your mouth shut.

Chronic anger is hard on the circulatory system. It can manifest itself as high blood pressure and other cardiovascular disorders, whether the person has a Type A personality or not.

RESTLESSNESS. Often, the first noticeable sign that anger is brewing is the inability to sit still. Angry people sometimes find themselves up, pacing around, looking for something to do even before they realize that they're feeling keyed up and on edge.

INCREASED MUSCLE TENSION. Blood and adrenaline flowing to the muscles makes them expand and tighten. People who are getting angry usually feel tense. Sometimes the tension is generalized, but often it shows up as clenching and unclenching various muscle groups as if warming up for a fight. Actually, there's no *as if* about it. The muscles that are most often involved are in the arms, shoulders, and the jaw. Frequent sources of referrals for anger treatment are dentists, because they recognize worn-down teeth as a sign of chronic sympathetic arousal.

FLUSHING, SWEATING, TREMBLING, AND TINGLING. Remember how it felt when I had you experiment with hyperventilating, back in the chapter on fear disorders? Rapid breathing without corresponding strenuous activity causes all sorts of weird sensations that arise from changes in the chemical composition of the blood. A fairly typical pattern is for angry people to experience hot faces and chills down their spines, accompanied by clammy, tingling hands.

QUEASINESS. Remember that to get ready for action, the digestive system shuts down and tries to dump whatever it's carrying. Sometimes the first sign of anger are feelings of stomach upset.

Everyone gets angry in his or her own way. The important thing is getting an angry person to notice before it's too late to stop. In addition to the internal, physiological changes, there are several external signs of impending angry outbursts. Not everybody does them, but when people do, they are unmistakable.

MUTTERING.   It's surprising how many angry people play their self-incitements out loud, talking to themselves as if to other people, checking whether events warrant an angry response and answering with a resounding *Hell yes!* Muttering is merely rumination with the external speakers turned on. Often people are unaware that others can hear it. If you ask them what they said, they will answer *nothing,* then say it again.

TICKING OFF POINTS ON THE FINGERS.   Finger ticking is another external indicator of rumination. To the people who do it, finger ticking is such an integral part of the ritual that if you stop them, they're unable to maintain the emotion.

> *"Brandon," I say, "this may sound silly, but I do this with all my anger control clients. If you start ticking off points on your fingers, I'm going to ask you to sit on your hands. Is that okay?"*
>
> *"Yeah, sure," he says. His look suggests that I've confirmed his belief that psychologists are crazy.*
>
> *Later in the session he begins enumerating his wife's domestic misdemeanors. I ask him to sit on his hands, and he finds himself wagging his shoulders, unable to speak. I now have his full attention.*

RAISING THE VOICE.   How many times have angry people told you they aren't really angry, they merely have a naturally loud voice? It happens to me all the time. In a soft voice, I ask them to whisper, and enjoy their surprised looks when they forget what they were going to say.

Getting angry is so ritualistic that if you disrupt one part of the pattern, you can sometimes stop the whole thing. This is a risky technique; you probably shouldn't try it at home. I'm a trained professional, so people let me get away with more than they would you.

SARCASM, SNORTING, AND EYE-ROLLING.   Adolescent rebellion, at whatever chronological age it occurs, has its own customs and traditions related to the display of anger. When I see them in a client, I disrupt by pretending to be an anthropologist from Mars.

> *"Brittany," I say, "what does it mean when you quote your boss, then roll your eyes and make a kind of throat-clearing noise?" I demonstrate.*

* * *

> *"What is the significance of adding the syllable 'uh' to the end of the word 'no'?"*

* * *

> *"Does 'Yeah, right' mean you agree or disagree?"*

You get the idea.

WITHDRAWAL. Sometimes angry people don't do anything. They just walk away, or perhaps sit there conspicuously not talking. This is, of course, an unfair attempt at controlling the situation, but if you don't make a big deal of it, nothing further will happen. A cold shoulder may be better than a conflagration.

One of the most useful techniques in dealing with anger is taking a "time-out," but if it's taken unilaterally, it just looks like another way of expressing anger. The rules for time-outs must be agreed upon beforehand. The most important ones are: no following, no parting comments, and both people must agree how long the time-out will last. We'll discuss this technique in more detail later.

AN UNCONTROLLABLE URGE TO EXPLAIN. Angry people usually believe they've been mistreated or misunderstood. They will attempt to explain the situation so you'll understand it

> *At two a.m. you're completely exhausted, but David is just getting started. "You say you care about me, but if how I feel actually*

meant anything to you, you'd do a better job of keeping your promises. If I have an important appointment, I always arrange my schedule so I can be there at least 10 minutes early. It's just a matter of respect."

These "explanations" can be a form of torture. At best, they're a biased version of the situation with the details twisted and turned so they all point to the supposedly inescapable fact that you are completely and utterly wrong. Often, the explanations are interspersed with hostile questioning designed to elicit even more information to misrepresent.

The desire to "explain" your side will burn inside you. Keep it there. Most of us have an irrational belief that if we clearly explain situations to angry people, they'll realize they were wrong and we're right. This belief is nothing short of delusional. No matter how reasonable your explanation may seem, it will be perceived, correctly, as a counterattack. *Never attempt to explain anything to an angry person, unless you're willing to deal with the escalation that will surely occur.*

In the next chapters we'll discuss some more effective strategies. For now, be warned. Explanations may seem like a reasonable attempt to solve a problem by talking it over, but in angry situations very little is what it seems, and nothing is reasonable.

The first step in managing anger effectively is recognizing it, both in other people and yourself. For many reasons, psychological, physiological, or moral, people don't recognize anger until it reaches explosive proportions and it's too late to do much about it. Regardless of whose anger it is, the earlier in the process you intervene, the more likely you are to cool things down. It's much easier to pinch out a sputtering fuse than to contain an explosion.

Medications for Anger

Serotonin reuptake inhibitors and other members of the newer generation of antidepressants are the medications most frequently prescribed for anger control problems. They work quite well for some people, but for others they can be a disaster.

When SSRIs help, in addition to improving general mood, they break the cycle of rumination that is so essential to getting angry. Medications are most helpful to people who feel they're controlled by their anger. SSRIs don't make anger go away, but they seem to slow down the process enough that people can begin to recognize what's going on and interrupt it themselves.

The disasters are caused by the agitation that is a common side effect of SSRIs and newer antidepressants. It can sometimes make angry people *much* angrier, to the point that it's intolerable for them and the people around them. For depressed people, the agitation effect seems to peak at about the second or third day of treatment and then diminish. For angry people, this may be too long to wait. If an angry person in your life starts taking medication and begins to feel more agitated, call the prescriber immediately. Angry people are often far more aware of what is going on around them than they are of what's happening in their own bodies, so it's a good idea to let them know that the agitation is coming from the medicine, not a change in the universe.

Other medications, including anticonvulsants and betablockers, are sometimes used in treating anger, especially with people who can't tolerate SSRIs. Benzodiazepines are not a good choice for irritability. They may help initially, but they generally make the situation worse over the long run. In fact, benzodiazepines are not a long run solution for anything.

For various reasons, most of these medications are contraindicated with active substance abuse. At best, they won't work. At worst, they can lead to serious complications. Often, substance abusers neglect to inform their doctors of that particular problem. If there is one in your life, encourage him or her to come clean. Secrecy to substance abusers is as toxic as the drugs they take.

Chapter 11

The Instinct for Anger

WHEN PEOPLE EXPLODE INTO ANGER, we want to help them and get them treatment, but more than that, we want to protect ourselves. Medicine and psychology are less helpful in teaching us how to do this than is *ethology,* the scientific study of animal instincts.

Ethology is a new science. Konrad Lorenz, Nikolaas Tinbergen, and Karl von Frisch won a Nobel Prize in 1973 for pretty much inventing it. Their studies of birds and bees demonstrated that animals are capable of performing very complicated tasks without ever having witnessed them, and, given the correct situation, they are sometimes incapable of *not* performing them. These tasks are usually necessary for survival. They include finding food, courtship, and nest building, as well as how, when, and whom to fight or flee. We primates also engage in unlearned, ritualistic behaviors, especially with regard to sex and aggression. Our instincts are far more influenced by learning, and thus more controllable.

Instincts are hard-wired into the nervous system. Neurophysiologist Paul McLean suggested that the human brain is made up of three separate neural systems that evolved sequentially. The *reptile brain* is oldest. It's programmed with everything a dinosaur needed to know to survive in the jungle. The *limbic system* arose with mammals. It added emotion, rudimentary memory, and motivation by reward and punishment to the mix. The *neocortex* sits on top of the other two. It can think, but only if properly engaged.

McLean's *triune brain theory* is a gross oversimplification, but it describes aggression more fully than any model we've discussed thus far. In general, the higher the arousal, the lower the brain structure, and the more likely that people will follow their instinctive programming instead of thinking. In the animal world there are several kinds of aggressive instincts. They occur in different situations and follow quite different rules. If you want to keep from being hurt in angry explosions, you must know these instinctive patterns, since they describe the rules you'll have to play by.

Predation

Predators never think about whether their lunch has feelings. You could say they have disturbed object relations. Human predators share similar disregard for their victims. They *deserve* to be eaten. Life is a game you must win if you want to keep playing.

Predation is a no-brainer, or, more correctly, a reptile brainer. Words are no protection; you can't explain to a hungry dinosaur why it's wrong to eat you. All you can do is run, or shoot to kill. Instincts seldom allow much choice.

People think like predators when they're enraged. They're in contact with their anger and little else. Forget trying to figure them out or reason with them. They're not using the part of the brain that can be reasoned with. Get away, and deal with the situation at a later time. Anything you say will be taken as further provocation, so say nothing, just run.

If someone like Brandon is chasing you, go to the closest, brightest, most crowded place you can find, and make a lot of noise.

Being Cornered

It's not just dinosaurs—even rabbits will attack you if they're trapped. In dealing with angry people, keep your distance. Instinctive rage at being cornered often translates into a greater need for *personal space*, the bubble of air around us that we treat as part of our bodies.

This need is determined by various factors. Different cultures, for example, have different space requirements. Americans, especially those

lose face. This is bad enough at work, but worse where organizational charts are not so clear. Competing claims for dominance lead to countless unintended struggles.

> *You're slaving over a hot stove, making dinner. With both hands full of garbage, you kick open the cabinet under the sink. The can is overflowing. Again.*
>
> *Your husband, whose only household task is emptying the garbage, lounges on the couch, watching television.*
>
> *"Sweetheart," you say, "the garbage needs to go out."*
>
> *"Sure," he says. "I'll do it after the game."*
>
> *"Honey, I need it done now."*
>
> *He gets up, muttering something about working all day but still not being allowed to relax in his own house.*
>
> *"What?" you say. "You don't think I work?"*
>
> *"Yeah, you work," he says. "For $12 an hour."*
>
> *You look down at the frying pan, wondering what kind of sound it would make bouncing off your husband's head.*

This argument, like most I referee in marriage counseling, is not about garbage, work, or money. It's about dominance. Each of you is asserting ascendance over the other: You by "ordering" your husband to take the garbage out, and he by his declaration that his earning power places him above household responsibilities. It doesn't matter what you thought you meant, this is the way such actions will be interpreted.

Most fights, marital or otherwise, have an element of disputed dominance. Jenna believes that grammatical errors are tantamount to insubordination. Zack feels that lowly toasters may not refuse to work correctly. When you blew your horn at Brandon for cutting into line, you probably felt reasonable in reminding him that he was breaking the rules of the road. To him, how he drives is none of your damn business. Brandon is certainly not alone in this belief.

Instinct distorts. The very idea that arguments can end with one person being right and another wrong is a fantasy born of the urge for dominance. All being right gets you is the animosity of whoever has to be wrong for you. Good and evil work the same way. In the real world, there are precious few absolutes. Our instincts show them to us, regardless of whether they actually exist. Most battles for dominance begin with an arbitrary distinction, and never end.

The solution to the problem of unintended dominance disputes is *courtesy*, the anti-instinct. In many cases, courtesy involves ritualized deference, and apology for offenses both willful and otherwise. Which reminds me: I'm sorry about the blatant sexism of the garbage vignette. I'll try to be more sensitive in the future. Please forgive me.

Defense of Territory

Animals defend what is theirs, be it food, land, mates, or whatever. In the jungle, there is never enough to go around. If you share at all, it's only with those who are most like you.

> *In the mists by Gombe stream, a band of chimpanzees wanders into another group's territory. They know instantly. The air smells different here.*
>
> *In seconds other chimps approach, and pandemonium begins. All of them are hooting, shrieking, jumping, pounding the ground, and urinating all over everything. The activity builds to a wild crescendo, then diminishes as the intruders back away into the forest.*

* * *

> *It's lunchtime at Springfield High. Two long-haired slacker guys in baggy clothes are basking in the sun on the steps by the main entrance.*
>
> *The varsity posse bangs and thumps their way out the doors. "Look at these losers on our steps!" says a young mesomorph in a letter jacket. "What are you little girls doing here? This whole area is reserved for jocks."*
>
> *"Chill out, man. It's a free country."*
>
> *The jocks circle the slackers. "Oh, yeah. Well I guess that means we're free to kick your ass."*

* * *

> *You pull up a stool at Cassidy's and order a cold brew. There's an attractive woman sitting by herself two stools down. You*

make eye contact and nod. Just as you do, she knocks over her glass, spilling half a beer into her lap.

You grab some napkins and come to her aid, handing some to her and using some yourself, leaning in front of her to wipe up the beer that's still dripping off the bar.

A rough hand grabs your shoulder and yanks you back. "What are you doing, messing with my wife?"

The most common cause for violence is the defense of territory. The characters and the situations may differ, but the story is the same. Here are its elements:

INSIDERS AND OUTSIDERS. Insiders have something; outsiders want it. Usually, the distinction exists only in someone's imagination, but as we've seen, that doesn't matter.

The size of the stakes or whether they're really at risk have little relation to the strength of feeling. It's always the principle. You could tell Brandon (you knew it was him) that you had no designs whatsoever on his wife, and it wouldn't make any difference. Jealousy is in the eye of the beholder more often than in the actions of the beheld.

Sharing is never an option. The forest may be full of food, and the high school steps broad enough to hold hundreds of kids. None of it makes any difference.

ASSERTING DOMINANCE. The battle begins with the insiders signaling their dominance. There are a thousand ways this can be done; physical posturing and teasing are common among chimps, adolescents, and radio hosts. Among adults, a typical technique is using authority to intimidate whomever might flaunt it.

Ladies and gentlemen, the audit suggests that we lost almost $10,000 to employee pilfering last year. This is absolutely unacceptable. Based on the recommendations of our security consultants, the executive committee devised a new policy of zero-tolerance for theft. The details, to be distributed to your departments, are in the red folders at your places. I will go over the major elements now.

The CEO switches on the PowerPoint projector.

Punishing lapses of solidarity.   When territory is being defended, absolute loyalty is demanded, especially within the in-group. Suggestions of compromise are dealt with severely.

> *As the slackers slink away, Adam shakes his head. "I don't know what the big deal is," he says. "There's plenty of room on the steps."*
> *Jason responds immediately. "Adam, I didn't realize you were in love. Oh girls, come on back, we've got a gay guy who wants to kiss you." Everybody roars with laughter, except Adam.*

* * *

> *You watch the CEO's presentation attentively. The rules to prevent employee pilfering stop just short of strip searches. You cringe as you imagine how your team will react. Especially Brittany.*
> *As you look through the folder and do a little mental arithmetic, you realize that the zero-tolerance program will cost far more than the $10,000 it saves. You bring this up in a misguided attempt to demonstrate fiscal responsibility.*
> *The CEO scowls. "Money is not the object. The management team of this company—or at least most of it—will not be perceived as soft on crime!"*

No higher authority.   In most struggles for territory, might makes right. If you're part of the out-group, there is no one to go to for redress. The slackers know that the school administrators won't intervene, or if they did, it would be in favor of the jocks, who have much higher status. You won't risk your job by going to the board, and the chimps can't argue their case before the Lion King.

In the jungle, and in the free marketplace, you're on your own. Your only friends are tort lawyers. Or maybe guns.

Burning desire for revenge.   Can you think of an action movie that doesn't begin with in-group persecution and end with out-group vengeance? Whether this is art imitating life or vice versa, the idea of personal revenge sells. Who can blame people for fantasizing?

You've been on hold for 45 minutes, listening to inane music and recordings that say your call is important. Finally, a tech answers. You try to explain the strange things your computer has been doing just before it crashes. The words are scarcely out of your mouth before he says, "It sounds like a software problem. You'll have to contact the software manufacturer about that."

The software manufacturer's tech said it was a hardware problem.

MUTUAL PERCEPTION OF BEING WRONGED. In all instinctual struggles, both sides feel that they're the most aggrieved. This misperception is undoubtedly a software problem, but that doesn't make it any less real.

After you hang up, the tech leans back, looks at the guy in the next cubicle and shakes his head. "Another electronic moron. I don't know where these idiots come from."

The other tech nods. Then they press the button for another call.

So it goes. Ethology teaches us that the connection of anger and violence with certain situations is programmed into our very being. To avoid being hurt by angry explosions, you must recognize these situations in their many guises and avoid them, or at least avoid mindlessly playing out the internal scripts that were written on your brain before the dawn of civilization.

How to Defuse Anger

Following these steps will help you deal more effectively with explosions into anger, regardless of who or what causes them. This approach is based on understanding the instinct of anger as well as its physiology and psychology. The main goal is to protect yourself by avoiding unintended provocation. A useful side effect is winning arguments, not by beating your opponents and urinating on them, but by besting them in a battle of wits. The odds bear repeating: If they're operating by instinct, and you're using your neocortex, you'll have an advantage of about 50 IQ points. If you can't win with odds like that, don't play.

Ask for Time

Instincts are quick and dirty. All you may have to do to disrupt them is slow down. If someone is attacking you, say: "Please give me a minute to think about this." No one will ever get angry at you for taking them seriously. Delay may also subtly encourage them to do a little thinking of their own, which couldn't hurt. Most important, asking for time will prevent you from blurting out the first thing that pops into your head, which will likely be an instinctive response—some form of fighting back or running away, either of which will make the situation worse.

Instincts follow well-worn paths in the brain. Each step leads automatically and mindlessly to the next. Either fighting back or—unless you actually leave the scene—running away, no matter how well-disguised, will reinforce the pattern, and increase the anger. By doing the unexpected, you break the ancient rhythm of anger, forcing both of you to use newer brain systems to figure out what's going on and how to solve the problem. Anger becomes far less dangerous when people are thinking rather than merely reacting.

Listen to Your Heart

While you're taking those few seconds to think, monitor yourself for the signs of physical arousal we discussed in the last chapter. If you're revved up, ask for a little more time to wind down. Breathe deeply. Go through the basic calming sequence with yourself. The more aroused you are, the less likely you'll say anything constructive. If you're calm and thinking, you'll do just fine, even if you can't even remember the rest of the steps listed here.

Know Your Goal

The most important thing to think about in the few seconds you've bought for yourself is what you want to happen. This is a serious question, not a straight line. It's likely that each of the three parts of your brain is advocating for a different goal. You need to sort them out and choose the one that makes most sense. Sometimes you want to settle the situation, and sometimes you just need to get away.

The most important thing to remember is that you can achieve only one goal. It's impossible to simultaneously calm someone down, get him back, and convince him that the whole thing is not really your fault. If you send mixed messages, only the most aggressive will register, so choose carefully. In most cases, the goal you want to achieve is calming the other person down enough to have a rational discussion.

Speak Softly

In the Bible it says, "A soft answer turns away wrath." This is excellent advice, not just for the obvious reason that anger is loud, and speaking quietly makes you seem less threatening. Soft speech will also make you feel calmer because, as we have seen many times, internal state is strongly influenced by external behavior.

In the section on basic calming, I suggested starting your message loud and fast to synchronize with the jagged rhythm of anxiety. In defusing anger, your goal is to break the rhythm, not join in.

If you happen to be thinking about the *other* famous quote about speaking softly, the one by Theodore Roosevelt, bear in mind what I said about mixed messages. Angry people will ignore the soft words and pay attention to the stick. Teddy Roosevelt was never particularly effective at soothing people who were angry at him.

Take Some Distance

Often, angry people will step into your personal bubble of space. They'll stand too close or attempt to loom over you. Such aggressive gestures will automatically increase both your arousal and theirs. Moving forward, backing up, or cowering, even if done only with your eyes by locking contact or looking down, all signal fighting back or running away. Such expected gestures will turn up the heat, even if you want to cool things down.

To be cool, you need to do something unexpected. Luckily, your neocortex can come up with all sorts of options. Offer coffee, ask the person to sit down, or step away to get something relevant, like a file, a pen to take notes, or your glasses. All you need is a reason for moving; it doesn't have to be a good one. Remember, angry people are not too bright. Several times, I have solved this ethological problem by countering one reflex with another. I start coughing or act as if I'm about to sneeze. Even enraged psychotics step back.

The true master of doing the unexpected in aggressive situations is Bugs Bunny. Watch a few of his films and learn. One of my favorites is when Elmer Fudd is looming over him, raising a big stick, and Bugs says, "Say, Doc, was you ever in pictures?" Then he starts laying on the flattery, which, if you think about it, is absolutely the last thing an angry person expects. With the help of a few cartoons, the next time you're attacked, you won't have to act like a scared rabbit, you can act like a rascally one.

Do bear in mind that humor directed *at* people is an extremely aggressive gesture. Bugs never stoops to sarcasm. He uses his wit not to fight directly, but to distract. Learn from the master.

Never Reason with a Person Who's Yelling

Yelling and thinking cannot occur simultaneously. If an angry person is yelling, you need to get him or her to stop before you can go any further. If you ask people to stop yelling, they may yell back that they are not yelling but just have loud voices. You don't want to go there. Getting people to stop yelling is actually easier than you might think. Just keeping your own voice soft may do the trick.

Another way is by saying, "Please speak more slowly. I'd like to understand." Often, angry people will comply without thinking. Reducing speed will also reduce the volume. Have you ever tried to yell slowly? This strategy works particularly well on the phone.

When you're on the phone, also remember the *Uh-huh* rule. We usually respond with "Uh-huh" when the other person takes a breath. If you go three breaths without saying "Uh-huh," the other person will stop and ask, "Are you there?" This trick will allow you to interrupt a tirade without saying a word.

Validate the Problem or Emotional State

Repetition, both internal and external, is the heart of anger. If you can get angry people to stop repeating, that pounding heart may slow, or even stop.

Repetition probably comes from the limbic system, the early mammalian part of the brain. Mammals are usually social creatures, and as such have a drive to match their behavior with others of their kind. We do this unconsciously; it's what keeps us sane.

When we feel something that might make us different from the people around us, like a strong burst of emotion, we feel a strong need to check it out. Angry people are always doing this, asking if they're justified in feeling anger, and generally coming up with the wrong answer. Usually, they're asking themselves inside their own heads. This is what rumination and all that mental finger-ticking is about. The main reason they ask themselves is that they perceive other people as hostile, frightened, or simply as not listening. Angry people state their points, and the people around them don't recognize the implicit question, so the angry people repeat themselves, more loudly each time. Of course, this makes the people around them even less likely to answer the question in any useful way.

The way to stop this cycle is to listen, understand the question that's being asked, and answer, "Yes, you have a right to feel the way you do." The name for this process is *validation*. It is not the same thing as saying that angry people *are* right, only that they have a right to feel what they feel.

Validation is ridiculously easy, but it makes a tremendous difference. There are two ways to do it. You can validate the problem by restating it and saying, "That is a problem." You can validate the emotional state by saying, "I can see how you'd be upset about that." Don't use the word *angry* unless you want to quibble over semantics. Everybody will admit to being upset or concerned.

Validation is almost magical, but people who are confronted by anger regularly forget to do it. Their reptile brain tells them that giving anything is like giving in and letting the angry person be dominant.

Validation feels so great that it's easily worth its weight in gold. Validation is the real reason people pay big bucks for psychotherapy.

Don't Explain

Explanations are the way that primitive responses slither down from your reptile brain and out your mouth. Explanations are usually a disguised form of fighting back or running away. The typical explanation boils down to either:

- A play for dominance: If you know all the facts, you'll see that I'm right and you're wrong.
- A blatant attempt to run away: It wasn't my fault, you should be mad at somebody else.
- Worst of all, invalidation: You have no right to be angry.

Whether you recognize the provocative aspect of your explanations or not, angry people certainly will. Trust me on this if you don't want to get clobbered.

What Would You Like Me to Do?

This simple, unexpected question is absolutely the most useful tool you will ever find for dealing with anger. Angry people either do not know or will not admit what they want you to do. To answer this question, they'll have to stop and think, which is precisely what you want them to do. What could be simpler or more devious?

In the next chapter we will explore a number of ways to use this strategy as a way of opening up communication with the angry people in your life.

Say I to a Stranger, Not We

This suggestion applies to work settings in which you're dealing with angry customers, or perhaps coworkers you don't know. It will be easier for them to be mean to you if you define yourself as a faceless functionary by explaining your actions as company policy. Even if your company does have a policy, you'll be on safer ground if you make the situation more personal. Say something like, "I'd like to help, but there are only a few things I can do."

Negotiate

The opposite of fighting is making a deal. I give you something; you give me something. They even make deals in the animal world. If plovers can step safely into crocodiles' mouths to clean their teeth, you can figure out some sort of give and take arrangement with the angry people in your life. We'll explore some negotiating strategies in the next chapter.

Better Living Through Ethology

There it is, the basic defusing approach. Better living through ethology. The good news is that all of our instincts can be overridden by newer, more sophisticated neural structures. The bad news is that using them is much harder than going along with the evolutionary flow. Following instincts provides a feeling of moral certainty that is more intoxicating than any drug.

As we proceed into the next chapter, and an examination of psychological techniques for dealing with anger, remember this one warning from the distant past: When you feel the most right, you're in the most danger.

Chapter 12

The Psychology of Anger

FREUD, AT FIRST, THOUGHT that sexuality was the only human instinct. World War I convinced him of an instinct for aggression as well, but, being a lover and not a fighter, he was never quite sure what to do with it. Freud's ideas about the nature of aggression are still creating confusion among therapists in how to treat anger.

Freud conceived of instinctive urges as elements in a hydraulic system. Sexual and aggressive impulses accumulate in the Id, much like digestive gas in the intestines. Health at both ends requires *ventilation*. Freud reasoned that people could keep themselves from acting on indecorous impulses by, well, letting them rip in their therapist's office. Catharsis is an important component of psychoanalytic treatment, but as we have seen, cathartic venting of emotion is addictive. The more you vent your emotions, the more emotions you have to vent. This is probably why psychoanalysis takes so long.

To be fair, analysts do have a plan. They help their patients recognize that their angry feelings are based on irrational perceptions laid down in childhood. Over time, through many catharses, more adult perceptions dilute and finally dissipate the anger. With angry people, real psychoanalysts do no harm, and probably help, but slowly. The harm is done by would-be therapists who are influenced by psychoanalytic ideas but haven't spent the years of training it takes to become an analyst.

> *Brandon finally went into rehab for his alcohol problems. Just being clean and sober helped him to control some of his more flagrant explosions into anger. He stopped following drivers who honked at him, which was a definite improvement.*
>
> *In one of his treatment groups, Brandon learned that the source of his anger was growing up with an alcoholic, physically abusive father. His inner child was suffused with shame and pent-up rage that Brandon was encouraged to express by yelling at an empty chair. His outbursts were followed by tears, then hugs and words of encouragement from the group.*

Here's a secret that all therapists know: There's nothing easier than working people up to a fever pitch of emotion. Clients love it, and they come back for it again and again. They feel like they've done *really good work*, but it's mostly sound and fury. Cathartic approaches can make emotional control problems worse by endorsing excess as "getting out real feelings." Also, by convincing people that they're victims, these therapies may inadvertently give patients permission to victimize, or at least to take advantage of others.

> *"Brandon," his wife says, "don't forget we have the school program tonight at seven."*
>
> *"You know I have a meeting."*
>
> *"But you go to meetings every night."*
>
> *"Meetings are something I do for me. They keep me sober, and you know that right now my sobriety is the most important thing in my life."*
>
> *"More important than your kids?"*
>
> *"Quit trying to guilt-trip me! You were the one who made me get into treatment in the first place. Now I'm working my program, and you're still not satisfied. I don't know what it is with you. You're starting to sound just like my father."*

Brandon has always gotten angry when asked to do something he doesn't want to do. Getting sober hasn't changed that, and some of the counseling he's getting to keep him sober is actually making it worse by encouraging him to see his anger as having been caused by childhood trauma. Now Brandon perceives people making demands as doing the same thing to him as his father did.

There is no question that people who've been physically abused are more likely to develop anger control problems. Clearly, there's an element of imitation. However, it's usually not imitation of the anger itself, but of the thinking patterns that make angry outbursts inevitable. Brandon does not want to be like his father, so he projects his anger on other people, seeing them as attacking him. This is exactly what his father used to do. And his father before him. None of Brandon's forebears ever believed they started a fight, but over the years, they've finished more than their share. In a misguided attempt to help Brandon feel less guilty about his anger, his counseling program has also helped him continue the family tradition of blaming everybody else.

Anger is confusing. Many of our ideas about it—that the person who starts it is to blame, and that getting it off your chest makes it go away—encourage rather than discourage outbursts.

Speaking of confusing, you've probably noticed some inconsistency in my advice about the expression of anger. In the chapters on fear disorders and depression, I was *endorsing* it for people like Jane and Carol. Now I'm saying it's a bad thing. What gives?

The answer is, it's a matter of degree. Anger control problems are the extreme end of the continuum of aggression that begins with asking for what you want and ends with bashing someone in the head if they won't give it to you. Our society requires and rewards a good deal of personal aggressiveness. We like winners enough to downplay some of the unsportsmanlike actions that winning requires.

Freud believed that uncivilized aggressive urges could be *sublimated*, that is, channeled into more acceptable pursuits, like sports and art. This has been a longstanding belief in Western society. If it were true, athletes and rock stars would be the last people you'd expect to find in treatment for anger control.

In the sections on fear and depression, I pointed out fixed stars to help you sight a course through the swirling firmament of conflicting theories.

With anger, I can offer a similar useful oversimplification to light your way: *Repetition is the problem.* The first time people express anger, listen. They are talking to you. There may be a problem you can solve together. When they repeat themselves, stop listening and start using defusing techniques. Communication has changed to rumination. They are no longer talking to you, they're talking to themselves and making themselves angrier.

Steps in Treating Anger

To treat anger control problems, therapists have to step back and forth through the looking glass. To handle angry people effectively, you don't have to follow, but you do have to know which side you're on.

The biggest difference between angry people and most of the rest of us is that they're not in the least ashamed of operating in their own self-interest. They seldom make polite pretense of putting other people's needs ahead of their own. They don't play by the rules. They get to be selfish, but we have to be nice. It's totally unfair.

Angry people will always see self-interest in their own actions, and in yours. If you don't, they'll accuse you of hypocrisy. Believe me, that's a battle you do not want to fight.

Treatment must always be presented to the angry in terms of what's in it for them, even if a court is forcing them into it. If there are angry people in your life, don't think of therapy as sending them to the assistant principal's office. The cure for bullying isn't a referral to a bigger bully.

Morality is a dominance hierarchy based on right rather than might. The good are allowed to punish the bad when they don't do what they should. But when the bad attempt to punish the good, it's called an anger control problem, or worse, abuse. Unfortunately, we all see ourselves as the good— with the possible exception of depressed people. If we've been abused, we believe our suffering somehow makes us even more qualified to punish.

The goal of treatment is to persuade angry people to abandon moral evaluation of other people's behavior, to convince them that *nobody* does what they should, and that most of us are plugging along, doing the best we can. This crucial insight cannot be rolled down onto them from higher moral ground. If you argue with angry people about who's right or wrong, they'll always see it, correctly, as a struggle for dominance.

Punishment doesn't cure anger. On the other hand, it's important that angry people believe in the inevitability of consequences strongly enough to want to avoid them. Never threaten anything unless you're sure you can make it happen.

One other thing: Nobody is brave or saintly enough to follow all these recommendations all the time. We're all just plugging along, doing the best we can.

Brandon's wife told him that if he ever laid a hand on her, she'd call the police. Once, when he was drinking, he shoved her into a wall. She picked herself up, ran to the neighbor's house, and with trembling fingers tapped out 911, knowing that he would hate her and fearing that she might deserve it.

The most dangerous place to stand is between an angry person and the consequences of his or her behavior, but it hurts so much to step aside. That pain is the greatest gift you can give the angry people you care about, even if it is the least appreciated and doesn't always work.

Brandon's first offense landed him in the unsuccessful anger control class he joked about at Cassidy's. Shortly afterward, a family intervention got him into alcohol treatment.

To stop drinking was a tremendous improvement, but it didn't solve the anger control problem. His abused inner child was now making the moral judgments.

In desperation, Brandon's wife went to a psychologist I knew to get help in sorting out her tangled feelings. Should she leave or stay? She felt guilty, angry, and sad, but mostly confused. Brandon was better now that he wasn't drinking, but she couldn't see herself and her children enduring his temper much longer. But wasn't that being selfish?

"Yes," the psychologist says, "but what's wrong with that?" The psychologist goes on to reassure Brandon's wife that confusion is normal in such a confusing situation, and that doing what's best for her will also be best for Brandon. The psychologist comments on how much courage it must have taken to call the police, and ultimately how successful it had been.

"I had to," Brandon's wife says. "I told him I would if he ever touched me."

The psychologist also points out how "selfish" actions seem to be all that ever move Brandon forward, even if he kicks and screams the whole way.

Brandon's wife smiles. "I feel like I have three children," she says. "The two kids and Brandon."

"That just means you're doing it right," the psychologist replies. "So tell me, what do you want to happen?"

"I want him to stop being such an [expletive deleted]!"

"What would help most, staying or leaving?"

"I don't know."

The psychologist suggests that she calmly share her confusion with Brandon, along with a list of specific actions that would make him less of an [expletive deleted]. "You might tell him to get anger control treatment," she says.

"Been there, done that," Brandon's wife replies. "He had a class, but he just laughed about that. And now he's in a group that tells him it will take years for him to get out all the anger he's been carrying."

"I was thinking of something a little quicker," the psychologist offers. "I have a colleague who works with anger control dropouts." She writes my name on a sticky note and hands it to Brandon's wife.

The hardest step in anger control treatment is getting someone to go. Most people, like Brandon's wife, have very mixed feelings about the whole process. Her psychologist did a good job of helping her sort them out, without adding any more moral judgments to the mix. The word *abuse* was never spoken. The best therapists avoid the word because of its strong moral overtones, and focus on how their clients feel, how the angry people in their lives behave, and what they can do about it.

Here's one piece of advice on which every therapist would agree: If an angry situation gets physical, leave the premises and call the police. Unfortunately, the people who most need this advice seldom take it. If you're involved with an angry person who hits, shoves, or shakes you, please don't try to solve the problem by reading a book. Talk to a professional as soon as possible! The next chapter will give you some ideas about how and where to find one.

Step 1: Realizing That Anger Is *Their* Problem

This step is the sine qua non of anger control treatment. If you can't impart this critical insight, there's no point in wasting time and money on anything else. Imminent contingencies may get people in the door, but after that, the next step must be convincing them it's in their self-interest to be there.

I usually begin my first session by asking clients why they came in.

"My wife's shrink thinks I have an anger control problem,"
Brandon says.

* * *

Jenna takes a deep breath. "The managing partner says I need
some work on, uh, handling job stress."

* * *

David sits tall in his chair, an innocent man in the prisoner's dock.
"I'm willing to do everything possible to improve my marriage."

* * *

Zack smiles sheepishly. "I smashed a toaster."

* * *

"I don't know," Brittany says. "You're the doctor; you tell me."

I don't bother asking what they think of the charges against them. I already know. They're innocent.

Instead, I try and find out what drives them, what they want out of their marriages, their jobs, and their lives. People explode into anger because they believe it will get them something they value. They want love, respect, and sometimes adulation. For reasons they don't understand, they usually get fear and exasperation. The trick is to get them to realize that it's their anger that's getting them the opposite of what they want.

I ask them what they want, and go from there.

Instead of answering, Brandon launches into a sarcastic mono-
logue about his dealings with one S.O.B. after another, starting
with a ritual recounting of his father's offenses and ending with
the idiots on the road who made him late to my office.

I shake my head. "I can see why you'd be upset," I say.
"Sounds like your life can be summed up by an old saying: 'If you
[expletive deleted] with a truck, you're bound to get run over.'"

"You bet! I've got the tread marks to prove it."

"So, when are you going to stop [expletive deleted]-ing
with trucks?"

This little aphorism started a discussion of how Brandon, believing himself the perpetual victim, is always doing a little something to even the score. As a kid, he broke rules as a way of fighting back against his father, and he's been fighting back against everybody else ever since, usually getting the worst of it. Subtly, I suggested that in some cases he might be a victim of his own actions. I also said it was weird that he felt like the road kill, but people keep treating him like the truck.

Conflicts are always symmetrical. Angry people usually see themselves as being attacked rather than attacking. The therapist's job is to show them that the difference between road kill and truck is merely semantic.

Jenna knits her brow. "If people have a problem with me, I tell
them to talk to me about it instead of going over my head or
behind my back."

"Why on earth would they do that?" I ask.

"What do you mean?" she says.

"Let's say I'm a guy at your office and I come in and tell
you to stop picking on me. What do you do?"

"I don't pick on people. I do demand high standards."

"I think I see the problem," I say. "Rule one of human
behavior is you have to reward people for doing what you want or
they don't do it. When somebody comes to your office to com-
plain, do you reward him? Like by saying thank you and offering
to do better?"

"Not always." Jenna says.

"Can you think of a time you did?"

Jenna's eyes flash. "How should I know? I have a job to do, a department to run. I'm involved in hundreds of conversations every day. I can't remember every one. I don't have time to worry about every little comment people make."

I lean forward in my chair. "Jenna, would you be willing to talk about what you're feeling right now? My guess is you're thinking that therapy is a waste of time, and you're wondering how to convince your managing partner that you don't need it. Maybe you'll tell him it's keeping you from more important things."

She hesitates a few seconds before answering. "So?"

"So," I say, "I think it's interesting that you've been in my office ten minutes, and we've already managed to develop the same kind of working relationship you have with people in your office. Aren't you even a little curious about how that could happen?"

Usually, therapists don't try to make their clients angry, but sometimes it happens. With Jenna, I had intended a calm discussion of reinforcement theory, and how fear causes avoidance. What she gave me—a recreation of the very situation we were discussing—was far more useful. We were able to touch on a few of the thoughts that were fueling her angry outbursts. We talked about how hard she worked, how important it was for her to do a good job, and her feeling of constant time pressure. People problems, to her, were a waste of time.

I suggested that high achievers often define things they aren't good at as unimportant so they don't have to risk failure, and how their criticisms of themselves are so strong that even a hint of disapproval from outside is almost unbearable.

By the end of the session, we were back to what she said at the beginning—that she needed help with job stress—but with one important difference: She could see that she was creating at least some of that stress herself.

"Brittany, you say you want your boss to get out of your face, am I right?"

She nods.

I extend my middle finger. "Do you know what this gesture means?"

"Duh."

"How do people usually react to being flipped off?"

"Uh, let me see. Do they get pissed?"

"Right. Now let's talk about all the thousands of different ways to flip people off." I demonstrate a number of them, verbally and with body language, that I've learned from my teenage children.

Brittany laughs, despite herself, then returns to her mien of casual insouciance. "And your point is?"

Then it's my turn to laugh.

By the end of the session we were both laughing at the dumb things the authority figures in her life did, and the even dumber ways she reacted to them. I told her the saying about the truck too. If you have good material, you might as well use it.

Some of you may be wondering about my lapses into profanity and rude gestures, when it's fairly clear that I can express myself without them. I think it's important that a therapist speak his clients' language, rather than requiring them to learn psychobabble to talk to him. Profanity is the language of anger, so I use it. Please pardon my French.

"David," I say, "you want people to listen to you and pay attention to your needs. Have you ever noticed that the louder and longer you talk, the less people listen?"

Angry people often feel isolated. This is because they're so obnoxious that people avoid them. To be allowed to talk about the obnoxiousness, I must first show them that I understand the loneliness.

Once people realize that anger is *a* problem, the next step is convincing them that it's *their* problem, rather than something created for them by the insensitivity of loved ones and the unkindness of strangers. There are fairly standard tricks for this purpose.

"David, suppose you were meeting your wife for dinner at seven. It gets to be 10 after, and she still isn't there. How would you feel?"

"I'd think she was being inconsiderate."

"Okay, what if it got to be 20 after, and she still hadn't shown up?"

*David admits that he would be getting pretty angry,
because she does this all the time, and why can't people plan to
be somewhere early in case there are delays?*

"Now, what if you got a call saying that she was in a car
wreck and in the hospital?"

"I'd be there in a heartbeat."

"But would you still be angry?"

"Of course not."

"Why not?" I ask. "The situation is exactly the same. The
only thing that changed was what was going on in your mind.
When you think it's deliberate, you get angry; when you think
it's an accident, you forgive her in a heartbeat."

This is a typical lead-in to the idea that thoughts, not events, cause
anger, which we'll discuss in greater detail in Step 3.

Something I hope you've noticed in all these case examples is that I
do my best to avoid moral judgments. As far as I'm concerned, agreeing
that they have an anger control problem is not a condition of treatment.
I seldom even use the word *anger*. This is a good strategy to remember.
Try not to set up situations in which giving you what you want constitutes
an automatic admission of guilt.

Therapists tricks aside, the very best way to convince angry people
that anger is their problem is to make it stop working. Angry explosions
are an attempt to get something—usually dominance or territory—which
angry reptile brains deceive people into thinking are the same as the love
and respect they really want. Sometimes the explosions are set off for little
more than the excitement of a good fight. If angry outbursts get people
what they want or think they want, they will occur more often. It's the law
of anger.

If you know what an angry person is trying to get, you can make
informed decisions about when, whether, and under what conditions to give
it to them. Simple withholding will not work because it is an aggressive act
in itself. Withholding something else the angry person wants—in marriages,
sex and conversation are typical choices—is even more damaging. Few
marriages can withstand protracted trench warfare.

The best way to win a battle is to make it unnecessary to fight. Diplo-
macy allows both sides to achieve at least some of their objectives. Now

that you know some of the subtleties of defusing explosions, you can use that knowledge to avert a few battles.

The *Mine Field* Explosion

The most common explosion into anger is not a single blast, but a series of outbursts at irregular intervals that keep you away from territory the angry person has claimed. Think of it as a mine field. The idea is that after a few explosions, you'll stay far afield. This technique is often used by men to get out of doing housework. In the last chapter, I described a struggle for marital dominance that centered around garbage. The incident was just one of many small explosions that Zack's wife would set off in Zack when she came too close to asking him to help with household chores.

> Zack's wife looks at the clock and leaps up from the table. "I've got to change right now or I'm going to be late. This is bunko night."
>
> Zack's face signals a storm warning. "Well, who's going to do these dishes and give the kids their baths?"
>
> "I thought you—"
>
> "You thought! Did you ever think of asking if I had plans for tonight? You said you wanted me to change the spark plugs on your car."
>
> "You can do that tomorrow night. You know the first Wednesday of the month is bunko. I have it marked on the calendar."
>
> "Like I can even see the calendar with all the stuff you have written all over it."
>
> "All that stuff is there so we'll know where we have to go and what we have to do," Zack's wife says, inching toward the bedroom.
>
> Zack gets up and starts moving dishes from the table like a bulldozer clearing a construction site. Amid the clatter, he mutters loudly enough to be heard in the bedroom. "There's no way to win here. You work 10 hours a day, and then come home and work some more so her highness can go out drinking and gambling with her friends.
>
> Finally, his persistent pushing of her hot button about her job not being as valuable as his gets to Zack's wife. She rushes from the bedroom, still buttoning her blouse. "You don't think I work? I have a job just like you."

"Oh, sorry," Zack says "But I couldn't tell from the size of your paycheck. What did you make last month? Was it $800?"

"Zack, you know the girls were sick, and I was out almost a whole week."

Zack's strategy is simple. When asked to do something he doesn't want to do, he lashes out in as many directions as possible, hoping to engage his wife in an argument. In about two minutes he's brought up every contentious issue he can think of. The overall strategy is to make it so unpleasant for her to ask him to do anything that eventually she won't bother.

This strategy is not conscious. Zack feels a rush of adrenaline when his plan for an undisturbed evening of tinkering and TV is threatened, and immediately, in response to his internal validation check, the cassette tapes in his head start rolling, playing back every annoying thing his wife has ever done. All he has to do is turn on the outside speaker and he has a prerecorded argument, full of tried and true hooks to pull her in. He doesn't have to think about any of it.

What Zack is doing is blatantly unfair and manipulative, but it works. If his wife points out how unfair and manipulative it is, it will work even better. If an angry person has laid mine fields in your life, it's time to develop some strategy of your own. Here are some ideas:

MAKE YOUR PLAN BEFORE THE ARGUMENT STARTS. Once the shrapnel is flying, it will be hard to communicate with your neocortex, so do some thinking in advance.

Map out the mine field. What actions and issues bring on explosions? In Zack's case, the mines are thickest around any suggestion that he should help with housework. You can spot a danger zone by asking yourself what subject you're most afraid to bring up. Most marital mine fields are laid around spending money, sex versus affection, the uses of free time, and, the all-time favorite, one partner's perception that the other is trying to be the boss. Once an argument gets going, all of these issues are usually hauled in like ammunition to the front. In the smoky din of battle it's easy to get confused about what you're fighting for.

PICK YOUR BATTLES, AND FIGHT ONLY ONE AT A TIME. Think about what you want to happen, and stay focused on that. Objectives should be phrased in terms of what you want the angry person to *do*, not what you want them *not to do*. Zack's wife will have far more success getting him to do housework than in having him stop getting so angry whenever she brings it up.

Positive goals imply that you need to take some action to achieve them. Negative goals are often merely a wish that you can continue doing what you've always done, and the other person's response will miraculously be different.

The best defense is a good offense. Once you know your objective, you can choose how and when to ask for it. Make sure there is sufficient time and space to maneuver; you can't negotiate with a cornered animal. Don't bring up important issues when the other person is going out the door, and *never, ever, discuss inflammatory issues in the car or in bed!* If there is an angry person in your life, negotiate to have these areas declared demilitarized zones.

The best way to get Zack to do housework is to ask him in advance, and bargain for specific tasks at specific times. It's been my experience that women have a hard time with this. For women, household tasks are an ongoing process without beginning or end. They see something that needs doing and they do it, then move on to the next thing. No one tells them to wash dishes, vacuum the carpet, or put in a load of laundry. They see the task and do it with little separation between the two, almost like Zen.

Men are generally unable to achieve this level of awareness. They can be taught to do housework, but need to be told what, where, and when, *but never how*. The goal you will not be able to achieve, at least all at once, is for men to do household tasks as well as you would. This is a completely separate objective. You must get them *doing* before there is a prayer of having them done correctly. Remember, one battle at a time.

> "Zack," his wife says, "I need about 15 minutes to talk over an important issue. Is this a good time?"
>
> Zack's face is already beginning to grow red. "What is it?"
>
> She smiles. "If this is a good time, I'd be happy to tell you, but I don't want to start if you're getting ready to do something else."
>
> "What kind of manipulative game are you playing?" he says. "Just tell me what you want to talk about."

Note how Zack's wife has neatly closed at least one of the back doors to discussion. By asking her to tell him what she wants to talk about, Zack is conceding that he has time to listen. Even angry people will usually play by these conversational rules. The other thing to note is that in dealing with the angry, every word seems to move the situation in one direction or another. To be effective, you have to be deliberate, paying close attention to what's actually being said and choosing your responses carefully.

DON'T LET AGGRESSIVE HOOKS PULL YOU OFF COURSE.   The favorite strategy of angry people is getting you angry too. They're much more experienced at fighting than you are, so they're more likely to win. Zack's wife did well to ignore his facial display and his accusation of manipulation. They were merely feints, and had nothing to do with her objective. As she gets closer, the flak will get heavier. If things get too hot, she may decide to withdraw, and live to fight another day.

ASK QUESTIONS, DON'T MAKE STATEMENTS.   In a battle, you need to take the high ground as quickly as possible. In discussions with angry people, there are several forms of high ground to go for. Be careful; most of them will not be useful in achieving your goal. If you go for the moral high ground (I'm good and you're bad, so you should do as I say) or the organizational high ground (I'm your boss, therefore you must obey me), rather than a discussion of issues, you'll provoke a dispute over your place in the dominance hierarchy and what, if anything, that entitles. By pulling moral or organizational rank, you will have set up a situation in which an angry person must pay obeisance—by doing what you ask—or admit he or she is wrong. Both outcomes will create a need for the next battle.

It's much more useful and far less noticeable to take the conversational high ground by being the one who asks the questions. If you ask a question, it's almost a law that the other person must answer before going on. If you keep asking thought-provoking questions, you can keep control of the conversation and perhaps encourage the angry person to think. This cannot hurt.

Questions can also help by making unconscious assumptions conscious. When spoken, these assumptions are often far less defensible than when they're merely acted upon. Zack's actions say he shouldn't be responsible for any work around the house, but he can't say this aloud or he'll sound like a male chauvinist pig even to himself.

Asking questions is a simple and effective tactic, but you'll find it surprisingly difficult the first few times you try it. You'll discover that every angry person on earth already knows and uses it.

> *"Zack," his wife says tentatively. "We seem to be getting into a lot of arguments about housework. I think we need to make some ground rules about who does what."*
> *"And why do we need to do that?"*
> *"Well, to keep from getting into arguments."*
> *"We could keep from getting into arguments if you stopped nagging me about taking out the garbage right in the middle of the playoffs."*

Oops! To keep control of the conversation, you need to start by asking the first question and then resisting your own reflexive answering.

Another caution: A favorite tactic of dominant people everywhere is to ask you why you feel something or want something. Never answer a *why* question! You will suddenly discover that the discussion has changed to a critique and defense of your reasons, and your original statement has suddenly changed to a tentative proposition that you will only be allowed to keep if your reasons are good enough. When this happens, it will feel, correctly, as if your words are being pulled out of context and twisted around. The purpose of a *why* question is never to understand your reasoning, it's to elicit words that can be twisted. If you don't give them, there will be nothing to twist. Remember, the answer to a why question is an explanation, and explaining always makes angry situations worse.

It may take a number of attempts to clear a mine field. If you step on a mine, don't stay to argue irrelevant issues. Withdraw and fight your own battle another day.

> *Zack's wife holds up her hands and smiles as she backs away. "I can see this isn't a good time to talk about this. We'll try again another time."*
> *"And why isn't this a good time?"*
> *Zack's wife shakes her head, still smiling. "Do you really need to ask?"*

The person who asks is in control. Why do you think therapists are so fond of answering questions with questions? I can assure you that it isn't because we don't have all the answers.

It's another day:

> *"Honey, what do you think is a reasonable amount of housework for you to do?"*
>
> *Zack exhales loudly enough to be heard across the cul-de-sac. "I already do a lot around here. I take care of the yard. I fix things. I take out the garbage."*
>
> *"Yes, you do. But what percentage of the total amount of weekly work do you think that is?"*
>
> *Zack exhales again. "I don't know. Why don't you just tell me?"*
>
> *"Come on, I asked first. I really want to know what you think."*
>
> *Zack thinks for a few seconds. "About a quarter, I guess. Why are you asking?"*
>
> *"How much work in terms of hours per week do you think it takes to run this house?"*
>
> *"What is all this housework crap? What are you trying to do?"*
>
> *Zack's wife smiles and turns on the overhead projector. "This chart shows a list of household tasks and the average amount of time they take. Please look at them and tell me if you agree that these tasks need to be done, and that the time estimates are reasonable."*

DO YOUR HOMEWORK.   Okay, so you don't have an overhead projector in your living room. Use paper. The point is that taking mined territory back from an angry person requires as much poise and preparation as a presentation to the board of directors. You can't just speak off the cuff. Everything you say and do must be directed toward achieving your goal.

Here's a final question to see how well you understand what that goal is and how you can best move toward it. To answer correctly you need to take into account everything you've learned about anger up to this point.

Should the time estimates on Zack's wife's slides be:

a. overstated
b. accurate
c. understated
d. all of the above

This is the one of the few questions in the book to which the answer isn't *all of the above*. The answer is not *d*. As for *a*, if the figures are overstated, even slightly, it will lead to an argument about how the list is ridiculously padded. You might be surprised at how many people do overestimate. It's because they forget that the purpose of such a list is to get someone else to do more housework, so they succumb to the temptation of using the figures to demonstrate how hard they work.

If you said *b*, that the figures should be accurate, I agree in principle, but still don't think you chose the best answer. Without independent time and motion studies, you can't know what accurate is.

Remember how closely anger—both his and yours—is tied to beliefs about right and wrong. With angry people, you're always in the most danger when you think you're most right. Your estimate could be biased, and even if it weren't, it could seem biased. In order to look correct, the estimates should appear conspicuously low, at least to you. So the answer is *c*.

The estimate should be understated, if only to forestall arguments about padding, but there are reasons beyond that. If Zack thinks the time estimate for a task is overstated, his wife can agree to a test. Zack can do the job and time it to make sure the measurement is fair. Regardless of the outcome, she will win something. The most important prize is drawing him into the whole process of estimating task times with a view toward reassignment.

Another reason for understated estimates is that when Zack finally gets to the point of picking one, he'll end up doing more than he bargains for. Or if he goes for a bargain, his wife can make cleaning the bathroom a more attractive option by slightly *overstating* the time involved. If this is what you were thinking when you answered *a*, you get full credit.

If you're thinking that the process I'm describing is manipulative, you're absolutely correct. Everybody manipulates, but not everybody does it consciously and well. Manipulation is merely offering a deal in a way that makes the other person likely to accept it.

If you're thinking that you shouldn't have to go through a process like this to get a little help around the house, I'd also agree. Unfortunately, few people in this world do what they should. In dealing effectively with angry people, your own shoulds are your greatest liability.

MAKE A CONTRACT.   The reason for contracts is that people break them. When Zack finally picked his jobs, his wife demanded that they put it in writing. Of course, he asked why, and she just shook her head and smiled. Writing isn't always necessary, but a clear, firm agreement is.

Contracts should specify *who*, *what*, *when*, *where*, *how often*, and *if not, what happens*. Zack and his wife each agreed to put up $50 a month to pay at an agreed upon hourly rate for tasks not done within specified limits. Nagging turned into saying things like, "If it isn't done by noon, I get $15 for doing it."

Zack's wife thinks that the $50 a month she loses is the most useful money she's ever spent.

The Anger from on High Explosion

Anger from above you in the dominance hierarchy is more like a trial than a contract negotiation. Often, most of the angry person's energy is directed toward reading the indictment and convicting you of misdeeds, rather than figuring out an appropriate penalty. To deal with an anger-from-on-high explosion effectively, you have to do what any good lawyer would do: plea bargain.

Case 1: Anger from Your Actual Boss

> *Jenna sits behind her desk, scowling at your proposal and shaking her head. "I don't believe this!" she says. "Do you have any idea how much we could lose if this bid went out as you've written it?" Her eyes bore into you as she takes a deep breath, preparing to answer her own question.*

Before you start cringing, look at a chewing out as if it were an actual trial. Since you're a competent worker, the evidence is flimsy, but it doesn't matter. In this court you're guilty until proven innocent, but you won't get a chance to present evidence, and if you do, it will only be torn apart on cross examination; then, quicker than you can say *kangaroo*, you're convicted. If want to keep your job, there is no appeal.

Before you get worked up about the injustice of it all, consider this: The trial is usually far worse than the sentence, especially when the crime is independent thinking, which she can't legally punish nearly so much as it deserves. So the trial itself *is* the punishment.

Structuring the situation this way allows your persecutor to do, with some legitimacy, all the things that angry people do to work themselves up to cathartic eruption. Usually the centerpiece of this legal charade is repetitious reading of the indictment. Each retelling makes the offense more unpardonable. It's just plain old rumination dressed up in a black robe. Chewing you out generally makes the person doing it angrier.

It's not as if Jenna has been carrying around a load of anger, waiting to dump it on you to get it off her chest. She may have some basic points to cover, but she's manufacturing most of the anger as she goes along. Remember that before you say anything that will add fuel to the fire.

> *"Now," Jenna says, after an endless opening statement, "look at this paragraph. What kind of idiot would commit to this kind of pricing structure? It's ridiculous!*

Of course, the managing partner himself told you to do it, and Jenna gave you the figures. You have the actual memo! You now have a choice worthy of Jean Valjean. If you remain silent, you may be convicted of the one crime you can prove you didn't commit. If you speak, you may escape conviction only to find yourself damned.

The way to save your soul is to recognize that what looks like a trial is really no such thing. It's a trap, a great big *why* question, an excuse to draw you into incriminating yourself with your own explanations, which your angry boss will just twist around and add to the indictment, making it even more infuriating on the next reading. You can use the spurious legal structure to your own advantage if you plead *nolo contendere* and move on to the penalty phase.

Let's go back to the opening gavel.

> *Jenna sits behind her desk, scowling at your proposal and shaking her head. "I don't believe this!" she says. "Do you have any idea*

how much we could lose if this bid went out as you've written it?"
Her eyes bore into you as she takes a deep breath, preparing to
answer her own question.
Boldly, like Perry Mason, you say, "I'm really sorry. I'll fix
it immediately. What would you like me to do first?"

If you don't defend yourself, there's no trial. Jenna has to sentence you before she even reads the indictment. She will undoubtedly keep trying. Each time, you should contritely ask, "What would you like me to do?" Eventually, by the rules of her own court, she will have to answer. All you have to do is recognize that if it's not a real trial, you gain nothing by protesting your innocence.

HOW TO APPEAL.   No one should have to endure harassment on the job. However, in order to get it to stop, you must convince someone in authority that it's happening. Obviously, you have to present your case *very* carefully. You want to look like an emotionally stable professional with the highest regard for the company. Unless you intend to bring charges, don't use inflammatory words like *harassment, discrimination, retaliation,* or *hostile work environment.* Even then, let your lawyer do it.

If you're representing yourself, provide unembellished, understated facts and witnesses, if possible. Bear in mind that everything you say is on the record. It will be presented to your harassing boss and defended in private. The case will be judged by character as much as by facts. One provable exaggeration might get it thrown out.

Appeals for help are handled differently in every company. I can only offer a very general outline. Talk to a human resources person to find out the rules and procedures where you are. Watch his or her reactions closely to find out about rules that aren't written down. If the H.R. person is not enthusiastic, you won't get much of a hearing from anyone else.

IF YOU'RE THE JUDGE HEARING AN APPEAL.   Always remember two little details we learned in the chapter on ethology: First, that exclusion by the in-group, whether active (by bullying) or passive (by ignoring), is considered an aggressive act by out-group members. And second, that in-groups enforce solidarity.

The invisible pressure on you will be to side with the person closest to you in rank, automatically labeling the complainer as a malcontent like

Brittany, or to consider the whole issue as beneath your notice. Neither of these instinctive responses will be productive. Before you render a verdict, get some independent information from every level of the hierarchy, then think: *What would the Lion King do?*

Case 2: Anger from Someone Who Wants to Be Your Boss

Usually the person who most wants to be your boss is your spouse. Most marital bullying and nagging has simple control as its goal. The basic defusing technique or the mine field variation is often enough to render these explosions less effective, and therefore less harmful.

Attacks from the moral high ground are different, and, if you don't respond carefully, more devastating than mere attempts to boss you. The goal of moral attacks is to control you by using your own actions as evidence that you lack basic human virtues such as love, respect, and honesty.

> *Late at night following the restaurant debacle, David is still regaling his wife. "How many times have I told you how important punctuality is to me? I move heaven and earth to be on time for you or the kids. But does that make any difference to you? Not from what I've seen. Maybe you just don't care."*
>
> *"I told you I was sorry."*
>
> *"Sorry! That's all you ever say. If what I felt made any difference to you, I'd see some action on your part and not keep hearing one excuse after another."*

Angry explosions from the moral high ground are more like inquisitions than trials. Many, like this one, involve endless cross examinations, often followed by several days of cold shoulder, then another round of interrogation. The purpose of these explosions seems to be to get you to admit your unexpressed hatred, but their real function is to get you to prove your love.

People who explode in this way are often extremely distrustful and suspicious. They continually examine the behavior of others for signs of independent thinking, which to them is the first step on the road to betrayal. Any action that does not seem to place their needs first is dealt with severely, by holding it up as a sign of disrespect, dishonesty, or lack of caring. The higher the moral authority cited, the more cruelty is allowed. When angry people start talking for God, they free themselves of all earthly restraint. It will be up to you to prove your love by abasing yourself, admitting your wrongdoing, and promising never to make the same mistake again. Often, in marriages, having eager demonstrative sex after hours of browbeating is also a condition for forgiveness.

Explosions from the moral high ground can be dangerous. The more you participate, the worse they get. The techniques we've discussed so far will have little effect unless you're able to awaken the still, small voice in the angry person's heart that speaks of virtue first and human failings second. This is a difficult task, even for God. For you, it will require clean hands, a pure heart, and the courage of a saint. Divine intervention may also come in handy. At the very least, consult a therapist.

David's wife came in to see me by herself at first, feeling hurt and confused. She couldn't understand why David was always telling her that she didn't love him. It was getting to the point where she was beginning to believe it herself. Her own doubts, as you might imagine, made her situation even more difficult to handle. We talked for a long time. I tried to explain the dynamics of the interaction.

Explosions from the moral high ground are usually quite predictable. The point at which you have to intervene is when the angry person starts saying something to the effect of, *If you loved me, you'd never have done what you did.* If you do not dispute the connection immediately, you'll find yourself in for hours of torture to reassure your tormentor that your love is true.

Love must be felt; it cannot be proven. Look into your heart as your inquisitor approaches and take strength from what you know is there. Let love give you the courage to speak.

David's wife stands tall, like Joan of Arc about to be consigned to the flames. "David," she says, "I admit to being late to the restaurant, and even to not being as organized and punctual as you are, but I deny that those actions mean I don't love you and don't respect you.

"Before you say anything more to me, you have to look into your own heart and decide whether or not I love you. If you think I don't, you should leave me. If you think I do, you should ask yourself why you keep trying to prove to yourself that I don't."

That night, after much soul searching, David realized that his pain was caused by his own anger, not an uncaring wife. Transformations of this sort happen, but they take a good deal of effort to achieve—and raw, unmitigated courage. If you're set upon by anger from the moral high ground, and cannot say what David's wife said, it's better to say nothing at all. Go somewhere else for the night, and get help in the morning.

The Anger from Below Explosion

This explosion will occur almost entirely behind your back. It starts quietly, as whispering by the water cooler, perhaps by someone like Brittany, who wears her authority issues like a rock concert T-shirt. Immature, she may be, but underestimate her at your peril. The rumblings grow louder at happy hour gripe sessions. An eruption may be heralded by postings of Dilbert, the Che Guevara of corporate revolt. Just before the explosion you may see a list of the "seven habits" taped to your door, with ironies underlined in red. The blast itself may come as an ambush.

> Brittany, accompanied by what looks like a lynch mob, stands at your door. "We need to talk about morale problems," she says. Her henchmen wave their torches, muttering under their breath.

* * *

> "Got a minute?" your boss asks. "Sure," you answer.
> She steps into your office and carefully closes the door.
> "I've been hearing some disturbing things about you," she says.
> "I think we need to talk about them."

If you're a manager, I promise there will come a time in your career when you face an explosion from below, either from an angry mob at a "team building" session or hearing second versions of your actions blown so far out of proportion that you sound like a third-world dictator. When the explosion occurs, what you do next may determine the course of the rest of your career. There is only one effective immediate response: Listen quietly and think carefully about what you're hearing. Here are some ideas about what to do when the dust settles.

DON'T IGNORE THE PROBLEM. It's tempting to see the whole issue as caused by personality problems that will intensify if you pay attention to them. This perception is mostly wishful thinking. You cannot know whether the instigator is more like Brittany or you are more like Jenna unless you check the perceptions of people you trust to tell you the truth.

REMEMBER, IF YOU'RE A MANAGER, YOU'RE LARGER THAN LIFE. If you're the boss, everything you say and do, when talked about behind your back, will be distorted beyond recognition. This phenomenon is especially hard for newer managers to grasp. The tiniest criticisms will be described as verbal abuse. To your face, people will say you're great, but that you could maybe make a few tiny improvements. You should figure that reality is somewhere in the middle.

FIND OUT WHAT THE PROBLEM IS BEFORE YOU TRY AND SOLVE IT. This usually involves individual meetings with everyone in the department, getting everyone's views, and sifting through the information for common patterns. For a more candid response, ask people to talk about the problems others are having. Most people will not want to admit that they have any problem with your actions.

LISTEN WITHOUT TRYING TO CORRECT MISINFORMATION. This is hard. What's bothering people is usually based on errors, misconceptions, and incomplete understanding. The temptation will be strong to jump right in and clear everything up by explaining the real situation. DON'T DO IT! Your helpfulness will be seen as an attempt to cut off discussion. People have to be able to say what's on their minds. Remember that explanations intensify angry explosions.

If the explosion occurs in a group setting, your best bet is to let your detractors run on. If they're raging and you are calm and courteous, their support is likely to evaporate.

Listening is important, but it's very hard. Sometimes it's helpful to have a neutral party, like a consultant, do the listening and present the information to you for consideration before you make any response.

ACKNOWLEDGE AT LEAST THREE MISTAKES. This step should happen in your own heart, not necessarily in public. Based on everything you've heard, you need to take responsibility for at least three mistakes. Real mistakes, not misunderstandings. Unless the mistakes were explosions of your own, involving personal insults, apologies are probably not necessary. Instead, form an action plan to deal with the problem.

GET SPECIFIC. Finding out that your subordinates are discontented is embarrassing, but it's not the end of the world. If you handle it right, it may just be the beginning. Break the problem down into questions that need to be answered, decisions that need to be made, and actions that need to be taken. To do this, it may be useful to consult a therapist or consultant with a knowledge of your industry. It may take an unbiased outsider to help you decide who actually owns the problem, and to advise you about what to do to solve it.

Why We've Spent So Many Pages on a Single Step

The first step is the big one. There's little point in treating anger control problems unless the people being treated recognize that anger is their problem. Getting to this point, as we have seen, involves therapeutic skill, as well as courage and perseverance on the part of friends, family, and coworkers. The first step requires art. After that, the rest is merely science.

Step 2: Physical Control

The science involved in treating anger control problems is relatively simple. You teach angry people to do things that are incompatible with anger. As in other disorders, the control strategies start with external devices and move inward.

THE DUCT TAPE SOLUTION. Once angry people recognize that anger is their problem, I try and find out what sort of internal resources they have for controlling it. I call this applying "the duct tape solution."

> *"David," I say. "It seems to me that your problem with anger is like drinking for an alcoholic—once you get started, you can't stop."*
>
> *David hangs his head.*
>
> *"Now that you recognize the problem, we can do something about it. Over the next few weeks, we'll work on techniques to help you get some control. This next one is hard. It will take all the strength and courage you've got."*

David sits up a bit straighter.

I catch his gaze with mine and hold on. "You need to promise yourself and your family that from here on out, you will not raise your voice for any reason. Imagine that you have duct tape over your mouth and you have to rip it off before you say anything."

"That would hurt," *David says, rubbing his mustache.*

"That's the idea," *I say.* "If it hurts to open your mouth, you'll think carefully about what you say."

The essence of anger control for angry people, and for you, is thinking carefully about what you say. The duct tape solution helps by slowing things down, but that isn't the only reason I use it.

Most angry people have a good deal of pride. For most of their lives they have believed that speaking their mind was a strong response, requiring courage. The first step in treatment turns this perception inside out; they now suspect that anger may be a weakness. The duct tape solution redefines bravery as being strong and silent. Bold, competitive people need challenges in order to feel good about themselves.

I admit that just telling people to keep their mouths shut doesn't require much skill. To people who subscribe to Freud's digestive gas theory of anger, or the new age dictum of mental health as the ability to get feelings out, blatantly suggesting suppression may seem foolish, an invitation to bigger, more dangerous explosions in the future. It isn't. The research is clear on this point: The more people get angry, the more they get angry. The task of therapy is to break the chain, not add links.

Suppression is a good beginning, whether it actually works or not. It's a win-win situation. If angry people yell through the duct tape, it demonstrates the need for further external control, such as medication. When the duct tape solution didn't work for David, he agreed to try Zoloft. Medication can give an angry person enough control to move on to the next step.

Sometimes the duct tape solution is all that's needed to get anger under control. Zack never raised his voice at the office, which meant he was using something like duct tape already, even if he didn't realize it. At first he said it was because he didn't get angry at work. I asked him if this was because the people at work were more considerate than his family. He laughed, and talked about some of the difficult folks he managed and the cajoling he used to get them to give their best. I asked him why he never used his management skill at home. He didn't know. It had simply never occurred to him.

Angry people usually aren't equally angry everywhere. By looking closely at the areas of their lives in which they successfully control their anger, I can demonstrate that the techniques I'm trying to teach are down-to-earth strategies that they use every day.

TIME-OUT.   Another absurdly simple but effective technique is *time out*. When anger begins to smolder, people tend to throw on more fuel. The best thing to do is separate them and send them to neutral corners. Time-out is a good way to get friends and family involved in the treatment in a positive way.

> *Brandon's wife sits at the far end of the couch, shaking her head at his protestations that this time he's really going to change. She's heard it before.*
>
> *Brandon looks at me for support. "See what I have to deal with?" his eyes seem to say.*
>
> *"How do you expect her to feel?" I ask. "You've been in anger control treatment for three weeks, and she just told me how you blew up at the kids last night."*
>
> *"Well," he says, "that was because—"*
>
> *He stops when I make the duct tape sign across my mouth.*
>
> *"There's always a reason for being angry," I say, "but no reason is good enough to yell at your family. You've already agreed to that."*
>
> *He nods sheepishly.*
>
> *"Right now they're all avoiding you, which makes sense because they don't know when you're going to explode. I think they need some protection they can count on. Know what this means?" I make the time-out sign with my hands. "If either of you see this sign, it means that both of you need to go somewhere and take a 15-minute break."*

Time-out disrupts the sequence of anger. After I described the basic technique, we spent considerable time discussing exactly how it would be implemented in Brandon's family, under what conditions it would be used, where people would go, how long they would stay, what would happen if somebody called time out in the car, and so forth. This was one of the few times Brandon and his wife worked together on the anger problem. The ground rules that apply to all time-outs are: no discussion, no parting shots, no following, and if the sign is not obeyed immediately, the other person leaves the house.

For Brandon, I reframed walking away and letting his family have some control over him as a sign of strength. For his wife, I pointed out that using time out was the best way to help everyone she loved. I told them both that their typical way of settling differences wasn't working, and that before we could come up with a new one, there had to be a reliable way of disrupting the old pattern.

Time-out is a temporary solution, but it's an absolute necessity when there is anger that anger might become physical. When people use the technique even once or twice, they discover that walking away is hard, but when they do, it makes anger much easier to deal with. At the very least, it makes explanations and accusing the other person of starting the fight irrelevant.

RELAXATION AND EXERCISE. As you already know, I'm into duct tape. I appreciate simple tools that can fix a lot of different problems. Relaxation, exercise, and serotonin reuptake inhibitors are like psychological duct tape. They can hold situations together long enough to make more permanent repairs.

> *"Jenna," I say, tracing out a line in the air with my finger after explaining the fight or flight response "This is a normal level of physical arousal." I make another line about a foot above the first. "Here's you." I draw a third line an inch above the second. "Here's where you explode. To get your anger under control, we have to do everything we can to get your arousal down here.*

You already know the rest of this spiel. The short version is: If you're relaxed, there's no way you can get angry. Angry people need relaxation training more than people with other explosive disorders, not because they're more aroused, but because they're less aware of their arousal. Angry people focus on the external situation, and often do not notice tension building inside themselves until it emerges as a blast of depression turned outward.

*I'm waving my hands in the air again. "Brandon," I say. "Anger is
a chain of events that starts over here and builds up until you have
an explosion over here. It's a whole lot easier to control at this end."*

With angry people, it's important to integrate relaxation training with
awareness of the arousal cues we talked about in the last chapter. The earlier in the sequence you catch it, the easier it is to control. I begin by having angry clients listen to a relaxation tape, but once they've learned the
basic technique, I encourage them to develop procedures of their own that
they can use on the spot when situations begin to heat up.

*"Oh, like counting to ten?" Brandon asks. And, without hesi-
tating, I reply, "Yes, but in your case, make it 276."*

Relaxation is an important component of anger control treatment.
Encourage it, and participate with the angry people in your life. While
you're at it, encourage them to exercise, and do it with them. Almost any
kind of regular exercise will help, except for martial arts and heavy weight
lifting. The anaerobic bursts of activity involved in pumping iron and
breaking cinder blocks seem to maker anger worse. Better they should go
for a nice walk in the park.

Step 3: Psychological Control

Anger is made of negative judgments played over and over inside the head,
louder and more vehemently each time: internal cassettes of incendiary,
head-banging thoughts turned up loud and set on continuous replay. If
the music is turned off, the party is over. Cognitive therapy turns off the
music, or at least pops in a quieter tape.

Unlike the depressed, angry people resemble one another, at least in
the music they play in their heads. Here are some of the top selections.
You'll undoubtedly hear the angry people in your life humming along.

It's not fair! Angry people are always lamenting about not being
    treated justly. Of course, their idea of fairness is that they get
    what they want when they want it. Anything else is in
    violation of their contract with the universe.

I'm the victim. Angry people continually ruminate about how
they've been hurt, abused, misused, desecrated, and insulted.
When anything new happens, they add it to the list, then
repeat the whole thing, kind of like the 12 days of Christmas.

Idiots are everywhere. Angry people have internal rules about
everything, especially driving. They delight in pointing out
infractions to their passengers, and often to other drivers. To
an angry person, the rest of the world is also pretty much
like a freeway at rush hour.

You'll be sorry. Angry people lust after revenge. They stimulate
themselves with sensuous fantasies of sweet reprisal.

I don't have to take this. Angry people blow small frustrations out of
proportion. Outrage to them is 11 items in the nine or less line.

And, the number one hit:

Nobody loves me. Angry people only raise their voices to make
the world a better place. It never seems to work out because
you're uncaring and insensitive.

Cognitive therapy teaches angry people to recognize these tapes and
play other, less inflammatory selections. It is simple, and incredibly effective, but only when the other therapeutic steps have been achieved.

The Get a Load of That Moron *Explosion*

If you're close to an angry person, you will undoubtedly hear many indig-
nant tapes played through the external speakers. Don't waste your time
with lectures. You can help most by singing a soft, gentle lullaby.

> *Brandon pounds his hand on the steering wheel. "Can you*
> *believe this guy in front of me? This is supposed to be the fast*
> *lane, and right now he's doing all of 32 miles an hour. Now 31!"*
>
> *" He looks kind of befuddled," Brandon's wife says quietly.*
> *"Maybe he doesn't know how to get where he's going. Or maybe*
> *there's something wrong with his car."*
>
> *"Then he should pull off the road and get the [expletive*
> *deleted] fixed!"*
>
> *"Maybe he's trying to find a garage."*
>
> *"What are you talking about? Are you on this guy's side?"*
>
> *" No, sweetheart. Yours."*

Subtlety is the key here. All you need is enough disagreement to divert the flow of a developing harangue, but not enough to make you its target. As always, soft answers and well-composed questions turn away wrath.

For the next step in dealing with this kind of explosion, look back at the list of angry people's most popular cognitions, and ask yourself who habitually thinks this way. If you're a parent, you may already have a whole arsenal of techniques that will work when angry people start playing their internal tapes. Think *distraction*.

> "Oh, look," Brandon's wife says. "Jurassic Park IV is playing at the mall. Maybe we could go see it tonight."
> "If we ever get home."
> "Want some gum?"

If someone else is angry and you stay calm, you have a big IQ advantage. Use it.

Step 4: Inoculation

Believe it or not, doing therapy with angry people is relatively easy. Once they realize that anger is the problem, they're usually open to learning how to control it.

If a person you know is in anger control treatment, remember that changing troublesome behavior is not like flipping a switch. All explosive disorders improve, not by disappearing, but by decreasing over time in frequency, duration, and intensity. As my angry clients improve, I remind them that, though they're doing much better, it will take a long time for the people around them to notice. Regardless of how successful treatment may be, for months loved ones will see them as simply being on their good behavior, and will expect them to revert to their old ways sooner or later.

Eventually it will happen. If a recovering angry person hits his thumb with a hammer and yells out an obscenity, the people around him will be afraid that the bad old days are back, and will probably say as much.

At that moment, Brandon, David, Jenna, Brittany, and Zack will have to look deep inside to see the truth. So will you.

Chapter 13

Where to Get Help

IF THERE IS AN EXPLOSIVE PERSON IN YOUR LIFE, one or both of you may need help. Fortunately, treatment for psychological malaise is abundant in our society. Unfortunately, the quality is not uniformly high. Worse, the delivery system is completely disconnected; one component often has no idea what the other is doing because each believes it's doing what's most important. The kind of help you get will often depend as much upon where you go as on what you need.

The following are some ideas, based on more than 30 years experience in hospitals, crisis clinics, commitment facilities, mental health centers, and private practice, about where to find help and how to evaluate it. Not everyone will agree with my generalizations, but in mental health, who agrees? Let the buyer beware.

Emergencies

Call 911

If there is a chance of imminent physical harm, don't take chances; call 911, and let them decide. In most places, dispatchers are fairly sophisticated as to what their people can and cannot do. Calling 911 will send police or emergency medical personnel. What they call imminent is someone needing to be transported to hospital or jail, given lifesaving treatment, or immediately stopped from doing something dangerous. If someone is hurt, or you have any doubt as to whether an attack is panic or something more dangerous, or if a family dispute gets physical or a suicidal person is brandishing a gun, pills, or other means of bodily harm, call first and ask questions later.

In situations involving threat with no overt action, such as someone acting in a menacing way or just talking about suicide, 911 cannot offer much help. They may still come in such situations, but the police or emergency medical personnel might not have the legal authority to do anything.

Emergency Rooms

Emergency rooms are for people who need immediate treatment. If someone is having a panic attack or is otherwise severely agitated, you may have no choice, especially if the diagnosis is in question. Immediate treatment for agitation is usually a stiff dose of benzodiazepines, which may not be helpful in the long run. The second and third E.R. visits mean you should be going somewhere else.

Emergency rooms in large cities usually have a mental health crisis worker on call. Generally, it will take at least several hours to be seen. The wait may be necessary if you have no other resources for a suicide threat, or you think there might be a need for hospitalization. Many psychiatric units admit through the E.R. if the patient doesn't have an established relationship with an inpatient psychiatrist.

Urgency Care Facilities

Urgency care is not a good source of treatment for the disorders discussed in this book. Crisis treatments with no follow-up make explosive disorders worse.

Primary Care Physicians

The explosive person's primary care physician should be your guide in emergency situations. He or she knows the medical history and many of the available resources. Always call the family doctor first.

That said, I must point out that there is a good deal of variability among primary care physicians as to their experience with mental disorders. As you might expect, physicians lean heavily toward medical treatment. In an emergency, that's probably what you want. Longer term management should involve the psychological aspects of explosive disorders as well.

Crisis Hotlines

The crisis hotline number listed at the front of the phone book is a good resource if someone is considering suicide. Hotline volunteers will listen, and they often have some knowledge of treatment resources. Hotlines can be life-savers in the short run, but they are in no way, shape, or form a substitute for therapy. They require little from the explosive person except the desire to talk.

Mental Health Centers

Public-funded mental health centers are usually listed in the phone book as well. You may get an emergency appointment, but don't count on it. Often, funds are restricted to the chronically mentally ill, and centers cannot provide service except under certain clearly defined conditions. There is enormous variability across states and cities, so in an emergency, a mental health center might be worth a call.

If mental health centers will give an appointment, they usually have facilities for longer term care as well, especially if the person can't afford private treatment. Unfortunately, there may be long waits, considerable crowding, and many opportunities to fall between the cracks. If a person in your life is being seen at a mental health center, you'll need to make sure that patient and the center are maintaining regular contact.

Employee Assistance Programs

EAP programs provided by businesses are often an excellent source for quick advice and referral. Usually, there is a 24-hour hotline number to call. You may reach a person who is far away, but he or she will have a list of resources in your community and will know something about when and how to use them.

If an explosive person's company has an EAP program, or if yours does, make the call. EAP programs are especially good with substance abuse. They sometimes offer very short-term mental health treatment as well. Most EAPs are totally confidential; they give no information to employers. If you have any concerns about what will be shared, ask at the beginning of the call.

Insurance Companies

Believe it or not, your insurance company can help you out in an emergency. If, on the back or bottom of your card, there is an 800 number to call for mental health precertification, the person you eventually talk to will have some knowledge of mental health treatment in your area and which providers and facilities are covered by your plan. The person you talk to will usually have some training in triage, and can offer advice as to what level of care is most appropriate. In many plans, a call is essential to authorize payment for any form of mental health treatment.

If the situation does not warrant 911, and there is a mental health number on an explosive person's insurance card, always call it as soon as possible. If you don't, there may be a large, out-of-pocket expense. Do not make the mistake of believing that a referral from your primary care physician will ensure coverage!

Inpatient Treatment

Psychiatric Hospitals

Psychiatric hospitals used to offer extended treatment. People could go in sick, stay in tranquil surroundings, and come out well. At least in theory.

Psychiatric hospitals are now used for short-term stabilization, usually less than a week, or for long-term placement of people who cannot function in any other setting. There is little in between. I don't recommend hospitalization for any of the disorders in this book. Though there are some excellent short-term facilities, most do not provide much for nonpsychotic disorders beyond keeping people safe and starting them on medication. If a depressed person is actively suicidal or completely unable to function, or a fearful person is in a state of continuous panic, there may be no other place to go. For anyone else, think twice, and three times; you may be starting them on a very bad habit.

Hospital treatment is for people who are so severely disturbed that they're handicapped by their disorder. People who have been hospitalized are not expected to live normal lives. They're often told that they need heavy medication and readmission if symptoms recur. This is usually not true of the disorders in this book, but it can become true if it's what people believe.

People should not consider psychiatric hospitalization unless their lives are at stake, or unless such treatment is recommended by a therapist whose practice is primarily outpatient. In some cases the most therapeutic aspect of a hospital stay is convincing people that they aren't crazy enough to be there.

In most communities there is little integration between inpatient and outpatient treatment. The most common criticism of hospitals is that they discharge people as soon as the people cease being actively dangerous, with no provision for follow-up care.

Commitment

Even in this day and age, I've heard families talk about having a doctor sign a person into the hospital for treatment. In most places this has not been possible since the early 1970s, when involuntary treatment laws were revamped to protect patients' rights. Today, to be involuntarily hospitalized, a person must present a serious likelihood of harm to self or others.

A convincing suicide threat may constitute a danger to self, but usually it requires an attempt or a serious plan. Investigation for involuntary treatment is often a good way to get people to realize that they really don't want to die.

Your primary care physician will probably not know how to get someone committed. Calling the police nonemergency number, a psychiatric unit, the mental health center, or the emergency room of the largest hospital in town are better bets. One of them is typically in charge of local involuntary treatment.

Substance Abuse Treatment Programs

Because of cost, most substance abuse treatment is outpatient, involving daily groups, appointments with counselors, and Alcoholics Anonymous meetings. Urban areas will have several different kinds of programs listed in the yellow pages under *Alcohol treatment*. If you call, they'll give you information and set up an initial screening appointment at no cost or obligation. It is very important to check a program out carefully before signing on.

Substance abuse and mental health treatment occupy parallel universes, divided by law in many states. Each has its own version of reality. If an explosive person in your life is also a substance abuser, you may have to experience both. Be prepared for confusion, because each universe is largely unaware of the strengths of the other and of its own weaknesses.

Substance abuse must be dealt with first. Mental health treatment will not work, and many medications will become dangerous, if an explosive person is actively abusing alcohol or drugs. Psychotherapy that focuses on why people abuse substances can go on forever without much benefit. Likewise, 12-step programs have little success in treating mental disorders.

Outpatient Treatment

Primary Care Physicians

Primary care physicians are usually the first contact in treating the disorders discussed here. They establish a differential diagnosis, prescribe medication for the symptoms, and provide a referral for psychotherapy. Ideally, the physician and the therapist will work together to coordinate care.

As we have seen, some explosive disorders respond to medication and don't require therapy, some need therapy and no medication, and some need both. Primary care physicians sometimes perceive too many patients as falling into the first category. For people who explode into fear or anger, or depressed people who do not completely recover after about a month of medication, you should press for a therapy referral, or find one for yourself.

Most primary care physicians are adept at prescribing the medications we've discussed here. Unless the patient's response is atypical, there is usually no need for a psychiatric consultation. These days, most physicians do not prescribe regular doses of benzodiazepines for more than a week or two. If yours does, you should find out why, and possibly get a second opinion.

Psychiatrists

Psychiatrists usually have a *Medical Doctor* or *Doctor of Osteopathy* degree. Except in very large urban areas, psychiatrists are typically not the people who do talk therapy. In private practice, their primary concerns are diagnosis and medication. Their expertise is critical in managing medically difficult cases, which include patients who have psychotic symptoms, may require hospitalization, or have unusual responses to psychoactive drugs. Of the maladies we have discussed, bipolar disorder and medication-resistant depressions are likely to need psychiatric management.

People seeing psychiatrists should also be seeing a therapist, and should have a regular primary care physician. All the professionals should maintain contact with one another, because what each one does affects the work of the others. Always insist on regular contact, and sign the appropriate releases at each doctor's office. Patients should not be carrying messages from one doctor to another; there's too much chance for distortion.

Psychiatrists are usually quite busy and schedule appointments far in advance. They often spend an hour or two with patients in the initial evaluation, followed by 15 minute sessions to manage medication.

Psychiatric Nurse Practitioners

Psychiatric nurse practitioners are trained in prescribing psychoactive medications. Their skill level falls somewhere between primary care physicians and psychiatrists. They generally take more time with patients and are more available than either.

Psychologists

Psychologists have a Ph.D. (Doctor of Philosophy in Clinical Psychology) or Psy.D. (Doctor of Psychology) degree and a state license. Some states license at the master's level, but usually with a number of restrictions. Psychological specialties include testing and diagnosis, and, of course, talk therapy.

Being a psychologist myself, I am biased in favor of my own profession. I think there are two things that set us apart from other people who do therapy. The first is rigid, written ethical standards and, in most states, licensing boards that aggressively police those standards. The second is extensive training in research. In mental health, more than most other fields, it's easy to get lost in the internal world of therapist or patient. What feels good or fits people's expectations may not be the best or most appropriate treatment. Psychologists are taught that controlled studies are necessary to tell which therapy works best for which disorders, that the phrase *clinically proven* is an oxymoron. Psychological training pounds respect for research into the heads of practitioners. Not that we always remember.

Social Workers

Social workers have a Master of Social Work degree. Many use the desig-
nation LCSW after their names to indicate Licensed Clinical Social Worker.
To be fair, social workers do many of the same things psychologists do just
as well as psychologists do them. I don't know that there are any reasons
to choose one profession over another for therapy. The choice is more of
one individual therapist over another.

Other Counselors, Therapists, and Coaches

There are many people out there who have a master's degree in psychology
or counseling and various levels of licensure and ability; counselors, marriage
and family therapists, substance abuse counselors, pastoral counselors, and
life coaches are among them. Some are very good, but most are not qualified to treat the explosive disorders described in this book. The reason for
this is not that doing therapy is so difficult; the hard part is knowing when
you're not doing it. The best therapists, regardless of training, will always
clearly define their limits of their practice.

How to Find a Good Therapist

If there is an explosive person in your life, getting him or her into treatment
is an important goal. But treatment with whom?

There is at least as much variability in skill and ethics among therapists
as there is among attorneys or auto mechanics. As with other professionals,
there's no sure way to know in advance who will best meet your needs.
Over the years, I've trained and worked with hundreds of therapists, some
brilliant, others less so. I've thought long and hard about which personal
and professional characteristics differentiate the really good therapists
from the rest. Knowledge, of course, is essential, and sufficient self-aware-
ness to separate the client's needs from your own. The best therapists see
themselves as craftspeople rather than friends, parents, crusaders, spiritual gurus, or rescue rangers. Unfortunately, you may not be able to tell
in the first couple of sessions what a therapist knows, much less what he
or she thinks about him- or herself. To pick a good therapist, it helps to
think like one. The following are some quick indicators of a real pro.

Professional Licensing

Professional licensing assures that a therapist meets minimum standards of training and expertise. If a therapist is not licensed, pass them up—there's usually a reason for it.

Experience

When I first got out of graduate school in the early 1970s, I thought that the best therapists were the ones who knew the most up-to-date techniques. At that time, there was actually some reason other than my own bravado for believing that. In the last quarter of the 20th century, therapy went through two spectacular paradigm shifts in both psychology and psychiatry, with the advent of behavioral treatment and the availability of medications for most mental disorders.

Since then, there have not been radical changes. Though keeping up is still as important as it ever was, I now believe that the best therapists are the ones who have lived through enough fads and fashions in the field to recognize the central elements that have remained constant.

Exaggerated Concern with Confidentiality

Therapists cannot give out any information about clients without their permission. Usually in writing. Without appropriate releases, a therapist cannot even admit that someone is his or her client, much less tell you anything about treatment. This can seem frustrating and obstructive if you're a family member of an explosive person who is calling for advice. Don't mistake the therapist's unwillingness to give you information as a sign of incompetence.

But confidentiality does not cancel out accountability. The pros recognize that clients don't live in a vacuum, and will somehow involve the people closest to them, often inviting friends and family to a conjoint session. Rarely will a therapist see two members of the same family individually except for a meeting or two. The primary treatment relationship always takes precedence, though that may be with a couple or a whole family, in which cases everyone involved would be seen by the therapist together.

If an emotionally explosive person in your life is in therapy, you don't need to know every detail of the sessions. You should have an overall idea about what treatment involves and how it's going. If you don't, think like a therapist. Why should it be a secret? Who has something to hide?

Sense of Humor

All the best therapists I know have a sense of humor. Shrinks who take themselves too seriously encourage their clients to do the same. If your therapist would object to being called a shrink, he or she might be too uptight.

Therapists must maintain a balance between the client's internal world, their own, and external reality. Humor is one of the only forces in the universe capable of being in all three places at once. The hallmark of therapeutic skill is inspiring people to laugh at the abyss; it's impossible for therapists who can't laugh at themselves.

Humor is necessary, but so is sensitivity to the audience. If you don't think your therapist is funny, he or she is probably not appropriate for you, unless you don't think *anyone* is funny.

Looking, Sounding, and Acting Like a Regular Person

Therapists should have good contact with external reality, and should demonstrate this by seeming normal. A good therapist should not be recognizable as a therapist outside the office, except perhaps for the comfortable shoes. In the trade, one of the highest accolades we can bestow on another practitioner is saying he or she is a "regular person." This means having an identity beyond being a therapist.

Therapists, by virtue of their profession, are no saner or more spiritual than bankers or accountants. The greatest temptation is believing that we actually *are* the all-knowing, all-caring people our clients want us to be, and that our opinions are the standard by which sanity should be judged. God help you if your therapist has a God complex.

The Ability to Listen

Therapists have to be able to listen. It's the minimum requirement. Listening means being able to focus on the client's needs first. This starts with returning phone calls, keeping appointments, and remembering what was discussed last time. If you feel your therapist is not listening to what you have to say, or talks more about him or herself than about you, or seems to be spouting prerehearsed material about what people with your diagnosis are supposed to think and feel, you're probably in the wrong place.

The Ability to Do More than Listen

Important as it is, listening doesn't require much effort or knowledge. Gone are the days when therapists can get away with nodding, paraphrasing, and asking "What do *you* think?" when you ask a question. Clients are paying for expertise, not just attention. Obviously, there are some questions clients must answer for themselves, but there are several that therapists should answer after the first couple of sessions.

WHAT DO YOU THINK IS WRONG?   There must be some clear agreement between client and therapist about what is being treated. This can be expressed as a diagnosis with some explanation of what it means and how it works, or simply by a clear description of the problem. This question should never be answered with, "What do you think is wrong with you?" without the therapist eventually giving his or her opinion.

HOW WILL YOU TREAT THE PROBLEM?   Therapy for explosive disorders is active, focused treatment, not a fishing expedition. There should be a plan at the beginning, and a way of evaluating success. Treatment plans should show familiarity with both physical and psychological aspects of explosive disorders, and, though therapists go about things in many different ways, should still cover all the steps I have listed for treatment of the various explosive disorders.

Some very competent therapists may strongly disagree with my strategies. They may be right, especially since they've had a chance to actually talk to you. Listen to their reasons, and see what kind of case they make.

Boldness

Therapists must be respectful, but not nice. A therapist should not follow the same rules of politeness as friends or family. Pros ask difficult and sometimes annoying questions, and we will not take throwaway lines for an answer. Therapists are supposed make you think. Sometimes the thinking makes you squirm.

If you feel your therapist is being too insensitive, it's always appropriate to ask, "What are you doing and how is it supposed to help me?" A good therapist can stop on a dime, answer the question, and then go back to whatever he or she was doing.

Therapists may be tricky, but unlike stage magicians, they are obligated to explain their tricks when asked. Therapy does not require deception or blind belief.

Using the Past as a Tool for Change, Not Merely to Explain the Present

Everybody expects therapists to ask about childhood. The expectation is so strong that therapists sometimes do it almost without thinking. In my opinion, much therapeutic time is wasted trying to discover why people act the way they do. The most important question isn't *Why?* but, *What are we going to do about it?*

Flexibility

A therapist must be able reach out. He or she must go where clients are, think like they do, and speak their language, not just the jargon of a theoretical approach. Though many of my colleagues would disagree, I think a therapist is a therapist first and a psychoanalyst, Jungian, behavioral cognitive therapist, or whatever else second. One thing I hope you've gleaned from this book is that no single theoretical position can conceptualize the whole of any mental disorder. Good therapists, regardless of orientation, do pretty much the same things. Less skillful therapists cleave to their techniques and recipes as if they were therapy itself.

Therapy is a journey from one specific place to another. The destination should be clear, and agreed upon before starting. Techniques are merely a road map. If one path is blocked, there's always an alternate route. Good therapists know many different routes, but even they sometimes get lost. If they do, the pros stop and ask for directions.

What's Not Important in Choosing a Therapist?

Sex, ethnicity, politics, religion, or personal experience. People often think that therapists with certain personal characteristics will understand them better. This is not only not true, but at times harmfully false. A physician does not need to have kidney failure to treat it effectively. Therapists are trained to understand experiences very different from their own, and to put their needs and views aside to focus on the client's problems. Any therapist who cannot do this is in the wrong profession.

Again, think like a therapist. Why would clients believe that one kind of person would help them more than another? Perhaps they think that people with the same characteristics or experiences will share the same irrational beliefs, and so will not ask embarrassing questions about them. But then, it's hard to see how having a therapist with the same blind spots and prejudices could do anybody much good.

Good therapist or not, one day, you'll find yourself alone in the blast zone. Don't let the sound and fury confuse you. Through the dust and ashes keep sight of the fixed stars. What you do can make a difference. Take courage from your desire to help, and remember always that what's scariest usually works best.

Appendix:

Classification,
Generic and Brand Names
of Psychoactive Medications

BENZODIAZEPINES
Chlordiazepoxide (Librium)
Diazepam (Valium)
Flurazepam (Dalmane)
Chlorazepate (Tranxene)
Clonazepam (Klonopin)
Quazepam (Doral)
Lorazepam (Ativan)
Temazepam (Paxipam)
Oxazepam (Serax)
Alprazolom (Xanax)

ANTICONVULSANTS
Valproate (Depakote)
Gabapentin (Neurontin)

AZASPIRONES
Buspirone (BuSpar)

SEROTONERGICS
Tricyclics and other serotonin norepinephrine reuptake inhibitors (SNRIs)
Amitriptyline (Elavil)
Nortriptyline (Pamelor)
Imipramine (Tofranil)
Norpramin (Desipramine)
Venlafexine (Effexor)

Selective serotonin reuptake inhibitors (SSRIs)
Fluoxetine (Prozac)
Sertraline (Zoloft)
Paroxetine (Paxil)
Fluvoxamine (Luvox)
Citolopram (Celexa)

Serotonin antagonist and reuptake inhibitors (SARIs)
Trazodone (Desyrel)
Nefazodone (Serzone)

Norepinephrine dopamine reuptake inhibitors (NDRIs)
Bupropion (Wellbutrin, Zyban)

Norepinephrine antagonist serotonin antagonist (NASAs)
Mirtazapine (Remeron)

MONOAMINE OXIDASE INHIBITORS
Phenelzine (Nardil)
Isocarboxazid (Marplan)
Tranylcypromine (Parnate)

LITHIUM
Lithium carbonate (Eskalith, Lithobid)

Index

Albert J. Bernstein, Ph.D., is a practicing clinical psychologist, corporate consultant, columnist, speaker, and bestselling expert on difficult people. His books—*Dinosaur Brains, Neanderthals at Work, Sacred Bull,* and *Emotional Vampires*—have been translated into over 20 languages and have helped people around the world deal more effectively with difficult and dangerous situations. Dr. Bernstein lives with his wife and children in Portland, Oregon.